PRAISE FOR NETSOURCING

"In the early phase of the evolution of the ASP market, few pioneers were willing to acknowledge the importance of understanding the concepts of outsourcing as they launched their offerings. The strongest survive, and will benefit from reading this comprehensive analysis of the third wave of outsourcing. The authors have shown insight and wisdom that makes this a must read for any company that is on the periphery or in the thick of delivering application services."

Paula M. Hunter,
Chairman, ASP Industry Consortium

"The sourcing neophyte, expert, and supplier can all benefit from the wisdom of these pages."

Dennis McGuire,
Chairman and CEO,
Technology Partners International, Inc.

"An important book. It provides an insightful, in-depth analysis of exciting new markets in their embryonic stage. The authors spare no punches, but also show how fundamentally different modes of delivering infrastructure, services and applications are taking shape....If you want to understand the IT future, this is essential reading."

Ghobad Broumand,
Chairman, MainPass Technologies

"*Netsourcing*...makes essential reading for those wanting to understand the new marketspace."

Sara Cullen,
Managing Director, Cullen Associates

Netsourcing

ISBN 0-13-092355-9

90000

9 790130 923553

FINANCIAL TIMES

Prentice Hall

In an increasingly competitive world, it is quality
of thinking that gives an edge—an idea that opens new
doors, a technique that solves a problem, or an insight
that simply helps make sense of it all.

We work with leading authors in the various arenas
of business and finance to bring cutting-edge thinking
and best learning practice to a global market.

It is our goal to create world-class print publications
and electronic products that give readers
knowledge and understanding which can then be
applied, whether studying or at work.

To find out more about our business
products, you can visit us at www.ft-ph.com

Pearson
Education

NETSOURCING

Renting Business Applications and Services Over a Network

THOMAS KERN

MARY CECELIA LACITY

LESLIE P. WILLCOCKS

An Imprint of PEARSON EDUCATION

Upper Saddle River, NJ • New York • London • San Francisco • Toronto
Sydney • Tokyo • Singapore • Hong Kong • Cape Town
Madrid • Paris • Milan • Munich • Amsterdam
www.ft-ph.com

Library of Congress Cataloging-in-Publication Data

Kern, Thomas.
   Netsourcing: renting business applications and services over a network / Thomas Kern,
Mary Cecelia Lacity, Leslie P. Willcocks.
      p. cm. — (Financial Times Prentice Hall books)
   Includes bibliographical references and index.
   ISBN 0-13-092355-9
      1. Computer leases—Computer network resources. 2. Office equipment
leases—Computer network resources. 3. Industrial procurement—Computer network
resources. 4. Internet. I. Lacity, Mary Cecelia. II. Willcocks, Leslie. III. Title. IV. Series.

   HF5548.6 .K47 2002
   658.7'2'02854678—dc21

                                                            2002020125

Cover design director: *Jerry Votta*
Cover design: *Talar Boorujy*
Interior design: *Gail Cocker-Bogusz*
Manufacturing buyer: *Maura Zaldivar*
Acquisitions editor: *Tim Moore*
Editorial assistant: *Allyson Kloss*
Development editor: *Russ Hall*
Marketing manager: *Bryan Gambrel*

 ©2002 by Financial Times Prentice Hall
An imprint of Pearson Education, Inc.
Upper Saddle River, New Jersey 07458

Financial Times Prentice Hall books are widely used by corporations and government
agencies for training, marketing, and resale.

For information regarding corporate and government bulk discounts please contact:
Corporate and Government Sales (800) 382-3419 or corpsales@pearsontechgroup.com

Company and product names mentioned herein are the trademarks or
registered trademarks of their respective owners.

Printed in the United States of America

10   9   8   7   6   5   4   3   2   1

ISBN 0-13-092355-9

Pearson Education LTD.
Pearson Education Australia PTY, Limited
Pearson Education Singapore, Pte. Ltd.
Pearson Education North Asia Ltd.
Pearson Education Canada, Ltd.
Pearson Educación de Mexico, S.A. de C.V.
Pearson Education—Japan
Pearson Education Malaysia, Pte. Ltd.

FINANCIAL TIMES PRENTICE HALL BOOKS

For more information, please go to www.ft-ph.com

Thomas L. Barton, William G. Shenkir, and Paul L. Walker
*Making Enterprise Risk Management Pay Off:
How Leading Companies Implement Risk Management*

Deirdre Breakenridge
Cyberbranding: Brand Building in the Digital Economy

William C. Byham, Audrey B. Smith, and Matthew J. Paese
*Grow Your Own Leaders: How to Identify, Develop, and Retain
Leadership Talent*

Jonathan Cagan and Craig M. Vogel
*Creating Breakthrough Products: Innovation from Product Planning
to Program Approval*

Subir Chowdhury
The Talent Era: Achieving a High Return on Talent

Sherry Cooper
Ride the Wave: Taking Control in a Turbulent Financial Age

James W. Cortada
*21st Century Business: Managing and Working
in the New Digital Economy*

James W. Cortada
*Making the Information Society: Experience, Consequences,
and Possibilities*

Aswath Damodaran
*The Dark Side of Valuation: Valuing Old Tech, New Tech,
and New Economy Companies*

Henry A. Davis and William W. Sihler
Financial Turnarounds: Preserving Enterprise Value

Sarv Devaraj and Rajiv Kohli
*The IT Payoff: Measuring the Business Value
of Information Technology Investments*

Jaime Ellertson and Charles W. Ogilvie
*Frontiers of Financial Services: Turning Customer Interactions
Into Profits*

Nicholas D. Evans
*Business Agility: Strategies for Gaining Competitive Advantage
through Mobile Business Solutions*

Kenneth R. Ferris and Barbara S. Pécherot Petitt
Valuation: Avoiding the Winner's Curse

David Gladstone and Laura Gladstone
Venture Capital Handbook: An Entrepreneur's Guide to Raising Venture Capital, Revised and Updated

David R. Henderson
The Joy of Freedom: An Economist's Odyssey

Philip Jenks and Stephen Eckett, Editors
The Global-Investor Book of Investing Rules: Invaluable Advice from 150 Master Investors

Thomas Kern, Mary Cecelia Lacity, and Leslie P. Willcocks
Netsourcing: Renting Business Applications and Services Over a Network

Frederick C. Militello, Jr., and Michael D. Schwalberg
Leverage Competencies: What Financial Executives Need to Lead

Dale Neef
E-procurement: From Strategy to Implementation

John R. Nofsinger
Investment Madness: How Psychology Affects Your Investing... And What to Do About It

Tom Osenton
Customer Share Marketing: How the World's Great Marketers Unlock Profits from Customer Loyalty

Stephen P. Robbins
The Truth About Managing People...And Nothing but the Truth

Eric G. Stephan and Wayne R. Pace
Powerful Leadership: How to Unleash the Potential in Others and Simplify Your Own Life

Jonathan Wight
Saving Adam Smith: A Tale of Wealth, Transformation, and Virtue

Yoram J. Wind and Vijay Mahajan, with Robert Gunther
Convergence Marketing: Strategies for Reaching the New Hybrid Consumer

To Anna Psoinos and the Kern family
To Michael Christopher and all the Lacitys
To Leonard and Doris, Roger and Kenneth

CONTENTS

xi

FOREWORD

Today there is little argument that strategic sourcing is an important management tool that is being utilized on a global basis. Like any evolving management practice, it is fraught with pitfalls and problems exacerbated by the dynamic environment in which it functions. The triumvirate of Kern, Lacity, and Willcocks has brought their collective knowledge, experience, and research on an international scale together to create an insightful yet practical treatise on the developing landscape of netsourcing and its value.

During my twelve-year involvement in the sourcing advisory industry, I have come to know and respect the authors and their work. I have heard them speak on numerous occasions and have worked with them on various projects. I have followed their research and publications since their earliest sourcing work. I continue to be impressed with their thinking, the depth of their research, and the practical application they provide when it comes to the burgeoning global sourcing marketplace.

This latest offering provides some keen insights not only for the consumer of sourcing services but also for the providers of such services. This presentation of netsourcing is a well thought out and well organized comprehensive guide to the subject. Incorporated within the pages of this book are the basis for defining this wave of outsourcing, criteria for making sourcing decisions, sourcing options, and technical tradeoffs. In-depth case studies from the United States and Europe are also included, demonstrating how suppliers are changing to adopt to the evolving needs of more sophisticated customers. Mitigating the inherent sourcing risks, the customer business drivers, and a look to the future in the context of the past are also included to provide a comprehensive examination of netsourcing.

The sourcing neophyte, expert, and supplier can all benefit from the wisdom of these pages. Interwoven throughout are the findings from various leading IT research firms in the world that provide a broad basis for making the content relevant and readily applicable. It is uncommon to find a book with this caliber of research, business insights, and practical application. I heartily recommend this easy-to-read guide laden with many golden nuggets you can apply to your everyday sourcing needs.

Dennis McGuire, Chairman and CEO
of Technology Partners International, Inc.

PREFACE

For most of the twentieth century, business managers were able to focus on their core business responsibilities while delegating the technology support to inside or outside experts. But in the new millennium, nearly every product, service, process, and function is enabled by, and embedded in, networked information technology (IT). Product design, purchasing, scheduling, manufacturing, logistics, recruiting, inventory, customer orders, delivery, customer service, finance, and accounting are all enabled by networked IT. *This means that all business managers now have IT responsibilities—whether they want them or not.*

Among the most important decisions business managers make is to determine the most effective way of sourcing IT solutions, and beyond those, IT-enabled business processes. They ask: What should we buy? What should we outsource?

Should we find a technology partner? And most recently—what value does the explosion in the number of third-party suppliers offering business services over the Internet offer us? Is this *netsourcing* of my business services safe and reliable? Many business managers feel ill-equipped to answer these questions, particularly because they are intimidated by the vast amount of confusing supplier-driven hype.

We believe that every business manager will need to understand the principles of sound sourcing, with particular attention focused on the third wave of netsourcing. For managers within small to midsized enterprises, netsourcing will probably become a popular choice for sourcing business applications and services. For large enterprises, netsourcing will become part of an overall sourcing strategy, just one important option among many.

Indeed, netsourcing is already a growing phenomenon. The revenues generated in the netsourcing space—depending on which research firm's report you read—were between $1 billion and $2 billion in 2000. But research firms such as Gartner Group's Dataquest, InfoTech Trends, Phillips Group, International Data Corporation (IDC), and DataMonitor are predicting that the market will grow significantly over the next few years. Total netsourcing estimated spending ranges from a low of $7 billion to a high of $132 billion by 2006. Although nobody knows for sure how large this market will be, all research firms predict significant growth because the underlying value promise is too compelling for business managers to ignore.

The prediction for widespread adoption of netsourcing is also based on the history of information technology sourcing. Since the dawn of computing, customers have adopted the most economical, reliable, secure, and flexible sourcing options to meet their business objectives. Although customers are often slow to adopt new sourcing options, eventually they do so, provided that the underlying value proposition is compelling. Consider a snapshot of IT sourcing options over the past 40 years. During the early 1960s, many customers could not afford expensive mainframes and sourced business applications through the first wave of outsourcing, called *time-*

sharing. In those days, visionaries such as Ross Perot actually picked up reels of data from customers, drove them to a data center for processing, then drove the results back to the customer site. During the late 1960s and 1970s, the advent of minicomputers drove hardware costs low enough to justify customer ownership and control of assets in centrally managed internal IT shops. The trend of *insourcing* business applications was also bolstered in the late 1980s and 1990s with the introduction of personal computers and client–server computing. Often, the underlying economics of these sourcing options still favored insourcing, but they also promised to dismantle central IT functions in favor of locally deployed IT. Other economic drivers during the 1990s drove the second wave of outsourcing, such as the increasing cost of software, the global IT skills shortage, and fear of Y2K. Often, external suppliers were better able to leverage IT resources in this environment, and outsourcing also served to free customers to focus on their core capabilities. So ballyhooed was this option that global IT outsourcing spend swelled to over $1 trillion by 2000. With the explosion of the Internet, the third wave of outsourcing washed ashore with netsourcing. What netsourcing enables is another dramatic shift in the underlying economics of sourcing—it's essentially the time-sharing concept of the 1960s, but instead of Ross Perot driving customer tapes to a data center, everything is delivered over a network.

Lest this snapshot of sourcing options seems like a technological utopia, we do note that every sourcing option has a life cycle of early supplier hype, naive customer expectations, initial discovery of pitfalls, then a maturing of the option with clearly defined best and worst practices. For example, client–server technology did reduce infrastructure costs but did not truly deliver on the promise of employee empowerment and completely decentralized IT management. (Most large organizations eventually centralized their servers to ensure backup, reliability, and security.) In another example—outsourcing IT to a third party was also fraught with problems until customers learned how to identify outsourcing options, negotiate better deals with suppliers, and manage relationships once contracts were signed. The same will be true for netsourcing: The value proposition is extremely compelling, but early adopters will help us discover the pitfalls and identify the best and worst ways to netsource. As all other sourcing innovations over the years, netsourcing will take its place among the other options rather than replacing them completely.

Although netsourcing services will mature, the suppliers in the netsourcing area will change radically. As of third quarter 2001, more than 1500 companies claimed to be netsourcing providers. To the present time, though, most media attention has focused on the fast-growing U.S. application service provider (ASP) startups such as Corio, Futurelink, and Interreliant. But the marketplace actually consists of a diverse range of service providers, including Internet service providers (ISPs), telecommunication infrastructure providers (telecos), data-center operators, independent software vendors (ISVs), computer manufacturers (CMs), online software companies, systems integrators (SIs) and established outsourcing service vendors.

Nearly every analyst, however, predicts that the industry is in the midst of a tremendous shakeout, characterized by failures, mergers, and acquisitions. The Gartner Group estimated that 60% of service providers failed by year end 2001. Service providers that closed shop include Agillion, Hotoffice, eBaseOne, Red Gorilla, Pandesic, and Utility.com. Survivors continue to scramble to find strategic partners to expand their products, markets, and services. Dot.com service providers also continue to face stiff competition not only from their immediate rivals but from the large independent software vendors, systems integrators, telecos, and consulting firms entering the market. For these established suppliers, buying or merging with an existing netsourcing startup may define a market entry strategy. These firms will then be able to offer those kinds of resource capabilities, expertise, technology, and geographical presence that will make the netsourcing business model an attractive option to global 2000 businesses. And, of course, the latter suppliers have deep pockets to survive the shakeout.

Many people suggest that the netsourcing shakeout will result in a handful of players, much like the shakeout in automotive manufacturing at the turn of the century. We believe, however, that more than a handful of players will survive because netsourcing is not about a specific product but an entire new delivery mechanism for business services. Small service providers will probably target a niche set of products and services for a niche set of customers. Large service providers such as Accenture, EDS, and IBM will offer total business solutions, with netsourcing as a delivery option.

Given the instability in the current netsourcing space, business managers need tools to evaluate if, when, and how to adopt netsourcing. In this book, business managers are given tools to identify core and noncore IT capabilities, assess their in-house versus market capabilities, assess the total value added of sourcing options, mitigate sourcing risks, and implement flexible sourcing arrangements that adapt to business and technology changes. Each chapter has extensive lessons for both suppliers and customers (see Table 1).

The target audience for this book is all stakeholders involved in IT-enabled business decisions and management. On the customer side, senior business executives, business unit managers, government officials, IT directors, internal lawyers, and end users will learn how to leverage netsourcing within their overall sourcing portfolio. On the supplier side, service providers will learn key insights as to what early customers are experiencing with netsourcing, and more important, what reticent customers expect from suppliers before they are willing to rely on them.

The tools in this book are based on over 10 years of research by two recent recipients of the PriceWaterhouseCoopers and Michael Corbett & Associates' Global Information Technology Outsourcing Achievement Award, along with a third author who has extensively studied, published on, and worked in traditional as well as netsourcing options. Our research access and expertise and extensive practical experiences give us, as a team, distinctive, and in some ways unrivaled, in-depth insights into the way that the outsourcing market has developed and where netsourcing is now taking that market.

TABLE 1 Summary of Lessons Learned

CHAPTER	CUSTOMER LESSONS	SUPPLIER LESSONS
Chapter 1: *An Overview of Netsourcing*	Understand what netsourcing promises you in terms of value, products, and services. Understand the actual experiences of early netsourcing adopters.	Learn how to position your products and services within a service stack. Understand what reticent customers expect from netsourcing before they will adopt.
Chapter 2: *Principles for Effective Sourcing Decisions*	Understand sourcing options (of which netsourcing is only one option). Learn to evaluate your IT portfolio in terms of business contribution, costs, and technical capability vis-à-vis supplier offerings.	Understand how to market products and services based on the customer's view of the contribution of their IT-enabled systems.
Chapter 3: *Management Principles: Core Capabilities and Contracting*	Learn one of the most valuable models for identifying core internal IT capabilities. Learn the principles of sound contracting.	Help customers retain core capabilities to ensure that you can be a successful supplier. Prepare for the impending future where netsourcing contracts will hold suppliers much more accountable for performance.
Chapter 4: *Netsourcing Technology Guide for Customers*	Deconstruct the technical terminology associated with netsourcing into simple concepts. Understand the business trade-offs between various netsourcing technical platforms such as using the Internet versus a virtual private network.	Learn to approach customers by using simple explanations for the technical aspects of netsourcing.

TABLE 1 Summary of Lessons Learned (continued)

CHAPTER	CUSTOMER LESSONS	SUPPLIER LESSONS
Chapter 5: *U.S.-Based Netsourcing Case Studies*	Learn how netsourcing suppliers are providing customers with various services ranging from simple application access through to total business solutions with netsourcing as an embedded delivery option; the first five cases are U.S.-based: Corio, Host Analytics, EDS, MainPass, and Zland.	Learn how 10 suppliers are constantly adapting to changes in the emerging netsourcing space as customers become more savvy and demanding.
Chapter 6: *European-Based Netsourcing Case Studies*	Learn about five European-based suppliers and their customers: Lodge, marviQ, SAP, Siennax, and Vistorm.	
Chapter 7: *Mitigating and Managing Risks in Netsourcing Deals*	Understand how to mitigate and manage 15 netsourcing risks, demonstrated through a customer case history.	Understand the difference between *actual* risks experienced by netsourcing customers and the *perceived* risks of customers not ready to adopt netsourcing. The implication for suppliers is that educating the public continues to be a major requirement.
Chapter 8: *Netsourcing Drivers: Customer Decision Checklist*	Based on all the learning of previous chapters, this chapter presents the business, economic, technical, market, and relational drivers of netsourcing to help customers fully evaluate netsourcing.	Suppliers are given over 30 guidelines on how to deliver customer requirements.
Chapter 9: *Past, Present, and Future of Netsourcing*	Understand how, like any other new industry, netsourcing will evolve, and how to determine the right time of adoption for your company.	Understand how early "tough" customers are shaping the future of netsourcing. Their demands will require suppliers to alter their business models, including service offerings, pricing options, and contracting.

Thomas Kern has built a rich understanding of what makes relationships in outsourcing work in his five-year longitudinal study of major IT sourcing deals sponsored by Lloyd's of London, resulting in a D.Phil. at the University of Oxford. This research was published in late 2001 as *The Relationship Advantage: Information Technologies, Sourcing and Management* (Oxford University Press) and was coauthored with Leslie Willcocks. Thomas also draws upon three years of focused work on application service provision solutions and their strategic impact on customers, which led to a large-scale project on customer expectations sponsored by the European-based consultancy CMG Benelux. Thomas is currently CIO of KERN AG, an international company headquartered in Germany.

Mary Lacity and Leslie Willcocks are coauthors of some of the most referenced and widely read texts and papers in the IT outsourcing field. They are sought internationally for advisory work and speaker engagements. Before becoming an academic and professor, Mary worked in the IT industry as adviser and consultant, a role she actively continues with several major corporations and government institutions. In 2001, she and Leslie Willcocks published *Global Information Technology Outsourcing: In Search of Business Advantage* (Wiley), representing a state-of-the-art summation of IT outsourcing and their research study findings over 10 years. Leslie also has an international reputation for his work on IT outsourcing, e-business, and information management, having published 20 books and over 130 papers on these subjects. He also worked in management consulting for 12 years before taking up leading academic appointments, including Oxford University and most recently, Warwick University. Drawing on this expertise, all three of us are now busily engaged in advising client companies and supplier companies alike on their business, Internet, and outsourcing opportunities and options.

We have tested the many managerial tools, developed and refined in the heat of outsourcing developments over the last 10 years, against a new body of research in the netsourcing space, based on over a dozen detailed case studies (fully described in Chapters 5 and 6) and a major international survey of customers and potential customers (see Appendix A). This book represents the result of what has been an exhausting, but highly satisfying and rewarding year. Through our research, we have sought to make sense of the conflicting and confusing evidence being produced about an easily misunderstood, but on our evidence and analysis, highly important emerging market. It has been genuinely exciting to be in at the birth of some fundamental underlying changes in the marketplace and how technologies are going to be applied. These changes are as yet only just beginning to be understood, but their impact and significance are going to be truly considerable. Netsourcing is going to be a fundamental and lasting set of changes in the way in which business applications and services are delivered. Netsourcing alters the ways in which clients relate to IT service companies, the ways in which IT service companies will need to behave, and the sorts of offerings they will need to make to their customers. But if the idea is revolutionary in concept, we expect to see in practice a more evolutionary rollout than most forecasts have predicted.

ACKNOWLEDGMENTS

In the course of writing this book many people kindly contributed directly and indirectly, and it is here that we take the opportunity to heartily thank all of them for their help, insights, suggestions, and comments.

First, we would like to thank and acknowledge David Feeny, Director of the Oxford Institute of Information Management Templeton College, Oxford University, for his major contributions to the core capabilities model discussed in Chapter 3. In particular, David Feeny and Leslie Willcocks were the creators of the nine core IT capabilities model, which has been successfully adopted by several international organizations. David is a widely sought internationally known speaker and consultant on information strategy and management. His research on CEO and CIO relationships has won international awards. He has published widely, including the book *Manag-*

ing IT as a Strategic Resource (McGraw Hill, 1997) and articles in the *Harvard Business Review, Sloan Management Review, MIS Quarterly,* and *McKinsey Quarterly.*

Special thanks go to Ramses Zuiderwijk, who substantially contributed to Chapter 5 and the ASP Marketspace Report 2001 in Appendix A. His objective and often querying perspective on the complexity of the netsourcing approach led us to frequently re-evaluate our own judgments, opinions, and understanding. Thanks for a wonderful collaboration.

For financial support for this project, we wish to express our sincere gratitude to Dr. Wim J.M. Teunissen, Coos Keijser, Dr. Rob Labordus, Nico M. M. Waaijer, and Dr. ir. Peter Zuidema and all others at CMG Benelux who kindly championed the need for an in-depth ASP market study—the ASP Marketspace Report 2001. A special thanks, in particular, goes to Dr. Wim J.M. Teunissen for his continuing support, close cooperation, and kind friendship and humor throughout the research. Thank you also to the University of Missouri, with special appreciation to those who helped secure the UM Research Board grant—Dr. James Campbell, Dr. Marius Janson, Dr. Douglas Durand, Dr. Nasser Arshadi, and Dr. Douglas Wartzok.

Special thanks to all at Oxford Institute of Information Management—Pam, Jenny, Chris, David, Sue, Gerd—for making so much possible and for being such great colleagues, and to all at Templeton for making it the great working place it is. Also sincere thanks to the Vakgroep 1 at the Erasmus University Rotterdam, especially Prof. Jo van Nunnen, Prof. Han van Dissel, and Prof. Eric van Heck for their support and stimulating queries on the application service provision model.

We also wish to thank the visionaries of the netsourcing phenomenon, most notably Michael Corbett, Kevin Campbell, and Traver-Gruen Kennedy.

A huge debt is owed to the many participants we interviewed and surveyed. In particular, interview participants patiently endured our stream of questions and follow-up phone calls—Robb Early and Tom Schehr of EDS, Don Veenstra of Zland, Jim Eberlin of Host Analytics, Mike Spenser of Corio, Michiel Steltman and Pieter Bokelaar of Siennax, David

Edwards, Onno Schellekens, Chris Boule, and Robert Noteboom of marviQ, Olav Claassen of RealScale Technologies, Marten Dessers and Peter Lanting of SAP, Wouter Cortebeeck of Punch International, Corné Paalvast of Abz, and Hans Vets and Michel Demmenie of the Vision Web.

Finally, we wish to thank all the wonderful people at Prentice Hall. Tim Moore—you have been a thoroughly supportive editor, and we thank you for assigning so many resources to our project. Russ Hall, thank you for translating our academic diatribes into understandable English! We also wish to thank four anonymous reviewers for their suggestions, as well as Jane Bonnell, our production manager, and Kathleen Karcher, our permissions specialist. Our heartfelt thanks.

Finally, the most testing part of undertaking the research and writing the manuscript has been on family and loved ones. The value of their emotional strength, patience, and help over several years has been immense, and it is to them that we dedicate this book.

Thomas Kern

Mary C. Lacity

Leslie Willcocks

1

AN OVERVIEW
OF NETSOURCING

Netsourcing *is the practice of renting or "paying as*
you use" access to centrally managed business applications,
made available to multiple users from a shared facility over
the Internet or other networks via browser-enabled devices.
Netsourcing allows customers to receive business applications
as a service. Rather than purchase software directly from an
independent software vendor (ISV), customers may use netsourcing to access ISV applications such as personal productivity tools from Microsoft Office, e-mail/collaboration tools
such as Microsoft Exchange, Lotus Notes, Netscape Messenger,
and sophisticated enterprise resource planning packages from
Baan, Great Plains Software, Oracle, PeopleSoft, and SAP. Customers typically pay for the service with an installation fee and
a monthly subscription fee based on number of users, number
of transactions, or percentage of the value of the transactions.

The concept of delivering ISV business applications as a service—or *apps on tap*—was initially called application service provision (ASP). But that term has proved too narrow. Customers are also using netsourcing to hand over entire business processes to service providers, such as human resource management or accounting. In this scenario, access to ISV software to support these business processes is just one component of the total packaged service. In addition, customers are also using netsourcing to remotely host and manage customer-grown applications, reducing the expense and need for internal information technology (IT) resources. More broadly, then, *netsourcing can be viewed as an alternative delivery channel for business applications, services, and infrastructure provision.*

Early adopters are already netsourcing to validate credit cards, to send legal documents, to apply sales tax, to transfer funds, and to exchange currencies—just to name a few applications. Customers will have entire business processes netsourced, including front-end customer orders through to back-end processes such as payables, inventory, and commission compensation. Intercompany exchanges are also ideally suited for the netsourcing model, including supplier and customer matching, bidding, negotiations, and delivery.

Because of the variety of netsourcing options, one of the first tasks for potential customers is to better understand the products and services offered in this new market space. In this chapter we first categorize the types of netsourcing suppliers and the types of netsourced business applications. We outline 11 *general* benefits of netsourcing, called *value propositions to customers*. We also identify some *unique* value propositions of different service provider business models. But much of this information is based on supplier marketing—business managers considering netsourcing also want to know: Who is currently buying these services? Are early adopters satisfied with netsourcing? Is netsourcing just a fad or will the market grow substantially so that it cannot be ignored? As covered in this chapter, the answers to these questions all suggest that large and small organizations in both public and private sectors will adopt netsourcing within the next five years because the value proposition is so compelling. However, there are significant netsourcing risks to be mitigated. As for any other emerging business practices, business managers will have to learn the principles of sound netsourcing identified in this book.

NETSOURCING BY ANY OTHER NAME . . .

Potential customers are often perplexed by the proliferation of acronyms in the netsourcing space, including ASP, BSP, VSP, CSP, FSP, MSP, and SSP. Exasperated journalists have often given up on the nomenclature and more generally refer to the space as *xSP*. We have selected the term *netsourcing* as the overarching name, because the common element of any xSP is the delivery of a product or service over a network. Although there are no standard definitions for these xSP acronyms, we have placed them within a service stack based on the product or service, as shown in Figure 1.1.

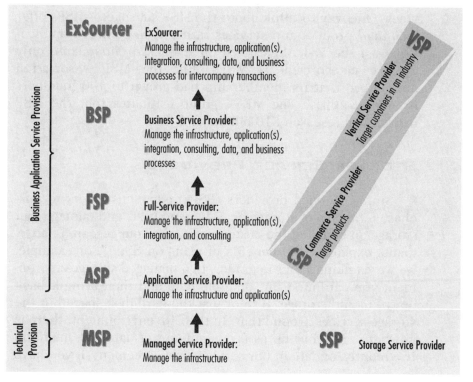

FIGURE 1.1 Mapping Netsourcing Options by Acronym

MANAGED SERVICE PROVIDERS

Managed service providers (MSPs) help customers manage their infrastructure, primarily by monitoring devices and network traffic for their clients. Larry Greenemeier, an Internet columnist, classifies an MSP as any company that provides monitoring services for network access, infrastructure, applications, storage, and security.[1] Typically, customers house their servers and workstations at their own locations, but the entire network may be monitored and managed from the MSP's remote network operation center. For example, Marconi Medical Systems in Cleveland, Ohio, uses the MSP Intellinet[2] to remotely monitor Marconi's wide area network (WAN), local area networks (LANs), and remote sites. Marconi's network includes 71 routers, 200 servers, and 1800 mobile users. Marconi pays Intellinet $3500 a month for the service.[3] Other MSP services could include high-speed Internet access, data and file backup, storage, and recovery services. One way to think about the MSP subspace—MSPs offer *technical* product and services rather than *business* applications. Of the 554 ASPs listed on *www.searchasp.com,* only 24 are categorized as MSPs. But the MSP Association announced that its membership had grown to 100 members by March 2001.[4] The META group estimates that the MSP market will research $10 billion by 2004.

STORAGE SERVICE PROVIDERS

Storage service providers (SSPs) allow customers to purchase terabytes of storage on a demand basis and manage that storage on behalf of the customers. One of our research participants explained the benefits of using an SSP: "For example, we were talking about upgrades. In a managed storage environment you can burst up some old data and then bring it back down. Liquid storage. It's not just the hard disk space but the storage services around that. In the ERP environment, there is nowhere to go but up as far as amount of data. We maintain two months of data in our service level agreement; if you have historical data you want to store, there is a data warehouse on-demand product to extract historical data." Thus SSPs and MSPs provide technical services primarily.

APPLICATION SERVICE PROVIDERS

Compared to the previous offerings, the primary product of an application service provider (ASP) is business applications, managed remotely by the ASP. Typically, ASPs do not even own their own data centers, but instead, lease servers from a third party such as Exodus. The ASP, however, serves as the central and primary interface between the customer and the application. ASPs may offer access to their own proprietary software and/or access to an ISV's software. ASPs may service primarily one application type (such as e-mail), or offer a full application portfolio, including enterprise resource planning, customer relationship management, and supply chain management software. In the embryonic stage of ASP, the one-to-many business model of vendors essentially prohibited any software customization. In the final chapter we explain how the ASP industry is moving toward customization to attract larger customers.

One example of an ASP is EasyLink Services (formerly called Mail.com). They offer e-mail and groupware services, including Microsoft Exchange, Novell GroupWise, and message delivery services such as EDI, telex, desktop fax, and broadcast. Their initial business model was to charge $5 per mailbox per month. The initial value proposition to the customer was cost savings because the average cost to license and support e-mail in-house was $100 per employee per month. Their business model has evolved over time. End customers now access e-mail free of charge, with EasyLink generating revenues from advertisements and direct promotions. In the corporate space, EasyLink provides full-service messaging solutions, groupware, firewall protection, virus protection, and content filtering capabilities for a monthly fee. They have been one of the first ASPs to attract large customers, including Chevron, Ford, General Electric, Mazda, Metropolitan Life, Siemens, Sunoco, and the U.S. Army. However, like many ASPs, EasyLink is still operating at losses and suffering a severe decline in stock price. When EasyLink was still Mail.com, the 52-week high for the stock price was $21 per share on March 28, 2000. The 52-week low was 41 cents per share on December 21, 2000, as reported on March 23, 2001.[5] Now trading on the NASDAQ under EASY, the 52-week low was 38 cents on June 21, 2001.

FULL-SERVICE PROVIDERS

Full-service providers (FSPs) manage infrastructure, applications, and services such as integration, consulting, implementation, and customization. Many FSPs are trying to differentiate themselves from merely hosting applications for customers by stressing their customer-care capabilities. In many cases, FSPs offer customer services via partnerships with consulting firms. Under this definition, Corio is an example of an FSP that hosts many ISV applications, such as PeopleSoft, SAP, and Siebel. Corio has a number of implementation partners, such as Cap Gemini/Ernst & Young, Cambridge Technology Partners, and eForce, to help customers implement solutions (see Chapter 5 for a case study of Corio).

Another example of a full-service provider is Host Analytics (see Chapter 5 for a detailed case study). This FSP does forecasting, budgeting, reporting, and analysis for strategic performance measurement, management, and planning. This includes customized reports, ad hoc reporting, and ongoing management and strategy support. This company's value proposition is to deliver business intelligence to smaller businesses comparable to larger corporations without investing hundreds of thousands of dollars in business intelligence technology. One FSP customer is Deloro Stellite, a St. Louis–based manufacturer of alloys and metal-related equipment. Host Analytics consolidates data from Deloro Stellite's manufacturing sites around the world, and creates and delivers the customized reports over a browser. The cost of hosting is $2000 per month.[6]

BUSINESS SERVICE PROVIDERS

Business service providers (BSPs) deliver entire business processes as a service by managing the infrastructure, applications, data, and processes associated with an entire business process. According to a research report on 304 multinational companies sponsored by PriceWaterhouseCoopers, the most commonly outsourced business functions were:

- Payroll (37%)
- Benefits management (33%)
- Real estate management (32%)
- Tax compliance (26%)
- Claims administration (24%)
- Applications process (21%)
- Human resources (19%)
- Internal auditing (19%)
- Sourcing/procurement (15%)
- Finance/accounting (12%)

But participants in the PriceWaterhouseCoopers study also identified several barriers to success, including:

- Organizational resistance (56%)
- Unclear performance measures (56%)
- Fear of the loss of control of the process (48%)
- Lack of prior outsourcing experience (43%)
- Lack of planning (42%)

Despite these obstacles, Input, Inc. estimated that the BSP market would assume one-fourth of the $2 trillion global outsourcing market by 2003.

Exult is an example of a BSP. Exult provides human resource management services, targeted at the entire human resources department for global 500 corporations. Exult delivers services via their Internet-enabled product, called eHR. Exult's eHR product, together with their comprehensive consulting services, enables the BSP to develop, refine, and implement HR best practices and realize lower HR costs for their clients. One of Exult's largest customers is BP Amoco, which signed a $600 million, five-year contract in December 1999. BP outsourced the administrative and IT burden, reserving for itself only "the things that require judgment and policy." The risks of such a big IT project—to standardize globally on and make accessible real-time human resource systems—were obvious. But BP's risk analysis concluded that project difficulties would not harm business directly and that the potential $2 billion reduction in operational costs associated with the venture warranted the risk. Other Exult customers include Unisys and Tenneco. Exult is one of the few players in this space that have enjoyed rising stock prices. Trading on the NASDAQ under EXLT, the 52-week high was $19.85 on June 27, 2001, while the 52-week low was $7 on July 5, 2000. But, by 2001, Exult was still not generating a profit (net loss of $94 million in 2000).

ExSOURCERS

A related evolution, enabled by developments in Web-based technologies and infrastructure, may well be what has been called *exSourcing*, here meaning "engaging a service provider to deliver and service business processes that connect external constituents with internal data and processes." As one example, firms needing back-end fulfillment to support their Web site could well go to such vendors like Ryder and FedEx, who will join hosted logistics applications with the logistics infrastructure and warehouses needed to fulfill orders, thus offering full services over the Net.

Another example of exSourcing is the Outsourcing Exchange provided by the Outsourcing Center. The Outsourcing Exchange is an Internet community where buyers and suppliers of both large and small companies can locate each other, post and respond to bids, and negotiate and award the buyer's work to the chosen supplier (see *www.outsourcing-exchange-center.com*). The Outsourcing Exchange is financed through annual registration fees from suppliers as well as success fees paid by winning suppliers based on the total contract value of a negotiated deal. Some sizable IT outsourcing deals have been made through the exchange, such as a $25 million CRM data warehouse project by a Canadian Bank. EDS won a $150 million deal in only 75 days from RFP to contract. Both customer and suppliers agree that the exchange shortens the purchasing life cycle and creates a level playing field. However, some suppliers are challenged to change their rules for sales compensation, which are usually based on region. In cyberspace, which region should get credit for the sale?

The term *vertical service provider* (VSP) has also been introduced in the media to describe ASPs targeting certain industries. The idea of VSP is to evolve the one-to-many business model toward a specific industry so that more requirements are met within the scope of parameter-driven software. The trend is also customer driven because customers want suppliers to provide customer references from their industry. A potential customer from an oil company may not be impressed by an ASP that has only dot.com customers—he or she wants to see industry-specific expertise.

Portera is an example of a VSP. Gary Steele, chief executive officer (CEO) of Portera, is vertically targeting the professional services market. Portera offers project collaboration, document sharing, Web meetings, as well as resource management and financial control to professional service firms such as consulting firms, advertising firms, or legal firms. Another VSP, Kliger-Weiss Infosystems (KWI), focuses on small to midsized retailers by hosting and providing access to data on cash registers, sales, and inventory. The CEO's family actually operates several Benetton stores, which provide a live laboratory for the KWI's systems and services.[7]

COMMERCE SERVICE PROVIDERS

Whereas VSPs focus on a particular industry, commerce service providers (CSPs) focus on a particular product. CSPs offer to manage online commerce operations from top to bottom. On some estimates the market will be $2.5 billion by 2003. Outsourcing retail operations could be attractive to midsized content sites looking to build a Web storefront and wanting to avoid the exposure from developing their own. The latter could, according to some estimates, cost between $2 million and $40 million plus another $2 million to $50 million in recurring costs. Between three and six technology partners would also be needed to build most sites. Enter the CSPs. The ideal range for these are sites that handle 50 to 250,000 transactions a year. Amazon would be too big and idiosyncratic, while AOL, for example, gets enough traffic to support expensive advertising sponsorships and affiliate programs. Within the midrange size, companies such as Escalate, Iconomy, CrossCommerce, and Vitessa are becoming store managers for businesses that are not solely e-tailers.

A CSP will manage every piece of the online store. This includes handling credit card transactions, order management, customer service through e-mail and call centers while keeping the Web site as the primary seller of goods, holding partial liability. A CSP will also help companies with merchandising and product sourcing, linking desired suppliers into the network, while further service can be e-fulfillment. CSPs will also help with customizing the commerce to the look and feel of their sites. Companies can choose which products to carry, design their own product catalog, set prices, suggest links, or develop a store with pictures and detailed descriptions.

CSPs also blend data analysis with CRM software. As one example, BellaOnline outsourced its retail operations to iSupplier and learned that 80% of sales were for goods between $20 and $25. iSupplier honed the company's catalog to fit with the pricing and product demands of its online audience.

The CSP revenue model depends on site complexity and volume. Providers tend to charge from $10,000 to $100,000 to set up the commerce operation. Further, they charge between $1000 and $100,000 a month for hosting and a 5 to 12% cut on product sales. Most CSPs launched online stores for their customers as late as 2000, and few have been forthcoming about their revenues.

Before CSPs, content companies that wanted to sell related products could build their own e-commerce engine or create a low-cost network of e-commerce affiliates selling through the same site. But some affiliates may be less than stable; there may be dilution of brand and loss of customer data. The rewards from the affiliate program may be small in terms of the percentage of overall revenue shared among members, and a company has no control over the pricing and products of other affiliates. Moreover, doing IT development work in-house often underestimates the amount of work involved.

An example of the alternative route is AutoMall.com, an auto shopping and resource site launched in August 2000 with the help of CrossCommerce. AutoMall needed to set up deals with distributors, project how much inventory to carry, and warehouse the product. Rather than build this capability in-house, Automall relied on its CSP, CrossCommerce. Automall also hoped that its CSP could move the company into selling books and accessories.

CSPs present a further twist in the e-outsourcing story. Although companies have been told to provide community, content, and commerce on the Web, the CSP model argues that if you are a content company, focus on that and outsource the commerce part. The model fits a certain size of content provider, although there were signs throughout 2001 of larger players becoming interested in this type of service. CSPs appeal to the logic of "focus on the core" inherent in outsourcing's attraction. However, an e-business using a CSP company must be prepared to surrender some control. For example, if a CSP mismanages an order, it is the Web site's brand that is damaged, not the CSP. There is also a trade-off between customization and cost; the more customization, the higher the price for the CSP service. Using a CSP does not avoid this trade-off dilemma, one that users also may experience.

NETSOURCING VIEWED AS A SERVICE STACK

Another commonly used framework to understand the netsourcing space is the service stack from an infrastructure perspective. Netsourcing can be viewed as a continuum of infrastructure services, beginning with connecting the customer to a network, through to hosting, application access, and application services. Service stack models help suppliers to position themselves in the netsourcing space, as well as to guide customers through the technical and business aspects of netsourcing. In Figure 1.2 we present our service stack from an infrastructure perspective, which contains the following five layers: network infrastructure, network services infrastructure, hosting infrastructure, application operations infrastructure, and application access. The service stack model immediately highlights that there are many ways to netsource. Customers may netsource only up to the hosting level, then manage their own applications, content, and business processes. Or the customer may look for a full-service provision, which includes all layers of the model. Because many novice customers feel unsure about what types of issues are involved in each layer, we have devoted Chapter 4 to defining all the technical issues associated with each level.

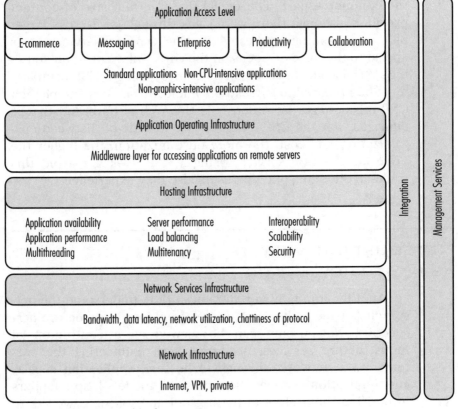

FIGURE 1.2 Service Stack Model: Infrastructure Perspective

It is also important for the reader to note that there are many variations of the service stack model besides our own. Table 1.1 contains service stack models from Oracle, Gartner Group, and IDC. In addition, EDS's service stack is presented in the EDS case study in Chapter 5.

To understand how the service stack can help suppliers position themselves in the market, we asked Mark Newton, branch manager at Oracle, to explain his view of Oracle's seven-level stack. For him, levels 1 through 3 represent hardware service provision, with only those companies operating in levels 6 and 7 being true business application service providers. According to this definition, an ASP is the organization that is on the hook for the customer's contract. Independent software vendors need to move quickly up the value chain by becoming ASPs themselves or by forming alliances with companies at that level. While those operating at levels 1 through 3 will form a vital provision, the interesting developments will be in the upper levels. Players in levels 6 and 7 are redefining types of market offerings and how best to deliver effectively to specific customer segments. Mark Newton suggests at least two overall markets at levels 6 and 7: as an application service provider, with a one-to-many relationship to small and medium-sized enterprises, or as a BSP aggregator offering a suite of customized capabilities and services to relatively few big corporations.

TABLE 1.1 Service Stack Models

ORACLE	GARTNER GROUP	IDC
Customized applications	Customer relationship, general contractor	Process execution
Standard applications	End services (integration, application management)	Process support
Management and support	Data center operations and hosting	Content
ISV applications	Applications and content	Applications
Hardware/infrastructure	Platform	Development environment
Colocation/hosting	Network	Systems infrastructure
Network		Network

However the netsourcing market develops, it is pretty clear that suppliers can use a service stack model to think through the ways to position themselves in the space

WHICH APPLICATIONS ARE CUSTOMERS NETSOURCING?

One of the ways in which the netsourcing space can be evaluated is by the types of applications being bought by early adopters. As of first quarter 2001, our online international survey (see Appendix A) found that the most commonly netsourced applications were e-mail and communications, personal productivity tools, customer relationship management, finance and accounting, human resource management, and business-to-business (B2B) e-commerce (see Figure 1.3). (E-commerce is actually the second most frequently purchased ASP application if the B2C (business-to-customer) and B2B results are combined.) Many people do not consider personal productivity or communication software as business applications, so these are not often listed in other surveys. But a study by IDC confirms our findings—60% of their respondents said they would probably use an ASP for collaborative services such as e-mail, groupware, document management, conferencing, and scheduling.[8]

In addition to our own survey work, a number of IT research and consulting firms are regularly monitoring the netsourcing space, including Forrester Research, Zona Research, Gartner Group, and the Yankee Group. They have found similar results. For example, Forrester Research identified the main netsourced applications as e-commerce, customer relationship management (CRM), manufacturing and logistics, finance and accounting, human resources, supply chain management, product development, and industry-specific applications. In February 2001, the ASP Consortium and Zona posted results of a survey of 137 U.S. senior IT professionals. They found that the most frequently purchased ASP services were communications applications (34% of respondents), finance/accounting (25%), e-commerce (21%), customer relationship management (19%), education/training

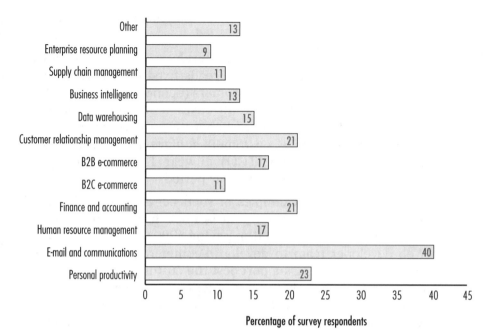

FIGURE 1.3 Most Commonly Netsourced Applications, First Quarter 2001

(18%), and human resources (13%). Applications such as e-commerce, CRM, and communications are ideally suited for hosting because they require unlimited access (ideal for Internet), are usually specifically written for Internet delivery (as opposed to delivering a client–server application over the Internet), and are usually not industry-specific. In the Zona study, less than 4% of respondents purchased ERP through an ASP. It is interesting to note that ASP spending patterns reflect overall application spending patterns. AMR Research estimates that ERP sales will increase annually by only 5%, whereas CRM will grow by 40% annually.[9]

WHAT IS THE PROMISED CUSTOMER VALUE OF NETSOURCING?

We have seen the types of suppliers and applications being offered in the netsourcing space, but what exactly is the value proposition to customers? In this section we introduce 11 general benefits promised to customers, which is explored more fully in Chapter 8 once readers are convinced to evaluate net-sourcing more closely.

1. *Lower total cost of ownership.* The cost is lower because the service provider spreads fixed infrastructure and software costs over many customers (economies of scale). In a Zona Research (2000) study of customers, this was cited as the most important expected benefit from netsourcing. Corio claims that on average, customers achieve a 70% reduction in total cost of ownership (TCO) in year 1, and a 30 to 50% reduction in TCO over a five-year period.

Two illustrative examples of such benefits being delivered are provided by Zland.com and USI.net. In the Zland case we found one manufacturing firm paying $200,000 to a two-person Web developer team to develop e-commerce and e-marketing capabilities. Ongoing support cost the customer $40,000 a year, representing primarily consulting fees. Zland.com demonstrated that they could provide the same functionality for a $10,000 set fee and a monthly subscription under $1000 (see the Zland case study in Chapter 5). In Table 1.2 the ASP USInternetworking compares the cost of a client's traditional application implementation with its actual USI billed costs. The main advantage from a TCO, then, would seem to be few or no upfront costs in software licenses, hardware, and implementation.

2. *Allows the customer to focus on core work.* We have seen this argument used for IT outsourcing generally. Packaged solutions was one move in this direction, but what netsourcing can achieve is a further move toward the commoditization of IT and its management, thus freeing up general employees as well as IT staff for more strategic activities.

3. *Scalability.* Another main advantage of netsourcing is that customers typically pay a monthly fee based on number of users or number of transactions. As such, some have called netsourcing a new "pricing model" because customers can adjust IT costs based on incremental increases or decreases in use. Customers can avoid capital investment costs when internal resources reach capacity, or avoid the expense of idle equipment if downsized.

TABLE 1.2 Traditional Implementation Costs versus USI-Hosted Costs

	TRADITIONAL IMPLEMENTATION COSTS	USI-HOSTED COSTS
LICENSE	$180,000	$0
HARDWARE	50,000	0
IMPLEMENTATION	480,000	0
INITIAL COSTS	710,000	0
OPERATIONS AND SUPPORT	20,000	
DISASTER RECOVERY	4,000	
BANDWIDTH	2,000	
MONTHLY COSTS	26,000	36,000

4. *Fewer in-house IT experts.* Fewer experts are needed because the service provider can spread expensive IT expertise over many customers. In addition to reducing a customer's internal IT head count, netsourcing can also provide skilled labor not otherwise available. Netsourcing providers can do this at a reasonable price because of economies of skill achievable by utilizing its staff over multiple clients. A service provider will also be more interested in keeping its staff's skills up to date and be able to provide a broader range of skills than most small and midsized enterprises (SME) could keep in-house. However, this advantage is not limited to SMEs. By 2001, even large organizations were experiencing problems retaining IT workers. For large organizations, however, the challenge is not the scarcity of IT people so much as the scarcity of specific skills. As one informant told us: "I was on the west coast with one of our existing large customers and I was asking this question about retaining skilled workers. They said they don't have this problem anymore because there is enough fallout from the dot coms. So they aren't struggling with the scarcity of people, but they are struggling with the specialization of skills."

5. *Faster implementation of business solutions.* With netsourcing, applications can be delivered in days or weeks rather than in months or years. For example, ERP and B2B exchanges are available much quicker via netsourcing than if they are installed as a customized solution within an organization. ERP may take between six months and two years on the latter process, whereas enterprise ASPs such as Corio and USI have been known to take 60 to 120 days. USI can also configure a PeopleSoft server with software in 4 labor hours versus 120 labor hours if done without an ASP solution. Such speed can be explained by the reduced degree of customization provided by the service provider but also by the fact that the service provider is placing the software on its own familiar hardware and is able to use software components across clients.

6. *Flexibility.* Because customers have less long-term commitment to hardware, software, and perhaps even suppliers, a TCO provides more flexibility. We have noted that the customer's total cost of ownership is reduced in part by investment avoidance. But investment avoidance also keeps the customer's options more flexible because they can easily switch hardware and software. Switching suppliers may be easier with netsourcing than with traditional outsourcing because contracts are typically shorter in duration and based on more commodity-type products and services.

7. *Provides bundled solutions.* The bundling of hardware, software, systems development, integration, infrastructure, and their management again simplifies the administrative and decision-making burdens traditionally associated with IT. In this sense the organization is buying not a product or a service but a bundled combination, which, following Shiv Mathur in his 1997 book *Creating Value*, we could call a *systems buy*.

8. *Provides powerful computing to geographically distributed organizations.* Customers may experience large managerial and technical challenges with mobile, dispersed workers. Netsourcing can simplify and centralize these issues, and provide technical solutions and access to a broad range of applications and computing power at a lower cost.

9. *Reduction of technical risks associated with a fast-growing business in times of rapid technological change.* Often, a customer will need to ramp up its use of IT considerably, and service providers can cushion the customer from the usual internal IT problems associated with the need for rapid adoption. Furthermore, service providers can take away the pain and cost of upgrading applications and keeping up with the technological trajectory as improvements and new technologies come onto the market.

10. *Transfer of ownership headaches and risks.* There are both financial and technological risks associated with IT, especially where the technology is unproven or is an existing technology in a new application to a specific organization. A service provider will reduce the investment risk, but also the technical risk, not least because it is easier to back out of a netsourcing arrangement if it fails technologically. Reducing such risks becomes particularly important where systems and application failure can have damaging consequences for the conduct of the client's business.

11. *Offers predictable level of IT expenditure.* Even where netsourcing does not turn out to be cheaper, large organizations may well be attracted to the stability of expenditure on IT offered by the rental model, especially where IT budgets are more typically volatile and future IT needs unpredictable.

Like all sourcing innovations, the promised benefits must be balanced against the risks. Netsourcing risks—at least as perceived by reticent potential customers in our international survey—include service quality, stability of service provider, security, reliability, and dependence on a third party. These risks, and how to mitigate them, are analyzed fully in Chapter 7.

WHAT OTHER VALUES DO NETSOURCING BUSINESS MODELS OFFER?

A business model is a service provider's plan for generating revenues based on adding enough value to attract customers while still earning a decent profit margin. Four business models are common in the netsourcing space: intermediaries, distribution channels, hosts, and portals. It is important for customers to understand a service provider's business model to assess the long-term viability of the supplier as well as the best sourcing options for their business needs. All four of these models promise the 11 customer benefits discussed previously. In addition to these common benefits, each of the four business models offers customers some unique benefits. Suppose, for example, that a customer needs an ERP system and has decided to netsource. Should the customer use an intermediary, go directly to the ISV's netsourcing subsidiary, purchase the software from the ISV and host it remotely with another service provider, or try netsourcing via a portal? The answer depends on a number of issues, such as whether the customer needs single or multiple applications, whether the customer is looking to avoid upfront software license fees, and whether one-stop shopping is important to them. Each of these four netsourcing business models is examined more closely below.

Service providers as intermediaries. In the netsourcing space, intermediaries host primarily third-party, best-of-breed ISV software and thus serve as retailers to ISVs (see Figure 1.4). Intermediaries can often provide a better deal to customers than if the customers purchased directly from an ISV. For example, the service provider Lodge (see Chapter 6 for a full case study) will refinance SAP licenses on behalf of customers, which allows customers to select a financing package to meet their needs, such as postponing any payments the first six months into the contract or paying fixed monthly fees.

Intermediaries may be *application specialists* by focusing on one type of application. For example, EasyLink (previously Mail.com) focuses on messaging applications and services. The additional value added to customers of application specialists

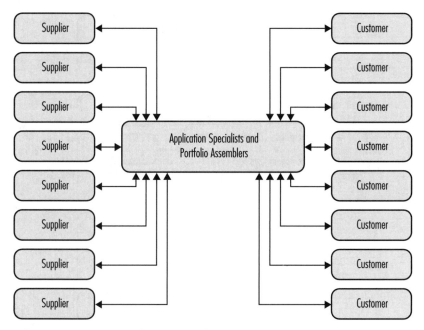

FIGURE 1.4 Netsourcing Provider as an Intermediary

is superior service because the service provider has focused expertise and resources on one type of application.

Intermediaries may be *portfolio assemblers* by offering several third-party, best-of-breed applications. Three widely known portfolio assemblers are Agiliti, Corio, and USI. The additional value added to customers of application assemblers is lower transaction and coordination costs because the customer has one-stop shopping for several applications and services rather than dealing with multiple ISVs.

Service providers as distribution channels. Many companies that write their own proprietary applications chose to deliver those applications to customers via an ASP channel (see Figure 1.5). The value added to the customer is direct access to a best-of-breed application with presumably superior technical support by the original architects, offered via a low-cost distribution channel. The value added to the supplier is that there are no payments to an intermediary.

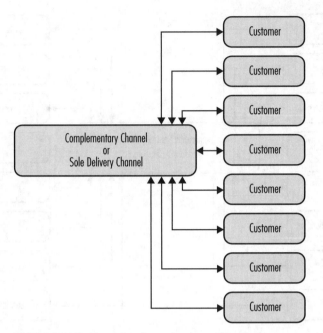

FIGURE 1.5 Netsourcing Provider as a Distribution Channel

The ISV may use the ASP as the only way that customers can access the software, or the ISV may use the ASP as a complementary channel to other distribution channels. In the case study chapters, you will see that Zland and Siennax are examples of ISVs that use ASP as their sole distribution channels. Most of the large ISVs, however, are developing multiple delivery channels, including an in-house ASP subsidiary. ISVs with in-house ASP channels include Oracle, PeopleSoft, SAP, and Great Plains. These companies also relicense to ASPs that act as intermediaries, as well as delivering through their own sales force, consulting businesses, and strategic partnerships. Multiple channels allow the ISV to market to large, midsized, and small firms across geographic regions and industries. Some people may question if the duplicate channels will cannibalize sales, but each channel adds different value to the customer. A customer may want to rent directly from PeopleSoft, for example, if that is the only application sought. But another customer may want PeopleSoft integrated with a customer relationship management package such as Siebel and therefore may prefer to rent both applications from an intermediary such as Corio.

Service providers as hosts. Some service providers host customer-owned applications, allowing the customer to avoid infrastructure investment and to reduce IT support personnel while accessing their own software (see Figure 1.6). For example, FutureLink hosts a customer's software provided that the application is MS Terminal Server or Citrix MetaFrame compliant. Microsoft certainly demonstrated its support in FutureLink's business model by investing $50 million in the company in the fourth quarter of 2000.

Probably one of the most widely known hosts is Exodus. Exodus offers Web-hosting services to 4500 customers and hosts over 62,000 servers worldwide. Many of Exodus's customers are actually ASPs that host their applications with Exodus to avoid building their own data centers, including Oracle Business Online. More traditional customers that host their

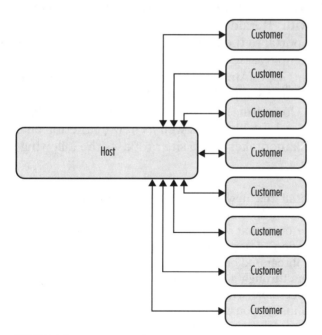

FIGURE 1.6 Netsourcing Provider as a Host

sites directly with Exodus include Lenox, Blue Cross/Blue Shield, L'Oreal, and U.S. News & World Report. Exodus reported 2000 revenues of $818 million, an increase of more than 300% from 1999 revenues. However, net losses were $256 million, primarily because of Exodus's heavy investment in new data centers. Consistent with the pattern seen in most ASPs, the stock price had fallen to a 52-week low of $1.18 per share on June 21, 2001 from a 52-week high of $69 on September 1, 2000. (Exodus trades on the NASDAQ under EXDS.)

Service providers as portals. Another netsourcing business model is the portal, which serves as a single point of accountability between multiple customers and multiple ASPs. The portal's added value includes one login and a single point of customer support for multiple applications (see Figure 1.7). The downside of the business model is that the portal does not typically have direct control over the service levels, although it is held accountable for them.

The most famous portal is Jamcracker, founded in 1999 by former Exodus Communications chairman K. B. Chandrasekhar, together with Herald Chen and Mark Terbeek. Jamcracker serves as a portal to the following ASPs: Connected, CriticalPath, diCarta, Employease, Entex, Icarian, iPass, Managemark, myCIO.com, OpenAir.com, OutPurchase, Talisma, UnitedMessaging, UpShot.com, USA.net, and WebEx. Accenture (formerly, Andersen Consulting) recently partnered with Jamcracker, which will lend credibility as well as new marketing channels to the portal. Jamcracker's Web site promises the following value to the customer:

> We test all the new web-based applications and services as they become available from a variety of partners, and offer only the ones that work best. We help you determine which combination of services is best suited to your needs. Everything is integrated onto a single platform and delivered to your end users through a simple, secure solutions delivery platform that's accessible with a single sign-on from anywhere in the world. Finally, you get continuous 24 × 7 support. Your end users get quick answers directly from us, by e-mail, phone, live online chat, or a service request placed through Jamcracker

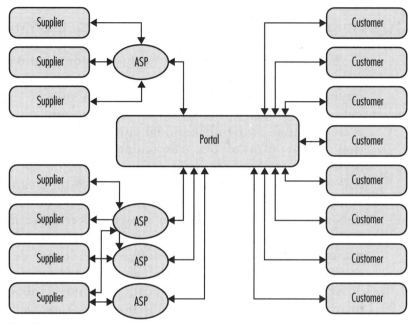

FIGURE 1.7 Netsourcing Provider as a Portal

Central. Your IT department, meanwhile, gets the time it needs to concentrate on more important things, like how to make your company even more efficient and profitable.

(Note that Jamcracker does not consider itself an ASP, but says: "We work closely with ASPs to integrate their services on our platform, offering our customers a broad range of different services.") During 2001, Jamcracker had about 40 active customers and was negotiating with another 40 potential customers. They actively seek companies with 300 to 5000 employees,[10] but, of course, know that their margins will be greater by selling to a few customers with many seats rather than selling to many customers with a few seats.

Another portal, Agiliti, decided to abandon this business model in 2001 because the market is not quite ready to purchase multiple applications from a single point of accountability. Instead, many customers instead prefer to test the waters by hosting one or two applications first before escalating their commitment.

CUSTOMER PERSPECTIVE: WHO'S BUYING?

So far we have seen the types of provisioning and applications typically offered in the netsourcing space. But who is buying? Most studies to date show that the netsourcing market has developed primarily around small to mid-sized enterprises (SMEs). Our international survey, for example, found that nearly 60% of our respondents generated revenues under $20 million per year (see Appendix A for details). SMEs are attracted to netsourcing because they can get big company solutions at small company prices. For example, a netsourcing provider might be a better alternative than the high up-front cost of a package software license. Although packages are a cheaper alternative to in-house developed solutions, it is still the case that many SMEs feel unable to cover the packaged solution costs. Second, a netsourcing provider can assist with IT skill shortages, especially in the development and software maintenance areas. SMEs may well be unable to attract, let alone retain and afford such IT staff. Third, packaged applications from e-mail to ERP and CRM require an established IT infrastructure and connectivity to ensure optimal performance. SMEs find it difficult to retrieve the necessary human and financial resources to support and continually develop such IT infrastructures. In particular, startup SMEs (e.g., dot coms) are attracted to the first generation of netsourcing, characterized by a one-to-many business model, because they have no entrenched infrastructure or business practices, making canned solutions easier to implement. Being new themselves, startup SMEs may also have more faith in the robustness of startup netsourcing suppliers. When you add in that SMEs are increasingly under pressure to become externally connected as extended enterprises, the advantage of an ASP-provided business Internet infrastructure becomes strikingly clear. (Of course, these and similar opportunities need to be weighed carefully against the potential drawbacks of a netsourcing solution.)

Netsourcing can survive in the long run, even if it remains an SME phenomenon because this market is potentially very large. Indeed, in the United States there are some 8 million businesses with fewer than 100 employees, while globally small businesses exceeded 40 million in number. Forrester Research has predicted that in 2004 over 90% of the ASP market revenues will be attributable to SMEs.

During 2000–2001 it was still the case that netsourcing generally did not appeal to large-company customers. Forrester Research found nearly three-fourths of large companies not outsourcing applications. A mix of the following reasons, in order of greatest citation, was given:

- *Software already in-house.* Basically, the customers have already made the investment.
- *Not cost-effective.* Customers have looked at the economics and found that they could still do it more cheaply.
- *Expertise in-house.* Customers could afford to retain their own IT staff.
- *Want to retain control.* Netsourcing was assessed as being risky given the importance of the applications.
- *Applications are business specific.* Customers perceive a lack of possible customization of netsourced applications.

Having talked with big companies and the suppliers targeting the big company market, our own view is that the large-organization market will pick up substantially over the next few years. Indeed, our international survey of netsourcing customers has already noted the presence of large customers in the ASP space. Over 30% of our respondents generate yearly revenues in excess of $500 million (see Appendix A). A study conducted in 2000 by the Phillips Group found that 19% of companies with 500 to 100,000 employees currently use an ASP. But more important, 65% of these companies said they plan to use an ASP for internal applications within the next five years, and 72% intend to use an ASP for e-commerce.[11]

Thus large companies are often the slowest to adopt innovations such as netsourcing, but eventually, they do adopt. For example, if we look back to the early 1990s, nearly all large companies initially rejected client–server applications because of their in-house mainframe capabilities. Eventually, the new applications that large customers wanted were written on client–server equipment, and the economics of delivery were often superior. In the end, nearly all Fortune 500 companies adopted client–server technology, even though many legacy systems still operate on mainframes. Thus although large companies may say that they will never adopt netsourcing, the more likely route will be a mixed-sourcing portfolio of in-house, outsourced, and netsourced. Some large companies (e.g., Monsanto) are already experimentally netsourcing for less critical tasks, such as image management. The trade press is also uncovering more Fortune 50 companies signing netsourcing contracts, such as DaimlerChrysler and Nestlé.[12] Other large companies will find that service providers can offer customized solutions because the size of their business can justify the supplier's investment in customization.

ARE EARLY ADOPTERS SATISFIED WITH NETSOURCING?

Very few surveys have been conducted of the early customer experience. Our online international survey is one of the few studies of early adopters. In our survey we asked respondents to indicate the overall performance of their netsourcing supplier using a 10-point Likert scale, with 0 or 1 indicating poor performance, 2 to 4 indicating satisfactory performance, 5 to 7 indicating good performance, and 8 to 10 indicating excellent performance. Thirty-two customers answered this question as of the first quarter of 2001. The mean response was 7.06, indicating a "good" performance rating overall (see Figure 1.8). The netsourcing performance rating is a little higher than we found for traditional IT outsourcing. Using the same scale, our prior survey on traditional IT outsourcing yielded a mean performance rating of 6.47 ($n = 113$).[13]

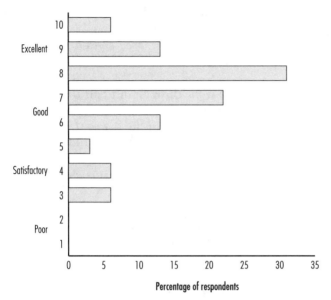

FIGURE 1.8 Customer Rating of Netsourcing Performance

However, this high performance rating does mean that ASP customers have not experienced problems with their service delivery. The two most frequently experienced problems were slow response time (41% of respondents) and application unavailability (25%) (see Figure 1.9). But only a small percentage of respondents experienced problems often cited in the press, such as lost sales or unanticipated costs, and no incidents of hacking were reported.

Early customers were also asked in the survey to share their most important lessons on netsourcing. Responses ranged from unbridled enthusiasm to strong caution:

> If it was available sooner, I would have done it sooner.
>> —*Customer buying services from a European telecommunications company*

> I can easily access everywhere I want . . . it saves me lots of time by not having to go to the office. We had no hard time installing software on my laptop. I only access via my browser, which always works. I always have access to information about

my customers. I don't need technical knowledge because they maintain the software and data for me.

  —Customer buying e-commerce software and services from a Dutch provider

In my ASP's case, we went through difficult times for quite a while through growing pains. I feel it is best for an ASP start-up to have sufficient capital from the get go. I had lost clients as a result of patches used until they acquired funds from an investor.

  —Customer buying Web hosting services from a U.S. provider

Some ASPs deliver bad quality, but it was a forced choice. Be objective when selecting an ASP. Don't buy their sales rap but compare services and ask for references from at least four other customers.

  —Customer using three ASP suppliers with varying success

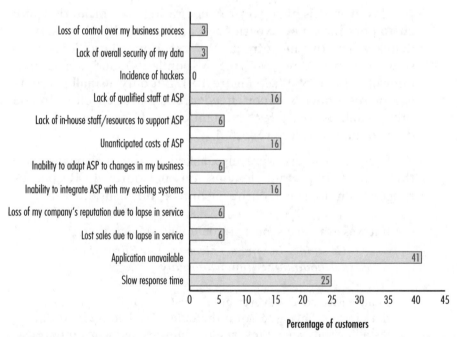

FIGURE 1.9 Customer Experiences with ASP

SUMMARY

The netsourcing value proposition to customers is compelling: no upfront investment costs in infrastructure or costly software licenses, faster delivery of applications (measured in days and weeks rather than months and years), scalable solutions that grow or contract with the customer's business, flexible solutions with minimal switching costs, and minimal expensive in-house support staff—to name a few. Given these benefits, who wouldn't want to netsource?

On the downside, *there are significant netsourcing risks that must be mitigated.* The netsourcing of business applications is still seen as an immature option primarily offered by unstable dot.com startups. Business managers worry about the reliability and security of the Internet, feel that their business requirements are too idiosyncratic for canned one-to-many solutions, and do not trust outsiders to supply mission critical systems. Many global 2000 companies initially rejected netsourcing on these grounds.

Despite these cautions, *our research has found that nearly all organizations—large and small in both the public and private sector—will netsource at least some of their business applications over the next five years.* Initially, netsourcing has appealed primarily to small and midsized enterprises (SMEs). The one-to-many business model offers SMEs low costs, little infrastructure investment, and rapid implementation. SMEs are willing to incur the downsides of the one-to-many model, such as lack of customization, to achieve these benefits. Moving to the global 2000—these customers will probably select noncritical, discrete business activities, such as document or image management, for their first netsourcing adoption. By "testing of the waters" in the netsourcing space, global 2000 players can gain the experience they need to exploit this option further. Global 2000 companies also have the clout to demand more services, customization, and integration from service suppliers than from SMEs. Thus the netsourcing model for these players will probably morph away from the one-to-many model. For the global 2000, however, netsourcing will probably always be viewed as merely one of the many sourcing options in their application portfolio.

Overall, research results on netsourcing are consistent with prior research on other IT management trends, such as IT outsourcing, business process reengineering, client–server technologies, and e-commerce strategies. Customer success depends on customer knowledge. Why are they adopting the trend? Are their expectations realistic? Have they evaluated the players properly? Did they mitigate the risks? Have they negotiated a clear, flexible agreement? Do they have internal capabilities to manage suppliers? As in any other new business practice, *business managers will have to learn how to net-source successfully.* Where does one begin? Throughout this book we provide business managers with tools to develop a sound sourcing strategy (of which netsourcing is merely one option), and to evaluate market options, mitigate risks, negotiate deals, and manage third-party suppliers. In Chapter 2 we step back inside the customer organization and describe the sound sourcing principles that serve as a precursor to a net-sourcing evaluation.

ENDNOTES

1. Larry Greenemeier, "Management Service Providers Mature," *www.PlanetIT.com*, November 8, 2000.

2. Intellinet also offers business intelligence and Web development services besides MSP services.

3. Michael Martin, "Early Users Give MSPs Thumbs Up," *Network World*, December 18, 2000.

4. Randy Scasny, "MSP Association Grows to 100 Members," *www.InternetNews.com*, March 12, 2001.

5. See *www.mail.com*'s Web site for product, service, and investor information.

6. Alan Jock, "Buying Biz Marts," *eWeek*, December 31, 2000.

7. Jennifer Hagendorf Follett, "Specializing Key to ASP's Future," *www.crn.com*, March 9, 2001.

8. Khali Henderson, "No E-Business Like C-Business," *www.a-cominteractive.com*, March 2001.

9. Julia King, "Forget ERP; IT Dollars Shift to Customer Applications," *www.computerworld.com*, June 5, 2000.

10. Edward Cone, "ASP Adjusts Customer Target," *Interactive Week*, on *www.zdnet.com*, February 19, 2001.

11. Eric Parizo, "Big Companies Will Be Big on ASPs," *www.searchasp.com*, September 20, 2000.

12. Ben Pring, "ASPs Finally Get Some Respect from the Big Boys," *www.asp-outsourcing.com*, January 2001.

13. For more details, see "Inside Information Technology Outsourcing: A State of the Art Report," by Mary Lacity and Leslie Willcocks, published by Oxford Institute of Information Technology. The report can be ordered by telephone to the UK 1865422515, by fax 1865422501, or by e-mail *Dave.Hall@templeton.oxford.ac.uk*.

CHAPTER 2

Principles for Effective Sourcing Decisions

2

When new IT or IT-enabled business practices are introduced, many decision makers seem to experience euphoria *and* amnesia. They are euphoric about the promise of a new solution but often forget to apply the sound management principles they have learned in the past to the new business practice. In the netsourcing context, we have seen customers sign very flimsy contracts with ASPs for their strategic e-commerce applications, yet they often sign very detailed contracts with traditional suppliers for routine data center management. We have seen customers select a netsourcing supplier based on a salesperson's pitch, yet those same customers regularly use rigorous and competitive bidding for traditional outsourcing. Much of the amnesia may be attributed to our culture's implicit belief in a technological utopia. Although experience constantly reinforces that new technologies and business practice cycle through early hype, rapid adoption, discovery of pitfalls, and reasoned maturity, we often forget history in the passion of the moment for the latest new, new thing. The overall message of this chapter, therefore, is that the sound principles behind sourcing have not changed with the emergence of netsourcing.

At this point it is important to distinguish between the sourcing of information technology (IT) and the sourcing of IT-enabled business applications. The sourcing of IT focuses on the ownership and management of underlying infrastructure activities, such as data-center operations, telecommunications, networks, and desktops. In short, the sourcing of IT provides *access*. In traditional outsourcing, the supplier often purchased the customer's infrastructure resources, often consolidated and standardized those resources, then delivered those resources back to the customer at a fixed unit price. Certain netsourcing options, such as MSP, SSP, and even ASP, address primarily the same infrastructure issues as traditional outsourcing—those of access. But rather than transfer customer resources to the supplier, the customer merely accesses the supplier's existing infrastructure, piggybacked on the Internet or other networks.

If IT provides *access*, the next question is: Access to *what*? Business applications encompass critical domain knowledge regarding specific business activities such as financial accounting, human resource management, inventory control, sales compensation, and procurement. In short, IT-enabled business applications are the *what*. Increasingly, these business activities are highly integrated and dependent on information technology, particularly on large packaged software products such as SAP, i2, and Siebel—thus the phrase *IT-enabled*. The outsourcing of IT-enabled business processes is a much trickier affair than the outsourcing of IT infrastructure. Customers have many more issues to consider, such as the extent to which their business applications contribute to competitive positioning versus competitive parity, the extent to which their business practices are or should be idiosyncratic versus standard, and the extent to which customer skills shortages are in a particular package (such as SAP) versus skills shortages in customer-specific knowledge. As you will see, netsourcing does not eliminate these strategic issues, it merely adds another option to the business manager's decision.

Four General Sourcing Options

An important lesson of this chapter is that *netsourcing* will earn its place among other feasible sourcing options, such as *insourcing* (use of internal resources and internal management), *buying* resources to run under in-house control (external resources and internal management), and *traditional outsourcing* (supplier-owned and supplier-managed resources in a one-to-one business model). In this context, netsourcing is the use of supplier-owned resources in a one-to-many business model; whether the supplier or customer manages the data content and business processes depends on which xSP model the customer adopts. See Table 2.1 for general sourcing options.

TABLE 2.1   Four General Sourcing Options for IT and IT-Enabled Business Applications

OPTION	RESOURCE OWNERSHIP[a]	RESOURCE MANAGEMENT	CUSTOMER–SUPPLIER RELATIONSHIP
INSOURCING	Customer	Customer	Not applicable
BUY-IN	Supplier	Customer	One-to-one
TRADITIONAL OUTSOURCING	Supplier	Supplier (with customer oversight)	One-to-one
NETSOURCING	Supplier	Varies depending on xSP	One-to-many

a. Infrastructure and headcount.

THREE PATHS OF OUTSOURCING

During the past 10 years of research, we discovered a rich picture of organizations taking one of three main paths to outsourcing IT and IT-enabled applications: (1) selective outsourcing, (2) total outsourcing of a necessary noncore IT function, or (3) total outsourcing of a strategic function through creation of a new business venture (see Table 2.2).

IN-HOUSE COMMITMENT

Many organizations have no significant IT outsourcing contracts (United States, 10%; United Kingdom 23%).[1] Here IT is perceived as a core strategic asset, with IT employees loyal to the business and striving to achieve business value in a way in which external providers are deemed not to be able to do. Or in some instances, total in-house commitment is based on historical precedent, entrenched labor unions, or other barriers to outsourcing. The risks of a mainly in-house function are that the service can become unresponsive and costs may escalate. To mediate these risks, business managers should continually evaluate market options to create an environment of competition. Netsourcing may be a feasible first option to examine given its low barriers to entry.

TABLE 2.2 IT Sourcing: Main Approaches

	IN-HOUSE COMMITMENT	TRADITIONAL AND NETSOURCING OPTIONS		
		SELECTIVE SOURCING	TOTAL OUTSOURCING	
ATTITUDE	Core strategic asset	Mixed portfolio	Necessary noncore cost	World class provision
PROVIDERS	IT employees loyal to the business	Horses for courses	Supplier	Strategic partner
EMPHASIS	Value focus	Value for money	Money	Added value?
DANGERS	High cost, insular, unresponsive	Management overhead	Exploitation by suppliers	Unbalanced risk/reward/ innovation

SELECTIVE SOURCING

By far the dominant sourcing mode is selective sourcing, especially in the United States (82% of organizations) and the United Kingdom (75%). Similarly, in the context of netsourcing, selective sourcing will probably be the most optimal route at first. A mixed-portfolio, "best source" approach typically sees 15 to 30% of the IT budget under third-party management, with other IT needs met through buying in resources under in-house management and through internal IT staffing.

One common underestimated factor of selective sourcing is the management overhead cost of IT outsourcing. This needs to be borne in mind when netsourcing is under consideration. After reviewing more than 250 case histories, we estimate this cost to be typically between 4 and 8% of total outsourcing costs.

TOTAL OUTSOURCING OF NECESSARY NONCORE COST

Outsourcing megadeals, for example those at Xerox, McDonnell-Douglas (now Boeing), and Continental Bank in the United States; Commonwealth Bank, Lend Lease Corporation, and South Australia government in Australia; and British Aerospace, British Petroleum, and Inland Revenue in the United Kingdom have received the most public attention. One could be forgiven for believing this type of total outsourcing of a noncore function to be the dominant trend. But total outsourcing (80% or more of the IT budget under third-party management to single or multiple suppliers) is a distinctly minority pursuit. In the United States some 8% of organizations took this route in 2000, in the United Kingdom about 2%; worldwide there are just over 140 such deals. Because most of these total outsourcing deals are of a necessary noncore cost type, a major driving force of these deals was cost reduction. We have found that total outsourcing deals focusing primarily on cost reduction can achieve such reduction, but sometimes at the expense of IT operational service and strategic inflexibilities. Alternatively, incomplete contracts or negligible profit margins through overtight contracts can promote hidden costs or opportunistic supplier behavior, or even come close to driving some suppliers out of business. Many of these relationships have experienced significant restructuring within a period of 18 to 24 months.

There arc very few netsourcing assemblers who could provide total netsourcing solutions at this stage. As you will see in the case studies, Corio and EDS are two examples of suppliers offering total solutions. As the market matures, more supplier options will be available, but obviously a total netsourcing strategy requires significantly more risk mitigation than selective netsourcing.

TOTAL OUTSOURCING
OF A WORLD-CLASS PROVISION
VIA AN EXTERNAL VENTURE

Although this too is a minority pursuit, external ventures have captured the attention of CEOs because of their strategic appeal. The initial intent is for the supplier not only to provide IT services to the customer, but for the IT supplier to generate and share revenues with the customer by selling the joint partnership's products and services to external clients. For example, in 1996, Swiss Bank signed a 25-year outsourcing deal with Perot Systems worth $6.25 billion. The partners planned to sell client–server solutions to the banking industry. Delta Airlines and AT&T(NCR) formed TransQuest to provide IT solutions to the airline/travel industry. In Australia, Lend Lease took a 35% holding share in ISSC Australia. Telstra (Australia's telecommunications company) signed a $2.9 billion contract and took a 26% stake in a new joint venture with IBM, Advantra, for network services. Commonwealth Bank of Australia and EDS signed a 10-year contract worth $3.8 billion in 1997. Commonwealth Bank paid $130 million for a 35% stake in EDS Australia. The deal was supposed to concentrate more on generating revenues than on cost reduction.

Tracking these deals over time indicates some failures with the equity model. In 1996, the Delta/AT&T joint venture was terminated. In 1997, the Swiss Bank/Perot Systems partnership was whittled down from 25 years to 10 years, from $6.25 billion to $2.5 billion, and Swiss Bank's investment in Perot Systems dropped from 26% to 15%. In 2000, the Telstra–IBM arrangement was also in the process of being revised radically.

The high hopes for external sales and joint profits were replaced with the realities of firefighting and understaffing. Strategically, the supplier argues that it is in both companies' interests that they focus on generating new business and profits; operationally, adverse impact of this finds customer users and contract managers complaining of poor service and loss of good supplier staff to new contracts. Bob Falthrop of supplier Logica argues that because the venture's primary customer is also an owner, there is an inherent conflict of interest in joint-equity deals. The customer has two competing goals: to maximize cost-efficient service delivery from the joint venture and to maximize the revenue of the joint venture. How can the party play the role of both customer and investor?

Joint ventures can work, but they must be based on a truly world-class provision. The Sabre reservation system is often cited as an example of a successful venture. The EDS spin-off from General Motors is another example.

The joint venture lessons are directly applicable to net-sourcing—many customers are being approached not only to become a provider's customer, but to invest in the venture. Some customers have decided to launch their own netsourcing companies. For example, Chevron started several netsourcing businesses, including Petrocosm, Upstreaminfo.com, and the Retailers Market Exchange. General Motors started Covisint and Project Emerald. The ideas are to isolate these netsourcing startups from the bureaucracy of established organizations, to provide some venture capital, to use company contacts and name-brand trust to attract more investors, to be the first customer, and to share in future revenue generation. Just like the challenges in such joint ventures discussed above with traditional outsourcing, some of these netsourcing ventures have already led to failure due to an inability to attract other customers and other investors. Petrocosm, for example, folded in

2001 when it couldn't find additional investors, even though 30,000 suppliers had put their catalogs on the Web site.

In summary, the routes to traditional outsourcing and net-sourcing are the same, which indicates that business managers can apply the lessons from traditional outsourcing to the new netsourcing options.

USING EXTERNAL IT SERVICES: THE TRACK RECORD

Too much of the discussion of the outsourcing track record is based on the opinions of interested parties, often arrived at before the ink on contracts is dry, or on research conducted without rigorous outcome metrics against which to assess the efficacy of IT sourcing arrangements. In Chapter 1 we found that in the netsourcing space overall, customers rated net-sourcing suppliers as providing a "good service." But this report card is based on a small sample of enthusiastic early adopters. It is also prudent to examine the immense evidence of performance in the traditional outsourcing market.

Here we present two sources of evidence that compare actual practices adopted against outcomes. The first is a case history research database of over 100 organizations assembled and studied across the 1990–2001 period. The second source of evidence is four European and U.S. IT/ASP outsourcing surveys carried out in 1994, 1997, 2000, and 2001.[2] This ongoing research base enables us to pinpoint the circumstances in which different IT sourcing practices can be effective or can contribute to disappointed expectations.

One of the first lessons to note from case histories is that outsourcing success rates have improved significantly over time (see Table 2.3).[3] This once again highlights that the adoption of new practices progresses from early enthusiasm, disappointments, and then reasoned maturity. Netsourcing lessons based on a significant track record of traditional outsourcing will be more robust than merely relying on lessons from early netsourcing adopters. By integrating lessons from both, business managers will have more confidence in the netsourcing prescriptions presented throughout this book.

TABLE 2.3 Outsourcing Success and Failure Rates over Time

Year Decision Was Made	Yes, Most Expectations Met	No, Most Expectations Not Met	Mixed Results	Total
1984–1991	14 (48.3%)	12 (41.4%)	3 (10.3%)	29
1992–1998	41 (73.2%)	8 (14.3%)	7 (12.5%)	56
Total Number of Decisions	55 (64.7%)	20 (23.5%)	10 (11.8%)	85

SOURCE: Lacity and Willcocks (2001)

First, surveys of traditional outsourcing found that 56% of U.S. and European organizations rated supplier performance as good or better. Many respondents were realizing benefits, primarily some mix of cost reduction (52%), refocusing of in-house IT staff (45%), improved IT flexibility (42%), access to scarce IT resources (42%), better quality service (41%), and improved use of IT resource (39%). The majority of respondents characterized problems/issues as minor, but some customers were having severe or difficult problems in some areas. Some qualifications are necessary, however. It is important to recognize that these results are positively conditioned by three characteristics of respondent practice: the vast majority pursue the selective IT outsourcing option; most use multiple suppliers, most have short-term contracts (four years or less in length), and respondents generally targeted infrastructure activities, mainly mainframe operations, PC support, help desk, network management, midrange operations, and disaster recovery. The least commonly outsourced IT activities involved IT management and IT-enabled business applications: in particular, IT strategy, procurement, systems architecture, systems analysis, and project management. Our conclusion has been that these are dominant practices, because they represent lower-risk approaches to using external IT services. Alternative decisions can be made, but additional, suitable risk mitigation practices will need to be adopted if the arrangements are to work.

The 79% of organizations using multiple suppliers pointed to several main advantages: the use of best-of-breed providers, risk mediation, and supplier motivation through competition. They also pointed to higher transaction costs and hidden post-contract management overhead in terms of time, effort, and expense. Multisourcing can also be disguised in the form of subcontracting. In some large-scale contracts, up to 30 to 35% of the work is actually subcontracted to other suppliers, especially in the areas of technical consulting, desktop hardware and installation, network specialists, and software specialists.

In traditional outsourcing arrangements, there was a noticeable negative gap between anticipated and actual benefits. In most cases, organizations were getting benefits but invariably less than they had expected. Only 16% reported significant cost reduction, another 37% reported some cost reduction. More worryingly, a number of organizations encountered severe or difficult problems in six areas as a consequence of outsourcing IT.

1. *Strategic:* supplier does not understand our business (37%); corporate strategy and IT no longer aligned (35%); poor strategic IT planning (24%)
2. *Cost:* costs for additional services (38%); cost escalation due to loopholes (31%); cost monitoring/control (27%)
3. *Managerial:* poor supplier staffing (43%); managerial skills shortage (28%); in-house staff resistance (26%)
4. *Operational:* defining service levels (41%); lack of supplier responsiveness (38%); getting suppliers to work together (35%)
5. *Contractual/legal:* too loose (41%); contract monitoring (41%); inadequate service-level agreements (35%)
6. *Technical:* suppliers' IT skills shortage (33%); outsourcing led to systems duplication (20%); failure to upgrade IT (17%)

These outcomes provide a fairly detailed worry list and preemptive agenda for action for any senior managers contemplating netsourcing. The results of the 116 case histories of IT sourcing are shown in Table 2.4.

TABLE 2.4 IT Sourcing Decisions and Outcomes [a]

DECISION	SUCCESS	FAILURE	MIXED RESULTS	UNABLE TO DETERMINE/TOO EARLY TO TELL	TOTAL
TOTAL OUTSOURCING	11 (38%)	10 (35%)	8 (27%)	4	33
TOTAL IN-HOUSE SOURCING	13 (76%)	4 (24%)	0 (0%)	2	19
SELECTIVE OUTSOURCING	43 (77%)	11 (20%)	2 (3%)	8	64
TOTAL	67	25	10	14	116

a. *The success measure used to assess the outcomes of 116 IT sourcing case histories across the 1991–2000 period were: organizational objectives against results, actual cost reductions achieved against those anticipated, and satisfaction levels established by the organization by, for example, user satisfaction questionnaires, level of disputes, or invoking of penalty clauses.*

Selective IT outsourcing emerged as the most effective practice, closely followed by the in-house route. Successful selective outsourcers embraced several distinctive practices. They had more limited and realistic expectations, signed short (two- to four-year) contracts for which the business and technical requirements remained relatively stable, kept in-house resource and knowledge to fall back on, resulting in less power asymmetry and lower potential switching costs, often leveraged competition through using multiple suppliers, and found ways to motivate suppliers through creative contracting.

The track record of total in-house IT sourcing has improved from that before 1996.[4] At that time, one-third were found to be unsuccessful due to an amalgam of in-house complacency, little sense of crisis, lack of external benchmarking, and lack of threat from an external supplier outsourcing bid. The evidence suggests that in-house functions have been responding actively to marketplace developments in the last six years and have been seeking to improve IT management, replicate supplier practices in-house, compete with potential supplier bids, and benchmark performance against market developments.

Total outsourcing emerges as a distinctly high-risk practice, a reason that most organizations have not been going down that route. As Table 2.4 shows, outcomes from 33 of the 140 or so biggest IT outsourcing deals in the world show a 35% failure rate. Unsuccessful deals shared certain characteristics. Virtually all sought primarily cost reduction. The organizations were in financial trouble and saw total IT outsourcing as a financial package to improve their company's position rather than as a way of leveraging IT for business value and keeping control of their IT destiny. All were 10- to 12-year single-supplier deals, initiated by the company board with little IT management input. The unsuccessful client organizations saw IT as an undifferentiated commodity, contracted incompletely, and failed to keep enough requisite in-house management capability. They incurred significant hidden costs, degradation of service, power asymmetries developing in favor of suppliers, and loss of control over their IT destiny. They did little to build and sustain client–supplier relationships, yet were reluctant to change suppliers because of the high switching costs.

The interesting group in Table 2.4 is that with mixed results. Typically, these are experiencing some success in one part of the deal, but little success in other major parts. Thus one U.S. aerospace company signed a $3 billion long-term contract, received a cash influx of $300 million, and transferred 1500 IT employees to the supplier. The infrastructure part of the contract was well managed, but some other sections had to be canceled after the first year. Subsequently, the supplier was found to lack idiosyncratic business knowledge needed for designing and running engineering-based systems. Serious service and cost issues continued to plague parts of supplier performance.

Success in total IT outsourcing has taken a variety of routes. It requires a lot of management maturity and experience of IT outsourcing, as exemplified by BP Exploration in the early 1990s. It needs complete and creative contracting; a shorter-term focus in the contracting arrangements, a longer-term focus in the relationship dimension, and very active and fully staffed postcontract management along the lines suggested in Chapter 3. Among the successes shown in Table 2.4, several were total-outsourcing long-term deals for IT infrastructure/mainframe operations. One involved a strategic alliance, where the company spun off its entire IT function in a shared risk/reward and joint-ownership joint venture with a software and services supplier. One involved a short-term contract to wind down a public-sector agency about to be privatized. Several went down the multiple-supplier five- to seven-year contract route, while several were single-supplier deals that took onboard the prescriptions noted above, had detailed contracts, and were also high profile, with the suppliers wary of adverse publicity in specific countries or markets.

CASE ILLUSTRATION: UNITED AIRLINES AND TIME TO MARKET

United Airlines (UA) has an annual IT budget of over $550 million and some 1500 IT staff. In 1999 it wanted to give its 28 million frequent flyers the ability to redeem mileage for free flights, to check account status, and to receive other third-party travel discounts. It outsourced this e-development due to issues of time to market and lack of internal capability. Internal Travel Network, in which UA had shares, was hired to develop advanced flight booking and to run the UA infrastructure and back-end systems. This involved creating a transaction server, based on BEA Systems' Tuxedo, running on an HP-UX server, linked to UA's Mileage Plus database running at the time on an MVS version of IBM's DB2 database.

The consulting firm Sapient was also hired to develop e-commerce software and to add navigation features to the online reservation system. This was launched in mid-1999. UA worked with Sapient on these developments, including on software that integrated customer profiles with tools that let users choose seats, rental cars, and hotels. The yearly results were promising, with a 25% increase in the number of Mileage Plus passengers accessing the site each month of operation. The site was designed to generate more sales through its travel discounts and reservations capability. By 2000 over 5% of UA's sales were through the online channel, and UA planned to make this 20% by 2002.

Learning points:

- Even large organizations with large numbers of IT staff increasingly find it necessary to use external partners to develop systems, in order to get the systems implemented quickly and due to lack of appropriate internal resources. For UA it resulted in an enhancement of its competitive position and a doubling of online sales in a year.
- UA took a selective, best-of-breed approach, choosing one supplier for infrastructure and another for the e-commerce software and front-end systems.
- UA made sure that it was heavily involved in the projects, an important feature of effective e-development projects.

MANAGING SUCCESSFUL SOURCING DECISIONS

Successful organizations carefully select which IT and IT-enabled activities to outsource, rigorously evaluate suppliers, tailor the terms of the contract, and manage the supplier carefully. We created a set of frameworks for thinking through sourcing decisions for IT and IT-enabled business applications, such as e-business projects. These frameworks embody a logic of first clarifying the sourcing options, then considering the critical business, cost, market capability, and technical factors influencing the effectiveness of sourcing decisions.

Concerning sourcing options, there are five distinct ways to contract with external service providers:

1. *Buy-in contract.* Companies buy and manage supplier resources to meet a temporary resource need, such as the need for programmers in the latter stages of a new development project. In these cases, companies are often unsure of the exact hours needed to complete the coding, so they sign contracts that specify the skills required and per day cost per person.

2. *Fee-for-service contract.* The supplier becomes responsible for managing and delivering the results of activities. This strategy is most successful when the companies can clearly define their needs in a detailed contract. Netsourcing providers initially tend to fall into this category but may well develop as a service preferred supplier or preferred contractor.

3. *Preferred supplier contract.* A company develops a close relationship with a supplier in order to access their resources for ongoing activities. The relationship is managed with an incentive-based contract that defines complementary goals. For example, one company engaged a preferred supplier to provide contract programmers whenever they were needed. The contract ensured complementary goals—the participant received a volume discount in exchange for not going out to tender when programmers were needed. The supplier was motivated to perform because they relied on a steady stream of revenue.

4. *Preferred contractor/strategic alliance.* Companies intend to engage in a long-term relationship with a supplier to help mediate risk. The supplier is responsible for the management and delivery of activities. To ensure supplier performance, the company tries to construct an incentive-based contract that ensures shared goals. The focus is on servicing the internal client.

5. *Strategic partnership/joint venture.* This is a joint venture in which the customer and supplier believe they have world-class capabilities to attract external customers. The customer and supplier create an inde-

pendent entity with shared risks and rewards, typically via joint equity ownership. The focus is on servicing external clients.

There remains the *in-house* arrangement. This option plays a critical role even when organizations were spending over 80% of the IT budget on contracting out or on preferred contractors. As you will see in Chapter 3, all forms of contract run larger risks if certain capabilities are not retained in-house.

BUSINESS IMPERATIVES

Selecting which activities to outsource and which to retain in-house requires treating IT and IT-enabled business processes as a portfolio. Successful sourcing begins with an analysis of the business contribution of various activities. Conventional wisdom has it that *commodity functions*, such as payroll or data center operations, are potential outsourcing fodder, whereas *strategic functions*, such as online reservation systems, should be retained in-house. This delineation is too simplistic. Companies that succeed consistently in their selection of what can be outsourced to advantage use a richer vocabulary. They distinguish between two ideas: the contribution that an activity can make to business operations and its impact on competitive positioning. The business factors matrix shown in Figure 2.1 helps managers to determine how these two business factors drive sourcing decisions. The following four categories of potential outsourcing candidates emerge.

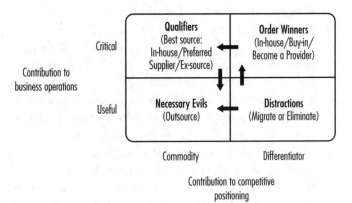

FIGURE 2.1 Strategic IT Sourcing Analysis by Business Considerations. From Willcocks (2000).

Critical differentiators: activities that are not only critical to business operations but also help to distinguish the business from its competitors. For example, a European ferry company considered its reservation and check-in systems to be critical differentiators and order winners (see Figure 2.1). The company had ships similar to those of its main rival and operated them from the same major ports across the channel between Britain and France. Its competitive strategy was to differentiate through improved services, including the speed and ease with which passengers and their cars completed the boarding process. It was constantly making innovations in this respect, and the systems were instrumental in achieving this. Although the company outsourced a number of its IT activities, the reservation and check-in systems were retained in-house, although the company was willing to buy-in expertise in short supply to support the in-house operation. This protected their ideas, expertise, and continuing ability to innovate rapidly.

Companies with critical differentiators would probably not outsource to a third party, but they might consider offering their critical differentiator as an outsourcing service to others. The revenues generated from selling a critical differentiator may be more than the revenues generated from attracting extra customers by keeping it in-house. The classic example here is always Sabre, American Airlines' reservation system. Of course, becoming a netsourcing provider would be one rapid way to distribute the critical differentiator to a wider market. For example, Sabre founded the netsourcing company Travelocity.com to expand Sabre to end customers. But many customers' critical differentiators cannot be turned into an independent, commercial product or service unless the customer is willing to invest up to 10 times the initial investment cost. Many customers will also need strategic partnerships to bolster skills in marketing and sales.

Critical commodities: activities that are critical to business operations but fail to distinguish the business from its competitors. A major British airline views its IT systems that support aircraft maintenance as critical commodities (whereas its yield management system for seat reservations is deemed a critical differentiator). Like its rivals, the airline must maintain its fleet to specification or face very serious consequences. However, the maintenance activity and supporting systems respond to the mandated requirements of the manufacturers and regulatory authorities. The IT activities are qualifiers in that they provide competitive parity. Qualifiers fulfill minimum entry requirements to compete in the sector, but no benefits accrue from overperformance. Although the airline has not yet outsourced these systems, it is in principle prepared to do so. Because of the risks involved for the business, such a decision would be based on clear evidence that an external supplier could meet stringent requirements for quality and responsiveness, as well as offer a low price. The policy is to "best-source" not to "cheapest-source."

Increasingly, competitors within an industry are realizing that each corporation is spending a significant amount of resources on critical commodities. Because critical commodities do not serve to differentiate competitors, there are strong incentives for competitors to collaborate to reduce everyone's costs. Netsourcing offers an ideal platform for interorganizational sharing, which was defined as ex-sourcing in Chapter 1. On February 25, 2000, for example, DaimlerChrysler, Ford Motor Company, and General Motors founded Covisint to serve as the world's largest online business-to-business exchange for the automotive industry. The vision for Covisint is for all participants to make gains by reducing new vehicle development cycles to a year and a half or less, reduce order-to-delivery cycles, and reduce costs through efficiencies from asset sharing. Although Covisint has not generated the projected revenues promised initially, investors such as Ford have declared that they did not lose money on their investment.[5] But other automakers, such as Volkswagen, have refused to do business on an open exchange because of the fear of competitor espionage. Despite the real or perceived risks of such ventures, netsourcing is clearly opening up new opportunities for managing critical commodities.

Useful commodities: the myriad activities that provide incremental benefits to the business but fail to distinguish it from its competitors. Payroll, benefit, and accounting systems are the first examples of useful commodities volunteered by most businesses. But sweeping generalizations cannot be made, even within industries. Useful commodities are the prime candidates for outsourcing. One CIO called them "necessary evils." Examples include personal computer support at a U.S. chemical manufacturer, accounting services at a U.K. oil company, and mainframe operations at a U.S. bank.[6] External suppliers are likely to have achieved low costs and prices through standardization. The business makes further gains if it can free up internal management time to focus on more critical activities. Useful commodities are natural candidates for netsourcing solutions because the customer is often willing to accept standardized products and services available in the one-to-many netsourcing model in exchange for lower costs. But the expectation of outsourcing must be validated through analysis of economic, market, and technical considerations.

Useful differentiators: activities that differentiate the business from its competitors but in a way that is not critical to business success. Useful differentiators should not exist, but they frequently do. One reason is that the IT function is sometimes relatively isolated from the business and subsequently, pursues its own agenda. For example, the IT department at a European paint manufacturer created a system that matched a paint formulation precisely to a customer's color sample. IT managers envisioned that the system would create competitive advantage by meeting customers' wishes that paint should match their home furnishings. However, senior management had established the company's strategy as color innovation. They failed to market the system because it ran counter to their strategy and the system became an expensive and ineffective distraction.

A more common reason for the creation of useful differentiators is that a potential commodity has been reworked extensively to reflect "how we are different" or to incorporate the "nice-to-haves." This was an extensive phenomenon at a Dutch electronics company, resulting in very problematic and high-cost software maintenance. The CIO of the company has now implemented a policy requiring that all needs for useful systems be met through standard software packages, with strict limits on customization. Of course, netsourcing standard packages rather than purchasing the software and running it on a customer's own equipment would also be a feasible way to migrate a useful differentiator into a useful commodity. Either way, useful differentiators are distractions (see Figure 2.1) and need to be eliminated from or migrated within an IT portfolio, but never outsourced merely to reduce their costs.

The business considerations are extremely dynamic. Customers may initially view a new IT-enabled business application as a critical differentiator, but as competitors quickly follow suit, the activity may evolve into a critical commodity. That same activity may then evolve into a useful commodity as the practices and technologies that enable it become increasingly standardized. Because of the dynamic nature of how activities contribute to competitive positioning, business managers must frequently review their entire IT and IT-enabled business application portfolio. In addition to business contribution, cost considerations, which are often prematurely assumed to favor the supplier, are an important consideration in confirming the feasibility of IT outsourcing candidates.

Cost Issues

Many senior executives assume that a supplier can reduce their IT-related costs because suppliers possess inherent economies of scale that elude internal departments. This may well be true where small and medium-sized enterprises are the clients, prime recruiting ground for netsourcing providers. But a distinctive feature of IT is that economies of scale can occur at a size achievable by many medium-sized to large organizations. If this is true, how can a supplier underbid current IT costs?

Often, the answer is that suppliers implement efficient managerial practices that may be replicated by large internal IT departments if empowered to do so. Suppliers may also claim economic advantages from experience curve effects, but in-house managers are not precluded from learning to operate more efficiently over time either. Two economic considerations—in-house economies of scale and adoption of leading practices—guide senior executives through these issues (see Figure 2.2).

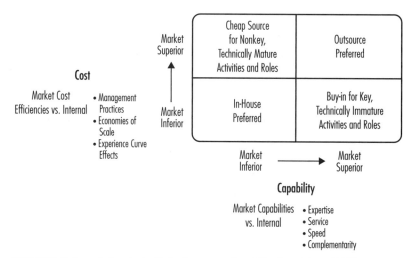

FIGURE 2.2 Strategic Sourcing by Market Comparison. From Willcocks and Sauer (2001).

If the internal IT department has reached critical mass and has adopted leading management practices, it is unlikely that a supplier will be able to reduce costs further because suppliers have to earn a 15 to 20% profit, whereas internal IT departments merely need to cover costs.

If the in-house IT department possesses theoretical economies of scale but has failed to implement efficient managerial practices, we recommend that senior executives allow internal IT managers to compete against supplier bids. The competition serves to empower IT managers to overcome user resistance to the idea of reducing costs. In the netsourcing context, Royal Dutch Shell Group serves as a good example of a company that has clearly achieved critical mass but had inefficient practices in managing applications for its operations in 130 countries. Shell liked the idea of netsourcing but opted to implement an *internal* application service provision rather than host completely with a third-party provider. Shell intends to consolidate all their applications to three data centers in Houston, Kuala Lumpur, and the Hague, and to offer standard applications to its divisions in 130 countries. Although the internal ASP will save Shell a projected 20% in TCO, Shell needs some outside expertise for the project and thus signed a $100 million contract with IBM for storage systems.

If the internal IT department is of subcritical mass but has adopted efficient practices, it is quite possible that a supplier's size advantage may be negated by its need to generate a profit. Best-sourcing is recommended in these cases. That is, test the market to determine the economic validity of outsourcing. Finally, if the internal IT department is of subcritical mass and has failed to adopt efficient practices, there is a strong economic justification for outsourcing (see Figure 2.2). But even companies that fall in this quadrant may wish to empower IT to implement whichever practices they can before outsourcing, to avoid giving the supplier the large share of easy savings. However, for many small to medium-sized enterprises, the nature of the price–service deal on an offer from a netsourcing provider may be sufficiently attractive to render this unnecessary.

But what happens when external supplier bids beat internal bids? Prudent managers question where and how the supplier proposes to earn a profit while still meeting the bid. In the most desirable scenario, suppliers clearly outbid internal IT departments based on a number of valid reasons: superior management practices that could not be replicated by the internal staff, inherent economies of scale or scope, or superior technical expertise. All these apply to the normal netsourcing offerings, too, and additionally, providers will often point to the savings on IT capital investment and head count that can be achieved by adopting their model. But in many cases, supplier bids may be based on "voodoo" economics (i.e., customers are offered long-term, set prices that are attractive in year 1 but will be out of step with price or performance improvements a few years into the contract). Or the supplier may be trying to buy market share in a fiercely competitive market. Once the contract is signed, the supplier may recoup losses by charging exorbitantly high fees for any change, realizing that customers are captive. Supplier bids may also contain hidden costs. Hidden costs might include items such as extra charges for services that turn out not to be in the contract, paying for the total cost of a five-year software license fee granted to the xSP when you have only signed a three-year contract, and high renewal or switching costs at contract end.

MARKET CAPABILITY ISSUES

Another set of reasons that make outsourcing attractive relate to supplier capability relative to an in-house IT function. Especially with moves to e-business, and among smaller organizations, organizations regularly experience a shortage of certain IT skills, difficulties in retaining staff, and difficulties in obtaining levels of service and expertise rapidly enough to deliver on fast-moving business requirements. In such circumstances, organizations regularly turn to the IT services market to assess the available capability there. Where the market has superior capability and offers a matching or cheaper price than the in-house option, outsourcing is an obvious decision, remembering, however that all outsourcing decisions also need to be checked against the business considerations described in Figure 2.1. But even where price may not be an attractive reason for outsourcing, it is often the case that an IT activity or skill is so critical—in terms of speed that is required and its importance to business performance—and so unavailable in-house that a buy-in strategy will be suitable. On the other hand, some organizations cheap-source. Having identified an IT activity or skill as non-critical, and wanting to reduce IT costs, they are prepared to make a cost–service trade-off, potentially willing to lower service and performance by outsourcing to an IT service provider who will do it cheaper and with lower quality (see Figure 2.2). On the other hand, in-house is an obvious preferred option if the IT function can perform both cheaper and better than the market, and we have found many organizations continuing to perform useful-commodity IT activities in-house for these reasons.

TECHNICAL ISSUES

Finally, the degree of technology maturity and the degree of technology integration are two key technical considerations that influence the effectiveness of IT sourcing decisions (see Figure 2.3). The degree of technical maturity determines a company's ability to define its requirements precisely to a sup-

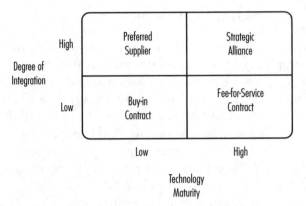

FIGURE 2.3 Strategic IT Sourcing: Technical Factors Matrix

plier. An IT activity has low-technology maturity when the technology itself is new and unstable, when the business has little experience with a technology that may be better established elsewhere, and/or when the business is embarked on a radically new use of a familiar technology.[7] Examples include an organization's first venture into e-business, first-time implementation of a large ERP package, or the development of a major network to support a new business direction of globalization.

Outsourcing technically immature activities engenders significant risk. Ironically, these are precisely the activities that many senior executives wish to outsource. Outsourcing technically mature activities provides less risk to organizations because they can define their requirements precisely. For example, a U.S. commercial bank outsourced its mainframe operations to a supplier. The chief information officer (CIO) was able to negotiate an airtight contract because of her experience and understanding of the requirements and costs of her mainframe operations. In the contract, she fully specified the service levels required, such as response time and availability, service-level measures, cash penalties for nonperformance, and adjustments to changes in business volumes. After three years into the contract, she achieved the anticipated savings of 10%.

A second important technical consideration is the degree of integration with other business processes. In cases where technical integration with other business processes is high, the risks from outsourcing increase. For example, when a U.K. food manufacturer outsourced the development of factory automation, managers soon realized that the new system had profound implications for almost every business unit in the company. Although the supplier was an expert in factory automation software, it lacked an understanding of business interfaces. The system took four years to develop instead of two. This again underscores the point that it is easier to outsource IT rather than outsource IT-enabled business processes.

In contrast, one financial services company successfully outsourced the development of a highly integrated system using a preferred supplier model. This company invested in imaging technology to replace paper records (such as customer letters) with an electronic file. The company first explored the technology through a discrete R&D project. Senior executives reached a point at which they were convinced of the benefits of large-scale adoption but realized that many of their existing systems would now be affected. At this stage, the company turned to its preferred IT supplier, a supplier with a very broad product line with whom it had worked for many years. Resisting the supplier's instinct to develop a detailed fixed-price agreement, the company set up an enabling, resource-based contract. The project was completed successfully, providing competitive advantages for both the business and its supplier, which had established a reference site for its own imaging products. In the netsourcing world it may well be that high levels of integration of IT with business processes make a move from application to business process service provision attractive to both client and the service provider. Customers may, in turn, also become reference sites for xSPs.

We have mapped the two technical considerations—technology maturity and integration—in Figure 2.3. Of particular note is the absence of the term *strategic partnership* from the contracting options. The strategic partnership contracting model has been widely recommended as the preferred governor of outsourcing contracts. But too often the rhetoric of strategic partnership was used as an excuse to sign poorly constructed contracts, leading to failure in several total outsourcing cases. We argue that strategic partnerships require shared—or at least complementary—risks and rewards, typically involving joint equity ownership.

Instead of the term *strategic partnership*, better labels are *preferred contractors* or *strategic alliances*. With a preferred contractor strategy, companies engage in a relationship with the supplier to help mediate risk. This strategy worked best for technically mature and highly integrated IT activities. Because of technical maturity, companies can negotiate a detailed contract in which the supplier is responsible for the management and delivery of an IT-enabled activity. Because of the high integration with other business processes, companies must develop a close relationship to maintain the integrity of interfaces. To ensure supplier performance, the company tries to construct an incentive-based contract that ensures shared goals.

As one example, in late 2000, Siemens, the German electronics conglomerate with some 440,000 employees worldwide, signed i2 as its preferred contractor in one of the world's largest e-business infrastructure initiatives at the time. Through this initiative, Siemens intended to reduce spending on materials, reduce inventories, improve product development and quality, and buying and selling efficiency, increase e-procurement from 10% to 50% of purchasing, develop a global knowledge database, and have all its employees Web- and intranet-enabled within 12 months.

Siemens created a central fund of some $800 million, with its divisions spread across 190 countries also providing further funds. According to CEO Heinrich Pierer, the plan was to run all processes electronically, from procurement to marketing, and from development to control. The company will use i2's software to manage its global supply chain and to standardize all its related customer and supplier processes. The company hoped to recover the central investment in the first 18 months of its e-business development and aimed to save up to 5% of its £42 billion net sales.

Siemens has a core capability on hand in Siemens Business Services, which, together with IBM, would manage the transformation using i2's Trade Matrix platform and integrated suite of e-business applications for designing, buying, planning, selling, fulfilling, and servicing. Siemens would also use i2 content management and consulting services. The e-business strategy would be driven from three centers—in Munich, Atlanta, and Singapore—forming the central platform for all of Siemen's e-business activities.

The plan was to use i2's architecture to integrate with Siemens' existing technology, including its 360 ERP systems, representing one of the world's biggest SAP installations. Siemens had already implemented i2 on top of SAP in its PC Division, an implementation that proved difficult. Interestingly, although Siemens is a major SAP user, it decided against using mySAP.com/CommerceOne to e-enable its business processes. Siemens also looked to develop further systems in association with IBM and CommerceOne.

The case points to three issues:

1. Siemens recognizes the significant advantages of having a standardized, global infrastructure for e-business in order to achieve its business targets. However, the criticality of these developments, going to the core of business operations, means that it must put at risk mitigating features in the implementation process, including parallel running of old systems and in the design features of the infrastructure.
2. The company has significant in-house infrastructure capability heavily involved in the development and implementation process.
3. The right technology partner is critical. It is clear that i2 architecture and applications have been judged superior, even though there will inevitably be implementation difficulties integrating these with the SAP and other legacy systems.

Making effective IT sourcing decisions involves carrying out the analysis prompted by each of these matrices, then comparing the results and making appropriate trade-offs. In practice there are inevitably trade-offs, which is where managerial judgment on the specific circumstances will play a key role.

CONCLUSIONS

We believe that all the sound sourcing practices discussed in this chapter apply directly to netsourcing. Sound netsourcing practices for customers can be summarized as follows:

1. Netsource incrementally to gain valuable experience in the space.

2. View netsourcing as an option in the sourcing portfolio.

3. Evaluate netsourcing as any other sourcing option, based on business contribution to operations and competitive positioning, costs, market capabilities, and technical issues.

As with any new business practice, a safe customer route is an incremental approach to adoption. By testing the waters, the customer gains experience with how netsourcing actually works and what customer capabilities are needed in terms of netsourcing evaluation, negotiation, and relationship management. We recommend this strategy to any organization, large or small, because netsourcing will probably be a dominant vehicle for distributing IT and IT-enabled business applications in the future. Even when a customer may not be able to justify netsourcing based on today's analysis of business, cost, market capability, and technology, it may make sense to netsource a discrete, useful commodity just for the learning benefits.

As netsourcing matures, we believe that netsourcing will become a standard option in the business manager's portfolio of sourcing solutions. Such sourcing decisions will be guided by the issues highlighted by the set of matrices provided in this chapter. Thus netsourcing will take its place among outsourcing strategies such as the buy-in, fee-for-service, preferred supplier, preferred contractor, and strategic partnership models. In Chapter 3 we focus on what we have learned about what management principles to apply once a sourcing portfolio strategy is identified.

ENDNOTES

1. M. Lacity and L. Willcocks, *IT Outsourcing: A State-of-the-Art Report*, Templeton Research Report, Templeton College, Oxford University, Oxford, 2000.

2. See M. Lacity and L. Willcocks, *Global IT Outsourcing: In Search of Business Advantage*, Wiley, Chichester, West Sussex, England, 2001; T. Kern and L. Willcocks, *The Relationship Advantage*, Oxford University Press, Oxford, 2001.

3. See Lacity and Willcocks (2001).

4. M. Lacity and L. Willcocks, *Best Practices in IT Sourcing*, Oxford Executive Research Briefing, Templeton College, Oxford University, Oxford, 1996.

5. See Carlos Grande, E-business correspondent, "Ford Recoups Investment in Covisint Web Exchange," *Financial Times*, July 1, 2001.

6. Lacity and Willcocks (2001).

7. D. Feeny, M. Earl, and B. Edwards, "Organizational Arrangements for IS: Roles of Users and Specialists," in L. Willcocks, D. Feeny, and G. Islei (eds.), *Managing IT as a Strategic Resource*, McGraw-Hill, Maidenhead, Berkshire, England, 1997.

3

MANAGEMENT PRINCIPLES: CORE CAPABILITIES AND CONTRACTING

Based on all of our studies of IT outsourcing, successful sourcing practices in the public and private sectors include the following:

- Base the sourcing strategy on assessment of business, cost, market capability, and technology.
- Create the sourcing strategy with senior executives as well as IT executives.
- Ensure that nine core capabilities are retained in-house, including the capabilities to buy and manage third-party providers extensively.
- For IT-enabled activities targeted for outsourcing, create a formal request for proposal.

- Invite external bids (and internal bids where appropriate).

- Analyze proposals, including risk assessment and mitigation.

- Negotiate detailed, short-term contracts.

- Actively manage providers to ensure success.

Whereas Chapter 2 dealt with the first item, developing an effective sourcing strategy, in this chapter we focus on the capabilities to retain in-house and negotiating effective contracts. The capability lessons are important because we have found organizations overfocused on what to outsource, as opposed to what to retain. This is particularly prevalent in netsourcing, given its claims to take away so much of the IT headache. One particularly weak and telling area of practice is to neglect to retain the right resources, in terms of skilled people who are able to manage and leverage the service provider while controlling the company's IT destiny and ensuring that the business side is exploiting IT successfully. We next present the principles of sound IT contracts, because many customers are signing flimsy netsourcing contracts, which leaves them extremely vulnerable to higher-than-expected costs or poor service.

It is important to note that lessons in this chapter are based on lessons from both large and small organizations. Some readers from SMEs may question the cost and value of some of the practices discussed. We have found that SMEs select netsourcing largely because they want big-company solutions at small-company prices. The same holds true for the success practices in managing netsourcing solutions: Even SMEs will need to retain capabilities in house for strategy, governance, market evaluation, and supplier management to ensure success. But SMEs may do so through different means than larger organizations. We have highlighted throughout the chapter some ways in which smaller organizations may be able to implement best practices efficiently.

CORE IT CAPABILITIES

In this section we deal with what is consistently found to be the outstanding and most neglected issue in IT outsourcing—that of retention of in-house capabilities.[1] Here we concentrate mainly on the emerging model of the high-performance IT function required to manage IT successfully in the modern corporation. The first step is to present the four faces of the emerging IT function (Figure 3.1):

1. The business face is concerned with the elicitation and delivery of business requirements. In the domain of *information systems strategy*, relevant capabilities are business-focused, demand-led, and concerned with defining the systems to be provided, their relationship to business needs, and the interrelationships and interdependencies with other systems. A further focus here is on a strategy for delivery, together with actual implementation of IT-enabled business systems.

2. The technical face is concerned with ensuring that the business has access to the technical capability it needs, taking into account such issues as current price and performance, flexibility, scalability, future directions, and integration potential. This is the domain of *information technology strategy* that defines the blueprint or architecture of the technical platform that will be used over time to support the target systems. IT presents the set of allowable options from which the technical implementation of each system must be selected. A further concern is to provide technical support for delivery of the IT strategy.

3. The governance face is concerned with *information management strategy*, which defines the governance, coordination, and human resource management of the organization's IT/IS activity.

4. The supply face encompasses understanding and use of the external services market. As such, it is the domain of *IT market sourcing strategy*. Particularly

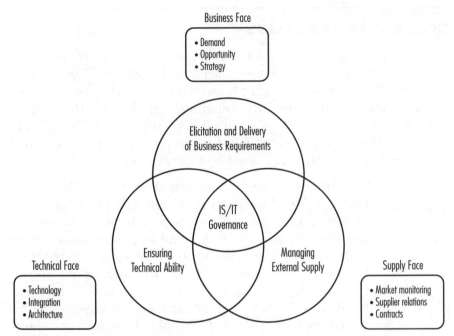

FIGURE 3.1 Four Faces (Tasks) of the Emerging IT Function

critical here are decisions about what to outsource and insource, which external suppliers to use, and how. A further concern is ensuring appropriate delivery of contracted external services. In this section we develop the model of the future IT function by detailing nine capabilities required to render it dynamic and fully operational.

These capabilities, expressed as roles, are shown in Figure 3.2. It should be noted that the nine capabilities populate seven spaces. These spaces are not arbitrary. Three of them are essentially business-, technology-, or service-related. One is a lynchpin governance position covered by two capabilities (see Figure 3.2), CIO and informed buyer. Finally, there are three spaces that represent various interfaces between the three faces. The capabilities that populate these spaces are crucial for facilitating the integration of effort across the faces. We now move to detailing each of the nine capabilities.

Capability 1: IT governance. IT leadership is required to integrate IT efforts with business purpose and activity. The central task is to devise organizational arrangements—structures, processes, and staffing—to manage the interdependencies successfully and to ensure that the IT function delivers value for money. Provision of IT governance capability is the traditional role of the centralized CIO or the CIO of the local business.

Capability 2: business systems thinking. This capability is about envisioning the business process that technology makes possible. In best-practice organizations, business systems thinkers from the IT function are important contributors to teams charged with business problem solving, process reengineering, and strategic development. The information systems strategy emerges from these teams' recommendations, which will have already identified the technology components of solutions to business issues.

Capability 3: relationship building. The need for relationship building is symbolized by the overlap between business and technical faces in Figure 3.2. Whereas the business systems thinker is the individual embodiment of integrated business/IT thinking, the relationship builder facilitates the wider dialogue, establishing understanding, trust, and cooperation among business users and IT specialists. The task here is *getting the business constructively engaged in IT-related issues.*

Capability 4: designing technical architecture. This is about creating the coherent blueprint for a technical platform that responds to present and future business needs. The principal challenge to the architect is to anticipate technology trends so that the organization is consistently able to operate from an effective and efficient platform without major investment in energy-sapping migration efforts.

Capability 5: making technology work. Operating in the overlap between the technical and supply faces of Figure 3.2 is the technical fixer. The fixer requires much of the insight found in the technical architect role, allied to a pragmatic nature and short-term orientation. In today's environment of high

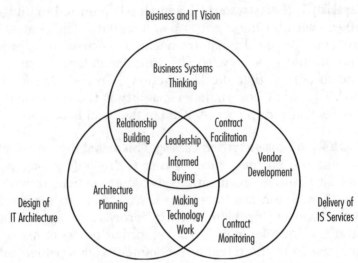

Business and IT Vision

Business Systems
Thinking

Relationship
Building

Contract
Facilitation

Leadership

Informed
Buying

Vendor
Development

Architecture
Planning

Making
Technology
Work

Design of
IT Architecture

Contract
Monitoring

Delivery of
IS Services

FIGURE 3.2 Nine Capabilities in the Emerging IT Function (From D. Feeny and L. Willcocks, "Core IS Capabilities for Exploiting Information Technology," *Sloan Management Review*, 39(3), 9–21, 1998.)

complex/networked/multisupplier systems, the technical fixer makes two critical contributions: to rapidly trouble-shoot problems that are being disowned by others across the technical supply chain, and to identify how to address business needs that cannot be properly satisfied by standard technical approaches. The need to retain technical "doing" capability is recognized even among organizations that have totally outsourced IT.

Capability 6: informed buying. This involves analysis of the external market for IT services; selection of a sourcing strategy to meet business needs and technology issues; and leadership of the tendering, contracting, and service management processes. In an organization that has decided to outsource most IT service, the informed buyer is the most prominent role behind that of the CIO. One respondent described his role in this way: "If you are a senior manager in the company and you want something done, you come to me and I will go outside, select the supplier and draw up the contract with the outsourcer, and if anything goes wrong it's my butt that gets kicked by you."

Capability 7: contract facilitation. It is important to ensure the success of existing contracts for IT services. The contract facilitator tries to ensure that problems and conflicts are seen to be resolved fairly within what are usually long-term relationships. The role arises for a variety of reasons:

- It provides one-stop shopping for the business user.
- The supplier or user demands it.
- Multiple suppliers need coordinating.
- It enables easier monitoring of use and service.
- Users may demand too much and incur excessive charges.

One contract facilitator noted: "They (users) have been bitten a few times when they have dealt directly with suppliers, and it's a service we can provide, so now we do."

Capability 8: contract monitoring. Another consequence of IT outsourcing complexity is the need for contract monitoring. While the contract facilitator is working to make things happen on a day-to-day basis, the contract monitor is ensuring that the business position is at all times protected. Located in the exclusive space of the supply face, the role involves holding suppliers to account against both existing service contracts and the developing performance standards of the services market.

Capability 9: supplier development. It is important to identify the potential added value of IT service suppliers. The single most threatening aspect of IT outsourcing is the presence of substantial switching costs. To outsource successfully in the first place requires considerable organizational effort over an extended period of time. To change suppliers subsequently may well require an equivalent effort. Hence it is in the business interest to maximize the contribution of existing suppliers, which is the role of supplier development. Anchored in the supply face of our Figure 3.2 model, the supplier developer is concerned with the long-term potential for suppliers to add value, creating the win–win situations in which the supplier increases its revenues by providing services that increase business benefits. A major retail multinational has a number of ways of achieving this, including an annual formal meeting: "It's in both our interests to keep these things going and we formally, with our biggest suppliers, have a meeting once a year and these are done at very senior levels in both organizations, and that works very well."

COMMENTS ON THE CORE IT CAPABILITIES MODEL

The model has been used effectively as an analytical device in over 16 corporations to date, to help organizations identify key IT management skills and appropriate human resource strategies. The model represents a number of serious human resource challenges. It requires high-level performers in each role. Furthermore, in contrast to the more traditional skills found in IT functions, there needs to be a much greater emphasis on business skills and orientation in all but the two very technical roles. There is a significantly increased requirement for "soft" interpersonal skills across all roles, and each role requires a specific set of people behaviors, characteristics, and skills. In the research, we regularly found that where a particular capability was missing or understaffed, problems arose. A typical issue was to conflate several of the roles and appoint one person to fulfill them. For example, at one large bank we found a contract manager responsible in practice for contract facilitation, contract monitoring, and IT governance. Not surprisingly, he underperformed in all these tasks.

The high-performance model also sets serious challenges for human resource policies. How do you pay these high performers at a level that is at least within striking distance of that provided by alternative employers in a tight labor market? How do you provide them with the consistent level of challenge they look for in the job? How do you create an exciting career path despite their very small numbers in the organization? Few organizations develop the necessary human resource policies in an anticipatory way, partly because many still enter outsourcing believing that it is an opportunity to shed labor and run IT in-house as something of a residual rather than a core function. Against this view, we would argue, from the evidence, that in fact building and retaining these core IT capabilities form an insurance policy for retaining control over the organization's IT destiny and will be the most likely source of any future competitive advantage the organization gains from its IT deployment.

In SMEs, unable to attract the skilled IT people needed to staff the core capabilities framework, one natural tendency is to give up and hand over their IT destiny to an application service provider. This would be an overly risky approach. Far better to make compromises and provide some degree of the internal IT capability required. High performers may not be affordable in these roles, and some roles may well need to be conflated. External contractors independent of the provider may well help to fill some of these capabilities on a temporary basis. Over time a stronger relationship may develop with the provider, so that its staff could come to operate more as a surrogate IT function, but this latter cannot be relied upon to happen. Far better as to evaluation, contracting, and core capabilities is to start tight and well staffed internally and allow a loosening subsequently if the relationship develops and provider performance consistently matches requirements.

PROVIDER EVALUATION AND CONTRACTING

For an organization contemplating outsourcing, a great deal of effort needs to be invested in understanding the costs and benefits of the existing IT operation so that these can be compared against supplier bids. Respondents found that this is best done before a request for proposal. Yet many organizations leave it until much later in the cycle. Their experiences suggest, though, that it is rarely a good idea to postpone this analysis to the period after contracts have been signed. This can promote both subsequent hidden costs and opportunistic behavior on the part of the supplier.

A consistent finding has been that outsourcing frequently carries hidden costs. In an extreme example, one petroleum company was being charged almost $500,000 in excess fees in the first month into a new contract. More often, the hidden costs are less dramatic but accumulate to a significant figure over time. As well as inadequate measurement systems, there seem to be six additional root causes of such hidden costs. They all relate to weaknesses in contracting:

1. Failure to define fully present IT requirements.
2. Failure to define fully future requirements or failure to create mechanisms for change.
3. Loopholes or ambiguities in the contract.
4. Not allowing the supplier a reasonable profit.
5. Rising (usually unforeseen) in-house contract management costs as a result of weak contracting practices.
6. A lack of prior specified management processes and essential information exchanges in postcontract management.

The first three weaknesses left client organizations open not only to additional costs for services not previously contracted for, but also to higher prices for those services. Loopholes or ambiguities in the contract may also trigger conflicts with, and also opportunistic behavior by, suppliers. That said, however, supplier opportunism can also be triggered by not allowing the supplier a reasonable profit. Supplier account managers then come under internal pressure to make their margins from the outsourcing deal.

There are two more important points to make concerning the evaluation process: (1) netsourcing decisions should be made jointly with business and IT executives; and (2) netsourcing proposals should be assessed against in-house bids under specific circumstances. First, in our study of traditional outsourcing, sourcing decisions made jointly with both senior executive and IT input had the highest success rate (76%). This compares with only 43% success for sourcing decisions made by senior executives without IT input. It appears that successful sourcing decisions require a mix of political power and technical skills. Political power helped to enforce the larger business perspective, such as the need for organization-wide cost cuts, as well as the "muscle" to implement such business initiatives. Technical expertise on IT services, service levels, measures of performance, rates of technical obsolescence, rates of service growth, price/performance improvements, and a host of other technical topics were needed to develop requests for proposals, evaluate supplier bids, and negotiate and manage sound contracts. In some cases, this mix of political power and technical knowledge was encompassed in one stakeholder group, as evidenced by some success by single stakeholder-led decisions.

In the netsourcing context, our international survey showed that CIOs were the most frequent netsourcing decision makers (see Appendix A) and that CEOs, owners, and partners were the second-most-frequent netsourcing decision makers. The telling sign is that at least senior people are involved in netsourcing evaluation, although the lofty titles may be indicative of our sample respondents, mostly from SMEs. As our survey did not ask a question on joint decision making, our assumptions here are limited. But the lessons from our prior research surely apply: that a netsourcing decision must be both business- and IT-directed.

Second, netsourcing proposals should be assessed against in-house bids in some circumstances. This suggestion is based on our prior research on traditional outsourcing which found that organizations that invited both internal and external bids had a higher relative frequency of success (83%) than organizations that merely compared a few external bids to current IT performance (42%). Internal bids enable the organization to access supplier proposals against what *could* be done as opposed to what has been done. Sometimes in-house IT teams were shackled by political barriers to change and a threat of outsourcing served to empower them. In other cases, in-house bids served to channel IT employees nervous about an impending outsourcing decision toward a constructive outlet. This advice is surely applicable to large organizations with established IT functions. But for startup companies and small organizations, in-house bids may be infeasible.

DETAILED CONTRACTS

A major finding in our research has been that if an organization outsources IT, the outsourcing contract provides the foundation of a good relationship. (Conversely, a poor contract provides the foundations for a poor relationship.) Based on our analysis of 85 customer–supplier relationships engaged in traditional, one-to-one outsourcing, by far the most successful contracts were detailed (see Table 3.1). These contracts included service-level agreements, pricing, mechanisms for changes in volumes, business, and technology, required skill sets, penalties for nonperformance, exit clauses, and transition clauses. In contrast, loose contracts (a few pages long), mixed contracts (detailed for the first few years, loose for the remainder), and supplier off-the-shelf contracts had the worst success rates.

TABLE 3.1 Most Successful Contract Types (%) Used in Traditional Outsourcing[a]

CONTRACT TYPE	YES, MOST EXPECTATIONS MET	NO, MOST EXPECTATIONS NOT MET	MIXED RESULTS
DETAILED CONTRACT	75%	15%	10%
LOOSE CONTRACT	0%	100%	0%
MIXED CONTRACT	55%	9%	36%
STANDARD SUPPLIER CONTRACT	50%	50%	0%

a. 85 case study results.
SOURCE: Lacity and Willcocks, Global Information Technology Outsourcing Search for Business Advantage, Wiley, Chicester, 2001.

One common concern in the netsourcing context is that most contracts are extremely loose and flimsy. Customers have shown us contracts which are less than five pages long for the provision on an entire enterprise system! Many SMEs who do not have experience with writing IT contracts tend to sign the supplier's standard contract, which of course is designed to protect the supplier, not the customer. Our international survey found that early adopters of netsourcing (primarily SMEs) are only systematically including application availability and data security clauses (see Figure 3.3).

In practice, weak contracting, based on inadequate assessment of a supplier bid and backed up by poor monitoring systems, not only results in unanticipated higher costs, it can create major problems for client organizations. It is all too easy for all parties to a contract to agree broadly on what is required from a supplier. We also found parties all too frequently relying on "partnering" notions to offset any difficulties arising from loose contracting. These rarely proved a sufficient base, in themselves, from which to run effective outsourcing arrangements. The issue, which is very pertinent for those considering a netsourcing option, has been summarized succinctly by one of our respondents: "Outsourcing contracts are agreed in concept and delivered in detail, and that's why they break down" (supplier manager).

When it came to drawing up effective outsourcing contracts, we found that indeed the devil is in the details. Large customers systemically hire experts such as Technology Partners International and outsourcing law firms such as Shaw Pittman, but these consultants may be too expensive for an SME. So where can the SME start to learn about effective netsourcing contracts? The ASP Consortium and the Information Technology Association of America (ITAA) have both published ASP service-level agreement guidelines to benefit both customers and suppliers. The ITAA guideline, for example, recommends 13 specific contract clauses covering service-level agreements, security, remedies, upgrades, and intellectual property indemnification. There are lawyers who specialize in netsourcing contracts, such as John Bonello, an attorney at McKenna & Cuneo, who charges clients anywhere from $500 to $5000 to help negotiate a netsourcing contract.

Clearly, specifying service-level measures is critical. Although this is done regularly, a common mistake is not to then stipulate 100% service accountability from the supplier.

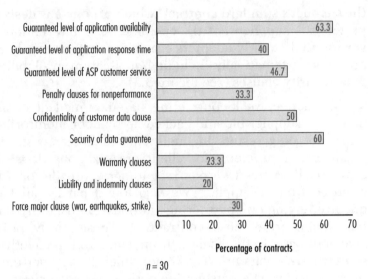

Percentage of contracts

n = 30

FIGURE 3.3 Specifics Included in Netsourcing Contracts

In one help desk support contract we researched in a major U.K.-based oil company, 80% of service requests had to be responded to within 20 seconds and 90% within 30 seconds. This leaves 10% of the service unaccountable . . . the provider could literally ignore 10% of all requests and still be meeting their service levels. Customers must also demand detailed service-level reports on the SLAs and specify the frequency of those reports (daily, weekly, monthly, quarterly) for each SLA. Also, customers and suppliers must agree in advance what happens when problems escalate: for example, by providing explanations. This must lead on to financial penalties for nonperformance for missing critical SLAs. Although financial penalties are now the norm in traditional outsourcing contracts, they are rarely seen in the netsourcing space.

Overall, it is important for client organizations to make contracts work *for* rather than against their interests. In one U.S. manufacturing company the contract specified a 2-second system response time for key applications such as order entry and customer service. It also specified supplier support for up to 20 users at a given time using a fourth-generation language (4GL). However, during the first week the 11 4GL users were taking up more than 30% of the machine cycles and making response times for critical applications unachievable. The supplier could have been forced to upgrade the technology provided, but the client, in this case, felt that the demand would have been unreasonable. A tight contract reasonably handled by both sides was felt to improve the supplier–client relationship and levels of satisfaction all round.

Despite all these guidelines, contracts by definition will be inherently incomplete because once signed, contracts often remain relevant only during the present and short-term future. The difficulty is one of defining the long-term future in the present so that both parties can use the agreements as the basis for the venture. The incompleteness in the long term of any IT outsourcing and netsourcing contract is really due to the volatility of information technology developments and the consistent shifts in users and company requirements. To accommodate these ongoing alterations, a common suggestion has been to focus efforts on the relationship and develop a partnering sense. But this does not serve to make the contract more complete and relevant. Once the agreements do not mirror the venture anymore, the resulting difficulties become those of enforcing what has been agreed upon. The best practice for contracting is to stick to the agreement by ensuring that the contract and SLA are frequently updated and revisited. The argument we put forward is that the contract and SLA have to be managed as a "live document" to prevent incompleteness and potential opportunistic behaviors. For this, a careful measurement system has to be devised that filters back any potential changes in both the SLA and overall deal that need incorporating into the agreements. This should potentially occur every six months and should not exceed a one-year period.

Another alternative best practice is to sign short-term contracts for which requirements are stable. In the netsourcing context, early adopters are certainly following this practice (see Figure 3.4). Over 56% of our netsourcing adopters have contracts that last for less than a year. One word of caution, however, is that suppliers cannot often generate a return on investment in such a short time and may have to elevate

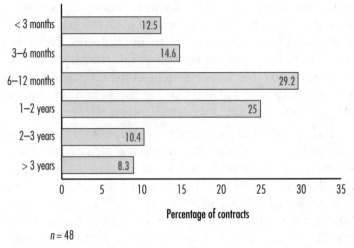

$n = 48$

FIGURE 3.4 Duration of Netsourcing Contracts

prices somewhat to compensate for the shorter contract. On the other hand, the supplier will be highly motivated to provide good service to win a renewal.

However, even good contracting, based on detailed IT evaluation and supported by comprehensive service measures and reporting systems, still did not avoid many problems arising during the course of any contract. This stresses again what emerges strongly from prior case and survey work: the importance of active monitoring and management of the supplier. As one respondent remarked ruefully about a particularly difficult outsourcing experience: "The one definite thing I have learned is that it's not like ringing for room service." This learning translates quite well into the netsourcing world, at least as a caveat.

CONCLUSIONS

In many countries in the world, private and public sectors are wading into a series of further potentially large IT outsourcing waves, stimulated by moves to e-business, application service provision, business process outsourcing, as well as more familiar forms of, and reasons for, outsourcing. It is useful to stand back and look at what has been learned so far about IT outsourcing practices. It should be said that good and bad IT outsourcing experiences, like everything else in IT and its management, is not sector specific. For example, financial institutions in all countries do not manage IT outsourcing any worse or better than do any other organizations or sectors. Organizations fail when they hand over IT without understanding its role in the organization and the supplier's capabilities. One rule of thumb is: Never outsource a problem, only an IT activity or set of tasks for which a detailed contract and performance measures can be written. Too many client companies see IT outsourcing as ditching their problems, not managing them. In fact, IT outsourcing requires a great deal of in-house management, but of a different kind, covering elicitation and delivery of business requirements, ensuring technical capability, managing external supply, and IT governance. A cardinal insight from our research is that organizations still expect too much from suppliers and not enough from themselves, or, put another way, suppliers are still much better at selling IT services than their clients are at buying them.

The key is to understand that the sound sourcing practices discussed in this chapter apply directly to netsourcing. These practices can be summarized as follows:

1. Ensure core capabilities are retained in-house or bought-in to buy, negotiate, and manage external providers.
2. Conduct a rigorous analysis of market options including a formal RFP and if appropriate, internal bids.
3. Negotiate a short-term contract.
4. Negotiate a detailed contract.

Practitioners must understand the IT services marketplace, the capabilities and weaknesses of relevant suppliers, and what their business strategies are and imply in any likely IT outsourcing deal with an organization. Two practices are proven to be effective. First, informed buying is a core IT capability for all contemporary organizations. Second, organizations that invite both internal and external bids achieve success more often than organizations that merely compare a few external bids with current IT performance.

Practitioners must also develop the ability to contract over time in ways that give suppliers an incentive and ensure that you get what you think you agreed to. Two proven practices here are that short-term contracts achieve success much more often then long-term contracts and that detailed fee-for-service contracts achieve success more often than other types of contracts.

Practitioners must also learn to postcontract-manage across the lifetime of the deal in ways that secure and build the organization's IT destiny and effectively achieve the required service performance and added value from the supplier. The evidence is that this is one of the weakest areas in IT outsourcing practice and is rarely adequately thought through at the front of outsourcing deals. Typically, a minimum of nine core IT capabilities emerge as necessary in response to problems confronted during contract performance. These cover leadership, informed buying, supplier development, contract facilitation, contract monitoring, technical fixing, architecture planning, relationship building, and business systems thinking. Institutions need to assess their capabilities against these vital components before outsourcing IT to any significant degree, and then build these capabilities where they are lacking.

ENDNOTES

1. D. Feeny and L. Willcocks, "Core IS Capabilities for Exploiting Information Technology," *Sloan Management Review,* 39(3), 9–21, 1998.

4

NETSOURCING TECHNOLOGY GUIDE FOR CUSTOMERS

Many current and potential netsourcing customers are unsure of the feasibility and security of netsourcing delivery. Our recent international customer survey (see Appendix A) highlighted that for potential and existing customers, security, business stability, reliability, service availability, and service levels are the biggest concerns. Many customers simply do not know if applications hosted by an outsider will perform well or whether data are secure. In this section we address the technical issues associated with netsourcing delivery, including application hosting suitability, application availability and performance, server performance, and network performance and choices. Our aim is to provide a technical primer for potential netsourcing customers, but it is by no means a substitute for the technical expertise required to negotiate successfully with a netsourcing provider.

TECHNICAL INFRASTRUCTURE

As a starting point, we outline in Figure 4.1 an overview model of an xSP's technical infrastructure and how the technical parts of the solution fit together. This forms the basis for subsequent discussion of the various technical parts. This model provides a helpful technical guide to visualize for yourselves and others what a netsourcing provider's technical infrastructure should comprise.

As evident, a netsourcer's key capabilities and business areas are the cross-integration and management of the various components of the netsourcing infrastructure, the ultimate goal being a solution for the customer.

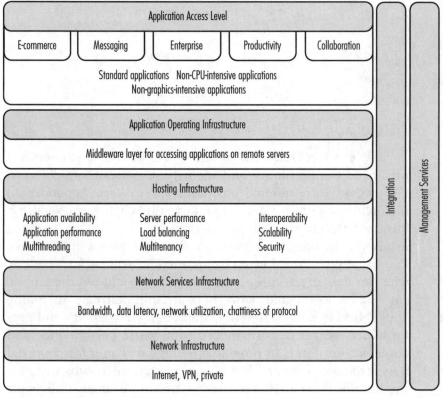

FIGURE 4.1 Netsourcing Service Stack

APPLICATION ACCESS LEVEL

Generally, most netsourcing is based on a one-to-many business model. That is, the netsourcer makes money by sharing standard resources with many customers. Presuming this business model, the applications most suitable for hosting are standard applications, non-CPU-intensive applications, and non-graphics-intensive applications because the supplier can earn a profit margin while still offering an attractive price to the customer:

- *Standard applications.* Web-enabled applications, for which the netsourcing provider does not have to customize source code. Instead, the netsourcing provider can meet a large number of customers' needs with the standard application. Commodity-type applications such as e-mail, personal productivity tools, end-user data access systems, and collaborative productivity tools are examples of standard applications that suit customers from a variety of industries.
- *Non-CPU-intensive applications.* Netsourcing providers gain their margins in part by sharing fixed computer processing power among many customers. CPU-intensive applications (e.g., weather forecasting) may consume too many of the netsourcing provider's resources to be cost-competitive.
- *Non-graphics-intensive applications.* Very graphics-intensive applications may consume too much computer processing power and too much bandwidth to make netsourcing a preferred option.

In the future, however, netsourcing providers may not base their profits on the one-to-many business model; thus the applications most suitable for hosting may change. (In Chapter 9 we explore how the future of netsourcing will probably be based on mass customization and customization.)

From a performance standpoint, thin-client applications are generally agreed to be more suitable for hosting than fat-client applications. *Thin-client applications* are applications written specifically to perform efficiently over the Internet by

minimizing the amount of data passed between the netsourcing provider's server and the client devices. (See "Server Performance" below for a more thorough explanation.)

> C/S apps are not necessarily network efficient because they
> were designed for LANs with lots of bandwidth. Internet appli-
> cations are fairly bandwidth efficient.
> —*Ashok Subramanian, chief strategy officer, Technisoft*
> *America*

Another commentator remarked that client/server applications typically do not lend themselves to a netsourcing provider model. Though some netsourcing providers were trying
to prove this belief to be inaccurate, more often than not it is
the truth.

But there is some debate among experts as to the general
application characteristics that do and do not lend themselves
to hosting. For example, some experts argue that netsourcing
is a logical extension of client/server, and that there should be
no performance penalty when moving to an ASP model, as
many local area networks are set up to work the same way as
ASP.

Because there is such debate as to the types of applications
suitable for hosting, a more in-depth exploration of the technical issues is warranted. Remember here that hosting becomes
more complex with differing application characteristics and
customers' system architectures. For example, ERP or e-commerce suites will demand more processing and storage power,
due to the diverse applications that will run in parallel when
using just the basic functionality of such programs. Similarly,
as the number of users who wish to access applications simultaneously increases, so will the need for more power and the
demand for increased maintenance and operational control of
the servers. Naturally, the hosting needs depend primarily on
the customers' system architecture requirements.

In the eyes of customers, however, good netsourcing service requires that applications are available to the customer
when he or she wants them and that the customer receives a

rapid response when he or she initiates a transaction. The hosting complexities are often overlooked. In turn, simple requirements are often muddied with such technical jargon as *multithreading*, *load-balancing*, *multitenancy*, and *scalability*. What do these capabilities mean to the customer in terms of availability and performance? Below we have defined the technical characteristics from the perspective of their effects on end-to-end customer service.

APPLICATION OPERATING INFRASTRUCTURE

All netsourcing providers rely on a middleware infrastructure through which their applications can then be delivered to and accessed by their customers. Simply put, it defines the infrastructure middle layer that needs to be in place to network- or Web-enable applications that are remotely hosted on server farms. Common middleware solutions here are Windows Terminal Server, Citrix, and Tarantella (by Santa Cruz Operations). These middleware solutions are essential as many, if not most, of today's applications were not intended to operate as Internet-enabled applications, but rather, were developed to operate on mainframes, stand-alone PCs, internal local area networks (i.e., intranets) or wide area networks (i.e., extranets).

The way these middleware infrastructures operationalize an application is simply by interfacing with the application and then making the functionality available over a network through a dedicated driver interface that needs to be installed on a desktop machine. Generally, the driver that is downloaded and installed has a data size in the region of 500 kilobytes to 1 megabyte at most. Once installed, a desktop user can access a specific application solution or portfolio from the netsourcing host.

The brilliance of this infrastructure solution is its multipoint access availability. The small size of the interface driver enables customers to log into their application solution through any data and Internet-enabled device that can store the driver. As shown in the Figure 4.2, examples can be per-

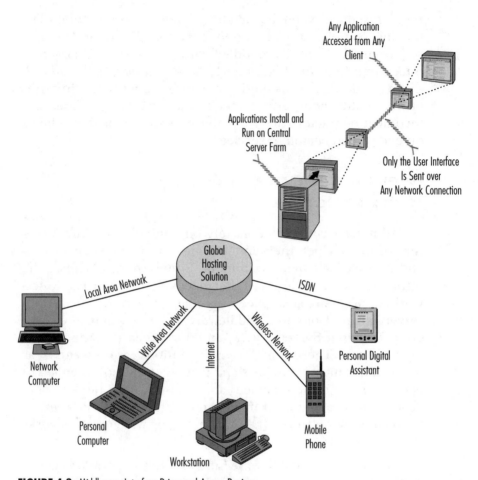

Any Application
Accessed from Any
Client

Applications Install and
Run on Central
Server Farm

Only the User Interface
Is Sent over
Any Network Connection

Global
Hosting
Solution

Local Area Network

ISDN

Wide Area Network

Internet

Wireless Network

Network
Computer

Personal Digital
Assistant

Personal
Computer

Mobile
Phone

Workstation

FIGURE 4.2 Middleware Interface Driver and Access Devices

sonal digital assistants (i.e., Compaq iPaq, Palm, Psion, Hand-
spring, etc.), mobile phones, network computers (generally
with no hard disks), desktop computers, and others.

In addition, these infrastructures are operating system–
independent. So you can operate your solution on a Microsoft,
UNIX, OS Warp, WAP, or Macintosh system since the necessary interface driver that is installed can be operating system–
independent (e.g., Citrix or Tarantella). Finally, the infrastruc-

ture necessitates only a limited amount of RAM and storage space, making it possible to operate such a solution often independent of the end user's computer power. All the computing and processing operations are done on the server, where the applications actually reside.

An example of an end user's interface module is presented in Figure 4.3. Structured as a browser front end, Citrix NFuse Application Portal Software® not only gives customers access to applications, their account information, current billing costs, and additional applications, but can also be set up to provide additional information about the company's stock performance, internal developments, and external press releases. This interface gives users flexibility to customize their desktop interface.

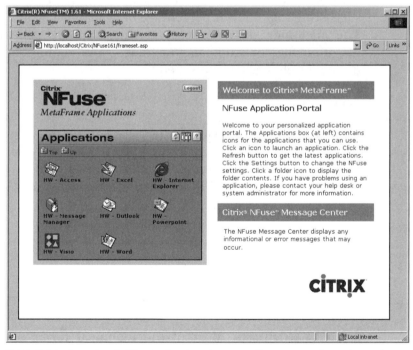

FIGURE 4.3 Citrix NFuse End-User Interface Example (Reprinted by permission of Citrix Systems, Inc.)

HOSTING INFRASTRUCTURE

Application availability. Most netsourcing providers guarantee some level of availability. For example, a netsourcing provider may guarantee that the application is available 95% of the time. What does this percentage mean to the customer? This means that the application could be down (i.e., unavailable to the customer) 8.4 hours per week! Table 4.1 quantifies the risk of unplanned downtime for each degree of availability.

Many netsourcing providers offer tiered pricing based on application availability. Thus the customer needs to determine how critical availability is to his or her business context. A customer's Web site that takes customer orders might require nearly no unscheduled downtime, suggesting 99.99+% service. An e-mail service used by employees might be less critical, suggesting that a lower percentage of availability would suffice. The customer should also have the supplier's schedule for maintenance, backup, and upgrades, and require advanced notice for changes in the schedule.

TABLE 4.1 Application Availability

	DOWNTIME	
APPLICATION AVAILABILITY (%)	MINUTES PER WEEK	HOURS PER WEEK
95	504	8.4
99	101	1.7
99.7	30	0.5
99.9	10	0.17
99.99	1	0.02

Application performance. Most of the technical terms associated with application performance have to do with the amount of data the application needs to send over the network. The more data sent, the slower the application will perform. For example, many netsourcing providers offer software that was initially written by independent software vendors (ISVs) for a client–server platform. The client–server architecture assumes that the servers, workstations, and networks connecting them were all housed locally on the customer's premises (this is called a *local area network*). Bandwidth was not a problem, so a large amount of data was constantly passed between the server and the desktops (client machines). An entire application and associated data may even be downloaded from the server to the client machine for execution. Or the server may send an entire screen refresh to the client machine every second even though the user had not changed anything. Such applications are called *fat clients*. Fat-client applications do not perform well over the Internet.

Netsourcing providers commonly provide two solutions. First, some netsourcing providers offer thin-client versions of ISV software. For example, Oracle has a thin-client version of its enterprise resource planning package. Thin-client versions are specifically written to perform rapidly over the Internet by minimizing the amount of data sent between server and client. A more common solution is to install middleware, such as Citrix or MS WinFrame discussed above. These products paint screens locally from software stored on client machines. This allows only *changed* data to be sent over the network, thus speeding application performance. Of course, these products must work with a Citrix server, and software must be installed on all client machines.

Multithreading is the ability of an application to execute program code simultaneously. Multithread capability increases the speed of application performance. Customers would want multithreading capability, for example, if they use a netsourcing provider to host a Web site that contains animation or video. The animation or video would be executed by the application as one thread while allowing the user to interface simultaneously with the Web site (e.g., scrolling) as another thread.

Server performance. Server performance means that once a customer transaction reaches the server, the server performs the task rapidly. The following issues affect server performance:

1. *Load balancing* is the ability to balance tasks on a single server with multiple processors or among multiple servers in a server cluster. Let's assume that a netsourcing provider has five servers. One server should not be overburdened while four servers sit idle. Load balancing would distribute customer tasks across the five servers to optimize performance.

2. *Multitenancy* is the ability to service multiple customers on one server. Multitenancy provides economies of scale for the netsourcing provider, but heavy loads from one customer might affect another customer's response time, especially in the absence of load balancing. Some customers prefer to incur the expense of a dedicated server for critical applications to avoid such interdependency.

3. *Interoperability* allows applications running on different operating systems to communicate. For example, a PeopleSoft module running on UNIX would be able to talk to another PeopleSoft module running on Windows NT if the netsourcing provider has interoperability capabilities. From the customer's perspective, the customer may have in-house systems written on one operating system that may need to interface with a netsourcing provider's application written for another operating system.

4. *Scalability* is the ability of the netsourcing provider to add capacity either by adding more servers with the same functionality (horizontal scalability) or by adding more processors within the same CPU (vertical scalability). From the customer perspective, the supplier should be able to accommodate customer increases or decreases in volume of transactions or users with no effect on performance. In addition, customers should still be charged based on volume of use regardless of whether a rapid decrease in volume would cause the netsourcing provider to have an idle server or whether an incremental increase would trigger the netsourcing provider to invest in an entirely new server.

Security. Security continues to be the principal concern of customers with respect to data confidentiality, service access, and general transmission security over networks. We have found that security is best discussed on three levels. The first level is the physical data and application security concerns of customers. Here customers want to be reassured that their data, wherever they are located, are sufficiently secure and protected. Application service providers commonly will colocate their servers and their customers' servers with a data center or colocator, who guarantees highest physical protection to the levels of governmental institutions, such as U.S. Department of Defense. These will be security-vetted regularly by independent auditors, for physical security. Additionally, customers want reassurance that data are sufficiently protected against viruses and external corruption. So the netsourcing provider will need to operate dedicated firewalls to avoid malicious parties from accessing particular customer data sets. Firewall access rules and/or architectures can be very complex, due to customers' different requirements.[1] Customers may, in turn, need to recheck that their netsourcing provider's firewall is properly configured and implements their security demands.

The second security-level concern is with data confidentiality and multilevel secure (MLS) operating systems.[2] MLS describes a classification system of unclassified, confidential, secret, and top-secret data that come from the military, but for the purpose of security within a netsourcing deal, the system allows customers to enforce data access and separation by user level. Clearly, it is not in the customers' interests to give, for example, shop-floor-level users access to the data destined for the CEO or CFO. There has to be a clear data separation and access level control by user according to the person's operational level within the organization. Additionally, confidentiality is a key concern when multiple customers are using the same centralized server and applications. For potential clients a paramount consideration will be to ensure that data generated by one user remains his or her private property and is never inadvertently revealed to another client.[3] For this, netsourcing providers will explicate not only physical but also software infrastructures developed to avoid possible data confidentially breaches. Users should inquire about access-level security to applications to provide adequate confidentiality among multiple users. However, there is no standard or common approach across netsourcing providers, and customers should clarify confidentiality and the multiple-level security issue with their netsourcing provider of choice.

The third level is the transmission security of data across the network infrastructure of a netsourcing provider. For customers, this is the heart of the security problem: sending information between the netsourcing provider and themselves, often, in their perception, on insecure networks, insecure in the sense that the computing system operates across networks that span the boundary of the firm. Hence data sent need to be protected to prevent competitors from capturing the data and using or corrupting and then sending the data on to disrupt their business.[4] There are a number of ways in which data transmissions can be protected. One way is by choosing, for example, a virtual private network (as discussed below) that provides authentication encryption through a 128-bit secure socket layer and hence data confidentially through encryption. Additionally, digital signatures can be employed that use one-way encryption to sign a document uniquely so that if anyone changes or tampers with the document, the digital signature will indicate these alterations. These two transmission securities may and often are used in conjunction to enforce data privacy.

Generally, customers need to remember that netsourcing providers spend significant amounts of time on developing and defining their security policy, which tends to be audited by a reputable independent agency for further reassurance. This approach to security often tends to be more comprehensive than that which customers themselves operate internally.

NETWORK SERVICE INFRASTRUCTURE

The speed of a network depends on many technical issues, including bandwidth, latency, utilization, and chattiness of protocol. *Bandwidth* is the carrying capacity of the network. Generally speaking, the greater the bandwidth, the faster and more costly the network. Most of the time, the customer selects a vendor's bandwidth package, such as a T1 line or a T3 line. The cost differences between vendor offerings may be hundreds of thousands of dollars; thus the customer needs to determine the most cost-effective bandwidth required for the type of data transmitted. Full-motion color video with voice would require about 6 megahertz of bandwidth, suggesting a T3 line, whereas voice and data would require significantly less.

Data latency is the amount of time the data spend in transit over the network. The shorter the data latency, the faster the response time for the customer. Delays in delivering data to a user can occur when traffic is heavy or when data packets keep getting rerouted across the network. One way to optimize network performance is to be able to identify and prioritize the type of data being sent. For example, a user who is downloading an immense file may be given lower priority than other users accessing e-mail. Customers want data latency measured in nanoseconds, but netsourcing providers will probably promise only 2 or 3 seconds of network transit time.

Network utilization is the amount of time elapsed actually transmitting data as opposed to transmitting control data or remaining idle. Network utilization depends on the *chattiness of protocol*. A *protocol* is a set of rules and procedures for sending data and control information required to transport data safely over the network. A chatty protocol might require that an acknowledgment be sent for every data packet transmitted. For example, Novell's SPX/IPX protocol required an acknowledgment for every packet sent. On a local area network, Novel's protocol did not slow response time, but on a wide area network, it did. Another example of a chatty protocol is the router protocol (RIP) part of the transmission control protocol for the Internet (TCP/IP), because it requires that routers talk to each other to adjust routing tables every 30 seconds. Another example of a chatty protocol is dial-up terminal emulation, which may have 30% overhead. This means for every dollar the customer spends, he or she is getting only 70 cents worth of actual data transmission. A nonchatty protocol, such as high-speed Ethernet, has only 2 to 5% overhead. Customers want high network utilization (low chattiness) to minimize idle time, overhead, and costs.

NETWORK INFRASTRUCTURE

Network performance varies greatly with the type of network selected by the customer. Generally, netsourcing customers may use the Internet, a virtual private network, or a private network. In our international survey we found that current netsourcing customers are accessing their service primarily via the all-pervasive Internet (see Figure 4.4). In fact, 55% of existing customers operate a technical infrastructure that is based on a secure socket layer (SSL) running 128-bit data encryption, which seemingly provides sufficient security for the majority of users. Of particular interest is the small number of existing customers (9% in total) that use a virtual private network, which ensures point-to-point network security. Unlike the expectations of many would-be customers who plan to access the provider service via a virtual private network (40%), 34% would be sufficiently happy with the security offered by an Internet connection.

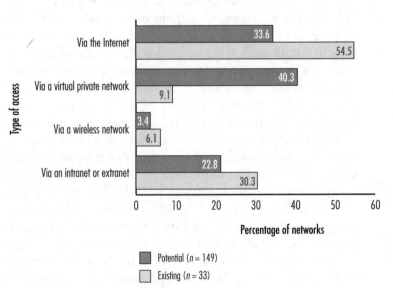

FIGURE 4.4 Netsourcing Networks of Existing and Potential Customers

EVALUATION OF OPTIONS

Next we look at advantages and disadvantages of network options. Netsourcing works by hosting the applications and data at a remote provider-managed site and by passing transactions to and from customer devices over a wide area network (WAN). Transactions can be passed over the Internet, over a virtual private network, or over a private network. The choice depends on the customer's need for connectivity, security, cost, implementation speed, and reliability (see Table 4.2).

The *Internet* is a public, cooperative, worldwide network of networks. The most distinguishing feature of the Internet is that no one owns it. The Internet has limitless connectivity— any computer can talk to any computer over the Internet. Because messages can be routed in many directions over the Internet, a failure in some parts of the network does not usually affect transmission delivery. (Exceptions sometimes occur; for example, the entire Internet was crippled in 1997 when a corrupted list of domain names was distributed to Internet routers.)

TABLE 4.2 Types of Networks Used in Netsourcing

CONSIDERATION	INTERNET	VPN	PRIVATE
COST	Low	Medium	High
SECURITY	Low	Medium	High
RELIABILITY	Low	Medium	High
CONNECTIVITY	High	Limited	Limited
IMPLEMENTATION TIME	Days	Week(s)	Weeks/months
SUITABLE APPLICATIONS	e-marketing; e-commerce traveling users	Stationary users; back-office applications	Stationary users; business-to-business

The Internet is well suited for public domain material because of the connectivity, low cost, and fast implementation. For these reasons, the Internet is the most frequently used network for netsourcing providers. For example, e-marketing sites that post public domain information such as product catalogs, press releases, and investor information are ideal for netsourcing delivery. But private information, such as individual data transactions and back-office systems, normally merits a more secure WAN.

A *virtual private network* (VPN) takes a slice of the Internet and treats it as a more private network by establishing firewalls, tunneling, and encryption. A VPN is frequently used for netsourcing because many applications require the additional security. In addition, a VPN can be implemented within weeks. But because a VPN must define the endpoints, it is not suitable for mobile users or retail customers. Experts also warn that customers must know their transmission requirements in advance:

> If you subscribe to a virtual private network, you subscribe to a data rate. If your traffic is below the data rate, the network is guaranteed as 100% reliable. If you exceed your contractual data rate, all bets are off. Thus, customers really need to know their stuff.
> —*Ashok Subramanian, CSO, Technisoft America*

Also, on VPNs:

> When reliability and cost are concerns connecting to security conscious clients, a VPN with encrypted tunnels is an excellent choice. We use a more open architecture on the front end to allow customers access to help desk, enterprise management and e-commerce technologies, but use the Internet, VPNs and encrypted tunnels for access to back-end resources.
> —*Mark Cook, VP Marketing, Center 7*

Loudcloud employs virtual private networks to provide a cost-effective and secure means to establish a virtual connection between the netsourcing provider's corporate office and its infrastructure. VPN's employ powerful authentication, key exchange and encryption technologies to build dynamic tunnels that allow for secure data transmissions, even over public networks such as the Internet.

> —*Jeff Kupietzky, general manager, Customer Solutions, Loudcloud*[5]

A *private network* is the most secure but is usually the most expensive network. Adding a customer to a netsourcer's private network entails laying privately owned wires and cables and can therefore take weeks to implement. Like a VPN, the ends of the network must be predefined and stable, again making this a poor option for a large number of disperse and/or mobile users. A netsourcing provider customer might consider a private network for back-office systems or for a business-to-business application for ongoing relationships among a limited number of users.

Some experts would recommend using a private network in cases where reliability and predictability may never be compromised, or the design of a legacy application requires that a guaranteed high-bandwidth connection be in place. This is typically seen with integration between Web-based exchanges and legacy ERP/fulfillment applications.

Netsourcing providers may deploy applications via all three network types or may deploy on only one type of network. For example, BlueMeteor helps the customer select the appropriate network during their rapid design process. Transchannel, however, offers only a private network:

> Network performance is not a problem in our ASP model. We dedicate a private T-1 for each client.
> —*Lorne Kaufman, vice-president of operations, Transchannel*[6]

Similarly, Technisoft America helps clients determine the trade-offs between high security and high application performance and response time:

> It is important to remember that security and application response time and performance are conflicting goals. Higher levels of security using firewalls or encryption are achieved at

the consequence of slower response time. Higher security requires additional layers of software that must be traversed between the server and the client. The same is true for interoperable applications—they require significant middleware layers in order to accomplish their goals.

—*Ashok Subramanian, CSO, Technisoft America*

Customers may even switch network types. To meet rapid installation requirements, eOnline starts with public networks. Most customers, however, are moved to a global network to promote better reliability and performance, for which customers are willing to pay.

It is important to keep in mind that there are always exceptions to general WAN guidelines. For example, some experts argue that frame relay[7] technologies can be deployed inexpensively over a supplier's private network, and that private is not always expensive nor public insecure. Sometimes frame relay technology is less expensive than a public network. One customer, for example, chose frame relay for a large project that included 1000 users in 15 states and over 400 locations.

Finally, many netsourcing providers often point out that poor network performance is most often attributable to the customer and not the netsourcing provider. One said that the network itself is not often the source of the slowdown. Rather, more typically it is the customer's connection to the Internet, or user access to the Internet. Another found the majority of challenges for network performance were with customers' local networks.

CONCLUSIONS

In the netsourcing context, there is an entire network between the customer's device (a desktop, a personal digital assistance, a Web-enabled cell phone) and the software and data remotely housed by the netsourcing provider. Netsourcing customers will want to ensure application availability, security, and response time. Because the networking issues can be very complex, many customers rely on their netsourcing providers to help them determine their needs. Although many netsourcing providers have suitably informed consultants to help customers make these tough choices, relying on a supplier can be dangerous for a naive customer. Based on our extensive prior research on traditional outsourcing, customers need to cultivate technical expertise when negotiating with a netsourcing provider. The customer and the netsourcing provider just naturally have conflicting agendas. Customers ideally want 100% availability, 100% security, and nanosecond response time for hosted applications for little cost. Netsourcing providers want to minimize performance commitments (especially over public networks which they don't control) and need to maximize their profit margins. Through the negotiation process, the customer and supplier need to negotiate the network type, and application, server, and network service levels. (These decisions should not be made in the sales process.) It is simply good business to have a technical expert represent the customer's needs during negotiations. The technical expert may be from in-house personnel for larger customers but will more likely be outside experts hired by smaller customers. Hiring an expert, even for a day, would be well worth the benefit to the customer in the long run.

ENDNOTES

1. "Secure Netsourcing Providers: Netsourcing Provider Security Best Practice," Jaws Technologies, Inc., Boston, 1999.

2. Ibid.

3. Ibid.

4. Ibid.

5. Quoted from *www.aspisland.com/panel/answers.asp*

6. Ibid.

7. Frame relay is a protocol for connecting devices on a wide area network, which is inexpensive but slower than other protocols such as ATM.

5 U.S.-Based Netsourcing Case Studies

In Chapters 5 and 6 we present 10 original case studies on netsourcing suppliers and their customers. Five suppliers based in the United States are discussed in this chapter: Corio, EDS, Host Analytics, MainPass, and Zland. Five suppliers based in Europe are covered in Chapter 6: Lodge, marviQ, SAP, Siennax, and Vistorm. The division of cases by continent is arbitrary, as suppliers based in one country often provide services to customers located elsewhere. Indeed, some of the cases—most notably EDS and SAP—are truly global players. The continental divide of cases is really to give you a breather. In the following introduction, we provide an executive summary of the five U.S.-based case studies by highlighting the lessons from customer and supplier perspectives. Next, the 10 cases are compared at a high level to further direct readers to the cases of most interest to them.

INTRODUCTION TO THE CASE STUDIES

CORIO OVERVIEW

Customers will learn how application portfolio assemblers such as Corio can provide access to best-of-breed software over the Internet on a rental basis based on the size of the customer organization. Customers from SMEs contemplating netsourcing for name-brand software such as SAP, PeopleSoft, and Siebel will be most interested in reading about Corio. Because Corio's successes and challenges are covered widely by the trade press, Corio will be a company that potential customers will want to monitor continually. Through this case study, readers will quickly understand how Corio got started and how it has evolved thus far. Customers may easily continue to track Corio in the future, because as a publicly traded company (CRIO on the NASDAQ), information is widely available.

For suppliers, Corio continues to be a barometer for the entire ASP space. It is a particularly good example of a supplier that has grown in product and service breadth through strategic alliances with established ISV and consulting companies. Corio is also an example of a good industry citizen because the company spends considerable time educating the public about the netsourcing concept, which in turn benefits all suppliers.

EDS OVERVIEW

Although the giant EDS has waded quietly in the netsourcing space, they are certainly poised to create a tidal wave. Because of EDS's critical mass of global expertise and existing global infrastructure, they are able to compete in nearly every segment of the netsourcing market. Like Corio, they can resell best-of-breed software in a one-to-many model or create customized solutions—or more commonly, provide a combination of both. They are particularly primed to service their existing customers, who already know and trust them. For people who still think of EDS as the regimented systems integrators, think again by reading this case.

HOST ANALYTICS OVERVIEW

Customers from SMEs who are interested in business intelligence capabilities will be most interested in reading about Host Analytics's products and services. Host Analytics software helps customers extract business intelligence from existing enterprise systems (although they also helped one SME select and install an enterprise system as a precursor to the delivery of business intelligence capabilities). The capabilities can be delivered via a netsourcing model (e.g., Host Analytics will house the software on a server it manages on behalf of the customer). Alternatively, Host Analytics allows customers to house the software on the customer's owned and managed servers. Customers who are intimated by technology will be pleased to read about a company that focuses on business solutions first, enabled by technology second.

As the founder of Host Analytics had seed capital from the sale of his existing business, suppliers will not find this case study to be a tale of investor-seeking woe. But Host Analytics is a good example of a company based on proprietary software offered through multiple delivery channels. Host Analytics keeps software development and maintenance costs low through their India-based employees.

MAINPASS OVERVIEW

As MainPass is still a startup company, there are no current customers. But there are ample lessons for current suppliers or people wanting to start a netsourcing business. By early 2002 MainPass's business plan was sufficiently robust to secure additional funding in an indifferent venture capital marketplace. Its niche strategy into the legal and similar professions made sense. It possesses in-house capability in the legal business that supports understanding of client requirements and appropriate customization of the support these clients require. It has allied with strongly branded, proven software providers. It has demonstrable, relevant, core technical competence, together with innovative, reliable wireless LANs and related products. It provides information and systems security levels appropriate to the legal environment and beyond what customers could achieve. MainPass demonstrates how to ride out a downturn by slimming costs, building core capability, and not hurrying to market but waiting for competitors to suffer cash burnouts. A further learning point is to scale revenue growth to what you can deliver. There are dangers in overcommitting and not being able to scale up fast enough to meet demand, especially if the pricing model involves long payback periods on initially slim margin contracts.

ZLAND OVERVIEW

Customers from SMEs interested in e-commerce capabilities, such as building Web sites with product catalogs and taking customer orders, will find the Zland case an example of a low-cost alternative to building it yourself. This case shows how customers can quickly implement e-commerce sites through Zland's proprietary templated software. The franchise model also helps the novice customer with significant handholding, as sales and marketing occur through 400 franchises worldwide.

Suppliers will be interested in Zland as an example of a franchise business model operating in the netsourcing space. The concept is to create high levels of service through local franchises while keeping costs low through centralized software development and management. The franchise model in the netsourcing space has had its challenges because widespread customer education is still needed. Unlike customers who readily identify a fast-food or retail franchise, many customers are still unaware of the equivalent of e-commerce retailers.

SUMMARY OF THE CASES

Taken together, these five cases, in addition to the five cases presented in Chapter 6, tell a story of how netsourcing suppliers are trying to adapt quickly to a rapidly emerging marketplace. Indeed, most of these companies do not even want an xSP label—they want to focus on the business solutions they deliver. The fact that some or all of their solutions are delivered in the netsourcing mode is becoming increasingly incidental. Part of the shift in focus away from netsourcing, and in particular away from the acronym ASP, toward business solutions has occurred because of the bad press and skepticism surrounding ASPs. But a more important reason for the shift in focus is that suppliers found that customers approached them for business solutions—customers were not interested in netsourcing per se. Often, the netsourcing component became relevant to customers only when discussing the options for delivering and pricing the business solution. This again highlights the notion that netsourcing is merely a delivery channel and a pricing model for applications and business services.

Table 5.1 provides an overview of the 10 cases, including their business products, services, revenues, profits, employees, and customers. This table immediately highlights that the suppliers range from very small startup companies such as MainPass Technologies to the industry giants such as EDS and SAP. The number of customers is still typically small, but growing. Products, such as those of Corio, EDS, and Siennax, range from single applications to total portfolio delivery. Some suppliers offer their proprietary software via netsourcing, including Host Analytics, Zland, and SAP. Other suppliers primarily resell best-of-breed packages from ISVs, such as Corio, EDS, Lodge, and Siennax.

TABLE 5.1 Profiles of Case Companies

COMPANY	FOUNDED	BASE	PRIVATE/ PUBLIC	PRODUCTS/ SERVICES	2000 REVENUE	2000 PROFIT	APPROXIMATE NO. EMPLOYEES	NO. CUSTOMERS (SEATS)
Corio	1998	California	CRIO	Portfolio of named ISV applications for back- and front-office applications	$44 million	Negative	400	80 customers
EDS	1962	Texas	EDS	Total portfolio management, including named ISV applications for back- and front-office applications in pure ASP space	In ASP space, $200 million in contracts	In ASP space, positive	130,000 (ASP head count is leveraged; thus an exact head count devoted to ASP is not possible)	50 customers; on average, 150 users per customer
Host Analytics	2000	Missouri	Private	Proprietary business intelligence software	$2 million	Positive	12	3 customers
MainPass Technologies	2001	California	Private	Proprietary technology desktop and e-commerce applications; wireless applications infrastructure provision	N/A (just starting)	N/A (just starting)	12	3 customers by early 2002
Zland	1995	California	Private	Proprietary e-commerce applications	$7 million	Negative	250	700 customers
Lodge	1999	Belgium and Netherlands	Private	SAP ERP application	$3.5 million	Positive	38	13 customers

TABLE 5.1 Profiles of Case Companies (continued)

Company	Founded	Base	Private/Public	Products/Services	2000 Revenue	2000 Profit	Approximate No. Employees	No. Customers (Seats)
marviQ	1998	Netherlands	Private	Java-based platform offering integrated ERP, CRM, collaboration, and workflow functionality from ISV applications	$2.1 million	Negative	120	5 customers
mySAP	1999	Germany	Public	Propriety ERP applications	$6 billion (company-wide)	Positive	22,000 (ASP head count is leveraged; thus an exact head count devoted to ASP is not possible)	4 million licensed users (June 2001)
Siennax	1998	Netherlands and Germany	Private	Offers a proprietary intranet suite, Microsoft Exchange 2000, Lotus Learning Space, electronic document management, and customer relationship management solutions	$2.5 million	Negative	109	15,000 licensed users
Vistorm (formerly eSoft)	1991	United Kingdom	Private	Full VPN and security services portfolio; full ISV desktop applications; infrastructure provision and service	$30 million	Positive	330	More than 1000 users

To get a better understanding of the exact nature of the applications being offered by the suppliers studied, refer to Table 5.2. Among our cases, the most frequently offered packages are in the e-commerce and customer relationship management (CRM) space, which is ideally suited for netsourcing. The next most frequently offered applications are in communications and personal productivity space, which customers increasingly are viewing as commodities. These frequencies correspond with our survey results, which show that communications and e-commerce are the most frequently netsourced applications. Thus, our case studies, although selected opportunistically, are representative of suppliers operating in the new marketspace.

The cases presented in Chapters 5 and 6 are based on interviews with senior executives, client care managers, and marketing and public relations staff on the supplier side, where these were available. We also gained customer perspectives from interviewing customer contacts. In addition, we gained views from industry analysts and utilized public sources where information was not forthcoming from these main sources. Our goal throughout was to achieve an objective and independent analysis in order to provide a realistic picture of application hosting in the context of overall business solutions.

TABLE 5.2 Products Offered[a]

PRODUCT	CORIO	EDS	HOST ANALYTICS	MAINPASS	ZLAND	LODGE	MYSAP	MARVIQ	SIENNAX	VISTORM
ERP	X	X				X	X			
SUPPLY CHAIN MANAGEMENT	X					X	X			
BUSINESS INTELLIGENCE	X		X				X			
DATA WAREHOUSING	X		X				X			
CRM	X	X				X	X	X	X	
E-COMMERCE	X	X			X	X	X	X	X	X
E-MAIL		X		X				X	X	X
COMMUNICATIONS		X		X				X	X	X
PERSONAL PRODUCTIVITY				X				X	X	X
DIGITAL SIGNATURE									X	

a. Authors' analysis, late 2001.

CORIO

Corio.com is considered one of the oldest ASPs, established in 1998, and is one of the founders of the ASP Consortium. Along with FutureLink and USI, Corio is one of the most widely recognized companies operating in the ASP space. As such, investors, potential customers, and industry analysts constantly look to Corio as the bellwether for the entire ASP industry. In many ways, Corio has the dual challenge not only of marketing its own company but also of proselytizing on behalf of the entire ASP industry. For example, the current CEO, George Kadifa, is also the chair of the Information Technology Association of America's (ITAA) ASP board of directors. In that capacity he is one of the few ASP zealots who still actively promotes the ASP nomenclature.

Corio has survived the dot.com crash and smaller-than-expected ASP demand by focusing on its core business proposition—to offer customers best-of-breed software and services for a monthly fee for less cost than if the customers managed it themselves. The company's model requires strategic partnerships with ISVs to provide access to best-of-breed software, infrastructure partners, and selling partners—capabilities they cannot afford on their own. In 2001, Corio added another major service offering, Corio Intelligent Infrastructure (known as Corio.Net), which offers hosting services for ISVs and customers. Corio discovered that its major investment in expertise for its core business could be better leveraged by extending these services beyond its own application offerings. Thus Corio's two major lines of business are pure-play application provision and infrastructure management.

Like many other ASPs, Corio has seen a steady growth in revenues (see Table 5.3) but is still operating at a loss. On April 21, 2000, Corio submitted forms to the Securities and Exchange Commission (SEC) for an initial public offering (IPO). Unlike some ASPs that pulled their requests due to a downturn in investor confidence, Corio's stock went public on Friday, July 21, 2000 and sold at $21.75 per share. But, by

TABLE 5.3 Corio.com at a Glance

FOUNDED	September 1998	
BUSINESS MODEL	Aggregator/integrator: rents a suite of hosted, integrated, best-of-breed business applications	
REVENUES	1999: $5,782,000	2000: $44,000,000
LOSSES	1999: $44,522,000	2000 (3Q only): $80,845,000
ASSET BASE	1999: $61,596,000	2000: $181,000,000
NUMBER OF EMPLOYEES	1999: 279	Dec. 2000: 498 June 2001: 420
NUMBER OF CUSTOMERS	Approx. 25	Approx. 80 as of summer 2000
NUMBER OF PRODUCTS	Approx. 20 applications	

December 21, 2000, the stock price had plummeted to $1.41. The stock price reflects the crash in the entire ASP market as well as the technology market overall. Gary Dean, a security analyst and ASP specialist for Robert W. Baird, an investment bank, feels that the technology press oversold Corio:

> [Corio] really first began to get attention back as early as late 1998 when it signed its first contract to host a PeopleSoft application with its site. You know, that company between then and now has received a tremendous amount of press and attention and subsequently went public in the middle of this year. And, as we talked to investors while that company was on their road show, we were uniformly surprised that almost every one of the investors we talked with was shocked at how small Corio was and the fact that they really only had 27 active customers at the time of the IPO. I think based on that amount of attention and press the company had received, most investors, certainly in the public domain, were under the impression that the company's maturity and its business model was further along than that. That's not a slap against Corio, that's just a reality of the fact that our technology press covers companies from the time the ideas are incubated and

speaks and writes about them in a way in which we believe that their business models are more mature than they are.[1]

Corio's stock had not recovered as of winter 2001, despite a first quarter 2001 report showing the company to be on target for 50% annual revenue growth and profitability by the end of 2002. Corio also has plenty of cash to survive until they are profitable, as they have nearly $120 million on hand. Until then, Corio has reined in expenses, primarily through natural attrition and a job layoff (announced May 2001).

PRODUCTS

In the application provision space, Corio rents and provides management of third-party best-of-breed software to customers. Corio offers ISV software in the following spaces: enterprise resource planning (current product offerings include SAP and PeopleSoft), customer relationship management (Siebel Systems), e-commerce (BroadVision, CommerceOne, Oracle, RequisteTechnology, and Moai), and business intelligence (E.Piphany). Customers pay a monthly subscription fee to access these applications using their browser over a virtual private network. Customers are typically required to sign a three-year contract.

From a customer perspective, the promised value added includes lower and more predictable IT costs, best-of-breed applications, accelerated implementation, good service and support, and business process integration. For example, Corio adds value by providing real-time business process integration among packages through their proprietary software called Orion. A salesman for Corio demonstrated that a purchase order from CommerceOne is immediately available to PeopleSoft's accounts payable system. Similarly, a sale in BroadVision is immediately available to an SAP invoice. Based in XML, Orion is a router, mapper, and integrator for Corio's application suite. One respondent compared Siebel:

> Siebel is a front-end customer relationship management tool which advertises 360 degree view of the customer. Function-

ality includes sales force automation, marketing, customer service, e-commerce, call center. If a customer calls, the person answering the phone sees every sale the customer ever made, mailings to his house, complaints. But Siebel needs to plug data in somewhere, such as PeopleSoft or SAP. So Siebel can take an online order, but they cannot generate a work order to fill the order. That's why Corio built Orion. To connect these applications.

Corio's fee structure is similar to that of other ASPs—customers pay an implementation fee and a monthly subscription fee. Some customers, such as Sportingnews.com, chose to hire KPMG to do the implementation rather than to hire Corio. The monthly subscription rate is based on number of users for some applications (such as SAP, PeopleSoft, and Siebel) and transaction-based pricing for other applications (such as CommerceOne and BroadVision). Compared to traditional outsourcing contracts, contracts are very short because service customization is minimal. There is about a three-page master-level agreement and two or three more pages appended to the contract for each application rented. Service levels are 99.5%, and clients access products using virtual private networks and IP tunneling.

Thus, Corio's business model is based on serving as a single point of accountability for third-party, best-of-breed application management, security, infrastructure, data center, and network management. Corio's application management center manages these activities 24 hours a day, seven days a week. However, Corio does not own and operate its own data center. Initially, Corio leased servers from Exodus (Exodus hosts over 27,000 servers worldwide), but Corio now owns its own servers, which are located in secure cages in outsourced data centers by XO Communications and iStructure. Corio's main competitor, USI, initially built and operated its own data center. But Corio felt that operating a world-class data center requires an enormous amount of capital and decided instead to host its applications elsewhere. In an interview with E. B. Flanagan, George Kadifa, Corio CEO, said that ASPs do not need to own their own data centers: "From day 1, Corio has believed that method to be a flawed strategy, so we executed our model without doing it. That decision saved us about $250 to $300 million in infrastructure costs."[2] Recently, USI followed suit by outsourcing data center operations for the same reason.

Despite the fact that Corio does not own its own data center, it does provide infrastructure services. Announced in December 2000, Corio decided to promote its proprietary infrastructure as a discrete service offering. Corio now offers infrastructure services including data center management (although iStructure and XO Communications own the data centers), technical services administration (such as backup), functional application support, service-level management, security management, and storage management. The primary target customers for Corio.Net are ISVs that wish to enter the ASP space. Corio.Net allows ISVs to offer software solutions to customers without building an ASP offering themselves. The ISVs will maintain the relationships directly with the customers, but the ISV can access Corio's sales and billing tools. Docent (an e-learning ISV) and Intershop (an e-business ISV) both selected Corio.Net to host their applications. A secondary market for Corio.Net is to upsell to existing customers who want to offload applications, as well as to offer hosting services to new customers who aren't quite ready for their off-the-shelf application offerings.

In both the pure-play and infrastructure provision, Corio aims to deliver cost reduction rather than in-house management by achieving economies of scale through their one-to-many business model. In its 2000 annual report, Corio describes its one-to-many business model as follows:

> Our business is based on providing an array of standardized services to numerous customers. We believe that we will be able to achieve the economies of scale inherent in this one-to-many model by being able to reduce the costs we incur in delivering our services. We intend to continue to develop implementation templates, innovative application management tools and integration models that can be used for numerous applications across a variety of companies and industries.

We believe this strategy enables us to leverage our IT resources to deliver cost-effectively high standards of service and support. By continually reducing our costs of providing service, we believe we can build a profitable business over the long term.

Given the one-to-many business model, the most likely customers will be SMEs. But as you will see in the next section, Corio is clearly trying to break into the Fortune 2000.

CUSTOMER PERSPECTIVE

Corio's original parent company was Data Systems Connectors, Inc. (DSCI), a professional services company. In September 1998, Corio founders acquired all the capital stock of DSCI. Thus Corio's first customers were inherited from DSCI, but all these contracts expired by the end of 1999. Corio's first non-DSCI customers were primarily new startup companies with plenty of cash, no entrenched business practices, and no legacy systems. On Corio.com's Web site, six of their customer success stories are from customers in Internet-related businesses: Enstar, Simplexis, Vertical Networks, Zentropy, MadetoOrder.com, and Excite@Home. This customer base could be seen as risky. Such companies were more likely to be merged, undergo financial difficulties, or even cease operations altogether. This potential volatility could affect Corio's business and operating results.

Corio soon realized that the viability of Corio depended on the viability of its customers. It became diligent about terminating customers who could not pay their bills, and marketed closely to financially stable customers. In 2000, Corio had only 20% of its revenues from dot.com startups, and that figure had been reduced to 10% by late 2001. Most recently, Excite@Home declared bankruptcy, highlighting Corio's need to find stable customers. Corio was also trying to market to larger companies; however, some of the ISV license agreements limit the customer size and geographic location to which the customer can market. Where Corio is not tethered, it has been using an incremental marketing approach to attract larger customers. It hopes to up sell to these customers after they gain confidence in Corio.

The strategy is to work with Fortune 500 organizations wanting to offload IT tasks such as procurement or supply chain management. Familiarity and good experiences may well then lead to outsourcing more strategic functions and activities to Corio.

Corio is making some progress in attracting larger clients. In their first quarter 2001 quarterly report, Corio noted that their average revenues per customer increased to approximately $40,000 per month from the average level of about $25,000 in the prior fiscal year. But marketing costs to customers—particularly large customers—proved high; Corio spent nearly $12 million in 1999 on marketing. So Corio sought a better way to attract more SMEs as well as larger customers. In April 2000, Corio entered into a strategic alliance with Ernst & Young (EY) Consulting. EY purchased 7 million shares of Corio stock at $6.50 per share. EY agreed to offer Corio services exclusively to its high-growth and middle-market customers in the Americas. In 2000, Ernst & Young merged with Cap Gemini, providing Corio with a potentially greater customer reach.

Concerning customers' experiences, Corio's current customers have received a significant amount of press, as the market craves stories on how to use an ASP successfully. In the November 30, 2000 issue of *PlanetIT*, reporter Jennifer Maseli interviewed the president and CEO of CommodiNet, Satoru Hirai. Hirai's company is an online trading CommodiNet exchange operating in San Francisco, Malaysia, Singapore, and Hong Kong. He wanted a third party to host and manage the online exchange, including multivendor catalogs, multiple auction formats, and dynamic trading capabilities. After evaluating several companies, Hirai selected Corio because of their consulting and 24-hour support. Corio had the exchange operating by September 2000. Currently, more than 300 CommodiNet customers buy and sell rubber commodities on the exchange in deals often worth in excess of $1 million. Corio satisfied CommodiNet's need for quick implementation, but Corio's EMarket Exchange package does not support multiple languages, which is crucial to a global commerce provider. If Corio does not support multiple languages by the time the contract expires in three years, CommodiNet will probably shop elsewhere.

Other customer success stories (provided by a Corio spokesperson) include Vertical Networks Corporation. The CEO, Alan Fraser, says that were he to run his business applications himself, he would need to spend $4 million straight off on hardware and software, and then have a staff of at least three engineers. By letting Corio handle the matter, he spends only $250,000 a year.

On Corio's Web site, Excite@Home (now bankrupt) is listed not only as Corio's first customer but as a resounding success story. Excite was an Internet portal company that provided broad-based content and navigation services to the consumer public. @Home was a broadband Internet access company for the consumer and commercial markets. In May of 1999, @Home Corporation and Excite merged to create a global media company that offered consumers content and interactive services across both narrow and broadband line networks. To make the merger work, Excite@Home needed to integrate its software applications quickly. Excite@Home chose Corio's offering of PeopleSoft modules for financial management, distribution, and human resources. Excite@Home had these applications live in 60 days. The company wanted to outsource this activity so that management members could focus attention on their core capabilities.

In part, Excite@Home had a preconceived notion that an outsourcing option was a better match, especially as IT support for a finance ERP system, at the time, was difficult to find. Moreover, in one quarter Excite@Home tripled its revenue growth over the period before. Thus it needed to focus its energies on projects and infrastructure that would have massive impact on its market performance.

Besides rapid integration and focusing on core capabilities, Excite@Home also required a scalable solution. If the company purchased PeopleSoft directly, too much cash would be required upfront. Corio's ASP pricing and scalability of product was a better option because, with the Corio model, Excite@Home could more easily scale the number of users and reorganize. In the event of an acquisition, for example, ERP expenses would increase massively using the old payment system tied to a revenue growth model. Corio's model was based on number of users and costs were much more predictable. Excite@Home could also put a new acquisition on to its enterprise system more quickly. With the Corio model, there were considerable advantages in efficiency and scale.

EDS

U.S.-based startup companies such as Corio, USInternetworking, and Interreliant have received the credit and spotlight for creating the ASP business model. Many startup ASPs, however, are losing millions of dollars because they are investing so much money on infrastructure while collecting only monthly revenues from clients. We have noted that many startup ASPs have already closed shop because they ran out of cash. But analysts have been predicting that large IT suppliers, such as Accenture, CSC, EDS, and IBM, will eventually dominate the ASP space. These players already have the infrastructure, customer relationships, trusted name brand, and global skills to deliver a customer-focused application hosting service. Although the press surrounding these larger IT suppliers has been surprisingly quiet, some of these major players have already entered the space in a big way. This case highlights one of those big players—EDS (see Table 5.4).

EDS already offers a wide variety of application hosting services, from a *one-to-many* resell of over 22 popular soft-

TABLE 5.4 EDS at a Glance

FOUNDED	1962 by Ross Perot
INCORPORATED	1994; split from General Motors in 1996
ASP BUSINESS MODEL	Full suite of application hosting services from one-to-many provision of packaged software to custom one-to-one solutions
TOTAL 2000 EDS REVENUES	$19 billion
TOTAL EDS PROFITS	$1 billion
ASP REVENUES	Signed $200 million in contracts by first quarter 2001
ASP PROFITS	ASP space is generating positive, yet undisclosed profits
TOTAL NUMBER OF EDS EMPLOYEES	125,000
NUMBER OF ASP CUSTOMERS IN ONE-TO-MANY SPACE AS OF SECOND QUARTER 2001	47
NUMBER OF PRODUCTS IN ONE-TO-MANY ASP SPACE	More than 20 packaged applications in the areas of messaging and collaboration, e-commerce, customer relationship management, and enterprise resource management

ware packages such as SAP, PeopleSoft, and Microsoft Exchange to custom application hosting in a *one-to-one* model. But the one-to-many and one-to-one dichotomy is not very useful. From an EDS customer perspective, EDS shows one face to the customer. The EDS manager for a client account can deliver business solutions for that client's particular needs by leveraging EDS resources worldwide. Thus, many of EDS's client solutions are actually delivered in a blended environment that includes both hosted applications (one-to-many model) and as traditional outsourcing (one-to-one model). For example, a major electric utility is an EDS customer that has a blended solution. EDS is delivering some applications (such as PeopleSoft) via a one-to-many ASP as well as providing one-to-one managed support on site at the client. Other customers with blended solutions include General Motors and Rolls-Royce.

EDS thus strives to provide total business solutions for a client's entire application portfolio (although EDS also provides services for a client wanting only a single application). As you will also see in the case of Host Analytics, EDS is not selling ASP, it is selling business services that may or may not be delivered to customers in a hosted environment. Although this case focuses on EDS's application hosting services,[3] it is important to keep in mind the breadth and depth of EDS offerings.

Compared with startup ASPs, EDS has the ability to leverage a global investment in ASP hosting and provisioning infrastructure and applications expertise. EDS assets poised for application hosting services include over 1 million square feet of data center capacity, a global network, 35,000 application specialists, established relationships with over 20 independent software vendors (SAP, PeopleSoft, Microsoft, etc.), varied sales and marketing channels around the world, and established relationships with current customers for cross/up selling in the ASP space. Thus EDS's ability to offer ASP services requires almost no capital investment, only a repackaging of solutions. By the first quarter 2001, EDS had $200 million worth of pure-play ASP contracts signed with nearly 50 customers, making them one of the largest ASP players in the space.

Although EDS shows a single face to the client, the EDS internal organizational structure is highly matrixed, allowing client-care managers to pull resources from over 100 global solution centers worldwide. In 1999, Dick Brown, the new CEO, reorganized EDS on a global basis into four lines of business: information solutions (representing nearly 75% of EDS revenues), business process management, e-solutions, and EDS's consulting arm—A.T. Kearney. But as you will see in this case study (particularly evident in EDS's care of Alpha

Corporation), EDS resources can be leveraged from any line of business to service any client.

The EDS corporate ASP offering is housed in the information solutions line of business located in Plano, Texas, and managed by the vice-president of application services marketing and portfolio management, who has global responsibility for application hosting services. The main task is to assemble or repackage global EDS assets into a coherent set of services to offer customers. This case study will closely examine those services. The sale of application services can occur through many channels: a customer may call EDS directly to rent an application, or sales can occur through and with EDS's strategic partnerships with ISVs or be initiated by an EDS client-care manager who needs application hosting services as part of a broader opportunity with a client.

To gain a better perspective on the latter sales channel, we looked at a large customer site, headed by the executive director of business services. We use the pseudonym "Alpha" to protect the customer's identity. This account is also housed in the information solutions line of business, but located on the customer site. The executive director and EDS communicated frequently on how best to leverage EDS resources worldwide to better service Alpha. Although the ASP offering to Alpha is still in the planning stages, in our view, EDS was clearly focused on delivering end-to-end digital business services for their existing customers.

HOSTING AND APPLICATION SERVICES

In the course of this research, we encountered many suppliers and consultants who view the entire application hosting space as a layered stack of services (see Chapter 1). EDS's view of the service stacks is as follows:

6. Extended enterprise services
5. Application management
4. Application maintenance and operations
3. Application enablement
2. Managed operations
1. Data center and connectivity

The first three layers of the EDS model—data center and connectivity, managed operations, and application enablement—are generally referred to as hosting and provisioning. This is what many ASPs offer today to clients: access to software over a network. EDS provides abundant evidence that they are world class in hosting and provisioning. Some of the standard services offered in these first three stacks include:

- Systems management, including backup, storage, capacity, and performance management
- Configuration management, including workload balancing, asset and procurement management, refresh services, and hardware support
- Client service management, including change management, continual operational support coverage, standard service-level management, and client-specific service-level management

These services are priced via a utility model using a tiered approach based on customer need, such as an entry price, basic price, an enhanced price, or a premier price.

Where EDS differentiates itself from other ASPs is on the top three layers of services: application maintenance and operations, application management, and extended enterprise services. In essence, these are services that many small suppliers cannot offer, such as integration, customization, and application functionality support. Examples of specific services offered within the top three layers of the service stack include:

- Predefined rapid implementation plan
- Checklists and templates for application data conversion
- Legacy systems integration
- Train-the-trainer guidelines for end-user training
- Software implementation tailored to a specific client's needs
- 24 × 7 toll-free level 1 support within 60 seconds
- Level 2 application expertise support
- Application performance tuning

A closer view of the top three layers of the service stack reveals that customers may have or want packaged applications, custom applications, or most commonly, a combination. Our limited research suggests that EDS offers application services described above for an entire portfolio of applications.

In the pure ASP space, most customers are looking for packaged applications. They want rapid implementation of named ISV products for a monthly fee. EDS currently offers many named ISV software items, arranged in four towers of functionality: messaging and collaboration, e-commerce, customer relationship management, and enterprise resource management (see Table 5.5).

TABLE 5.5 Named ISV Software Offered by EDS

MESSAGING AND COLLABORATION	E-COMMERCE	CUSTOMER RELATIONSHIP MANAGEMENT	ENTERPRISE RESOURCE MANAGEMENT
Exchange	mySAP.com	eSales	mySAP.com
Intermail	Oracle	PeopleSoft	Oracle
LearningSpace	Ariba		PeopleSoft
QuickPlace	eMerchant		TimeTRak!
Sametime			ExpenseTrak!
Notes			IdealHire
NexPrise			

EDS also offers at this date supply chain management, business intelligence, data warehousing, and digital signatures. Any product that EDS offers must pass a rigid certification process for application performance and interoperability in EDS's global hosted environment. Nearly 60% of the ISV software tested to date has failed EDS's certification on the first attempt.

The certification process is rigorous. In workshop mode, an ISV would be talked through how to move to a monthly revenue model, the cost model, and price curves. The ISV would then need to understand technical performance such as interoperability, latency, and how to create a template to roll out a global environment. A fitness test at the end of the two-week workshop would validate interoperability with the hosting and provisioning infrastructure, for example. The ISV then needs to fix things, come back, and get validated.

Eventually, EDS wants to offer generic business services such as messaging, distance learning, procurement, sales automation, call centers, financial, human resource, and workforce management, without specifically naming the ISV products. But for now, many customers ask for specific products such as SAP, so EDS continues to market along named applications.

EDS has tended to focus on the applications rather than on the basic services they should be providing. It is still useful to mention SAP and PeopleSoft because some customers are looking specifically for applications. But there needs to be a set of services behind these that span across any application, whether customized or packaged. The real value for EDS would seem to come from looking at a client's application portfolio and hosting these applications on a one-to-many or one-to-one model.

As noted previously, EDS differentiates itself from other pure-play ASPs offering these same set of applications based not only on the quality of the infrastructure (hosting and provisioning services) but on the application services, including application performance, customization, and integration. For example, most pure-play ASPs tweak or fine-tune performance for infrastructure components such as servers and networks. But EDS also tweaks application performance.

EDS actually monitors the application components, not just the underlying infrastructure components such as up time and response time. We found customers more interested in getting printed on their EDS bill the SAP response time, for example. Customers were much less interested in network availability figures. They wanted to know, for example, that if they hosted SAP or Microsoft Exchange on an EDS facility, they would get the same, or better, performance than if it were on their hard drive.

Concerning customization, terms must be better defined. Some EDS informants used the term *customization* in conjunction with their one-to-many ASP offering, which at first seems incongruous. Others, however, used the more apt term *personalization* to indicate that named software products can be personalized for a given client through templates. Earlier we used the term *mass customization* to describe what others term *personalization*.

The logic for the term personalization is this. In, say, SAP, there are template-like approaches that are highly repeatable and highly structured. This allows for some personalization, but it's hardly customization. These highly packaged, highly repeatable templates allow a one-to-many approach that can be priced quickly. Thus EDS can get up to 90% of requirements up in under 10 days and can personalize the rest. This ability contrasts with that of many pure-plays because they cannot do this last step.

Although personalization may meet the needs of SMEs, EDS also recognizes that global 2000 customers may need actual customization, that is, changing source code and building special components for integration. Many people believe that the main customers for ASP are small to medium-sized enterprises. However, EDS could see that there is potentially a much larger demand from the global 2000 companies. That makes customization, as we have defined it, a much more critical issue, along with integration, if such customers' needs are to be met.

Focusing now on EDS's pure-play ASP space, how does EDS compare to other pure-play ASPs as to price? There is at least one group responsible for developing a suggested retail price, which may or may not be negotiable with the end client, depending on the sales channel, the size of the sale, and the existing relationship with the customer. Establishing a suggested retail price as far as pricing services competitively can be difficult.

Let us consider this issue. Pricing is actually very challenging in the ASP space. Paid research firms have been known to attempt tasks on pricing for ASPs and came back admitting defeat. EDS does an annual 3P study across service lines. The three P's are price, packaging, and positioning. EDS has tried comparing pricing on a total cost of ownership in a non-hosted versus an ASP model. The ASP model might come out 40% less, but it's still very difficult to translate this into ASP pricing. Using competitors' prices is not always comparing like with like. For example, services might actually be different in content and quality. In a simple example like Microsoft Office, prices in 2000 might fall between $20 and $130 a month across competitors. EDS can be much clearer about the company's web hosting advantage, however, where, on some claims, it can offer twice the value at half the price. However, such claims would be much more difficult to substantiate in the ASP market space.

Besides pricing competitively, suggested retail pricing also entails ensuring EDS a reasonable return on their investment. For EDS, the margins in the ASP space have been positive because EDS already has the infrastructure. Thus, EDS can get away with making very little capital investment, which puts it in a very advantageous position relative to smaller ASPs.

Like pure-play ASPs, EDS's ASP prices are based on seats per module per month or transactions per module per month, depending on the application. Prices are also tiered, as mentioned previously, as entry, basic, enhanced, and premier, depending on the types of services the client needs. Some customer applications, for example, are back-office functions, and the service levels associated with the core price tier are acceptable. Other applications are mission-critical for customers and they may require a premier set of services. Prices may also be "blended" if a customer buys more than one application or if the services are blended with a managed solution.

To help salespeople develop a price quote quickly, one idea has been to create an engagement control sheet. The sheet helps the salesperson have a quick dialogue with the client concerning the number of workforce members on site versus remote, the number of users, the types of modules wanted, and so on. For example, the sheet can help a salesperson price SAP in a few minutes. The price may range from $70 to $400[4] per user per month, depending on the number of modules and number of users.

Although EDS is offering competitive prices and still earning a margin on those prices, one respondent pointed out that price is not the main customer criterion in the ASP space. He said that price is about fifth on the list after technical proficiency and skills, risk management and resource leverage, understanding the customer's business, and credible mass.

Concerning service-level contracts in the pure-play ASP space, the EDS contracts are about the same length as those of other pure-play ASPs. As noted previously, most ASP contracts have a two- to four-page master-level agreement and add about an additional four pages for each ISV module. For some of their partnerships with ISVs, EDS can put the contract on EDS letterhead to help maintain a single face to the customer.

To date, most of EDS's 50 customers in the pure-play space have rented only one application. They are, in essence, adopting an incremental approach and testing the waters. They might think, "let's investigate the messaging and collaboration space," and see if EDS can host Exchange, for example.

EDS has already seen early adopters calling to ask questions about renting additional modules or renting other software products. This is one of EDS's main advantages over small dot.com ASPs—it can afford to continue to build its application portfolio even if the majority of today's activity occurs in only three or four packages. The opportunity for up- and cross-selling is enormous in this space. EDS will be more likely to convince a customer to let EDS manage the customer's entire portfolio management if the customer experiences success with their first "testing of the waters."

EDS's Client Care for Alpha Corporation

Next, we describe how EDS is positioning application service provision within a total business solution for a large EDS client. To protect the confidentiality of the customer, we continue to use the pseudonym Alpha. Like many of EDS's global customers, Alpha operates in over 100 countries and employs over 100,000 people worldwide. The sheer size, global reach, and complexity of Alpha mandates a customized service from EDS. For the past decade, EDS has primarily served the roles of operations manager and systems integrator on behalf of Alpha. EDS has achieved efficiencies by consolidating Alpha's data centers and has found new ways to link computer-aided design, manufacturing, and engineering technologies to shorten lead times and improve manufacturing. Despite these improvements, the customer was increasingly becoming concerned about relying too much on EDS. Alpha's CIO decided to multisource to reduce reliance on one IT supplier and to reduce IT cost via best-of-breed packaged vs. build solutions.

The CIO wanted to set strategy, move to multi-vendor sourcing, and achieve a number of objectives, not the least of which was to reduce IT costs. Here IT costs were some 3 percent of revenue, and this needed to be driven down to 1.5 percent. In practice the CIO made a lot of progress on these fronts and also found the multi-vendor environment drove EDS to be more responsive and more aggressive for business. Alpha now has major IT outsourcing contracts with four other major IT suppliers as well as EDS.

On the buy vs. build front, Alpha has purchased many solutions worldwide, such as SAP for financials, PeopleSoft for human resource management, and I2 for supply chain management. Although the commitment to commercial off-the-shelf software (COTS) has reduced Alpha's costs and speeded application delivery, integration of these packages has remained a challenge. Alpha's IT department is officially responsible for integration, but they rely heavily on EDS for technical exper- tise, integration, and operational support. But the use of EDS as systems integrator of these packaged solutions is often piece- meal and based on firefighting. In our view, EDS would like to be more proactive in helping Alpha realize their vision of a best-of-breed COTS. Also, in our view, EDS could add more value to Alpha by being the officially recognized system inte- grator, allowing EDS to better plan for COTS implementation and integration.

Probably Alpha did not recognize well enough the need for a system integrator at this stage. There was little emotional and contractual commitment, though the concept was accepted. Alpha's own IS team has resumed integration responsibility, without the critical mass to accomplish the task. In fact, very few of the Alpha IS team had experience with Alpha systems. They had recently been brought in from outside. A logical step, and one EDS would probably suggest, is for EDS to become global integrator for Alpha on a formal, contractual basis.

More strategically, EDS could offer Alpha a more compre- hensive end-to-end business service rather than focusing on operational support. One idea is essentially that EDS would propose value-added solutions to functional areas such as cus- tomer relationship management, workforce management, or supply chain management. The proposed full-service delivery model is based on a construction metaphor (see Figure 5.1). Included in this full-service model, EDS could provide thought leaders and functional domain experts to serve as the "archi- tects" of an Alpha business solution. EDS could then serve as the "contractor" to implement the solution, including the management of "craftspeople" such as independent software vendors, systems engineers, and middleware providers. The ASP concept comes into play because as part of the delivery of the solution, EDS could host and integrate any IT package that supported the business project.

Let us look at this idea more fully. It would seem that EDS was developing a strategy resembling a construction model. An

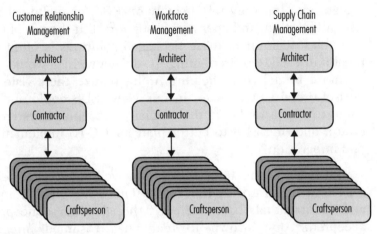

FIGURE 5.1 Full-Service Delivery: Proposed End-to-End Service Model

architect works with a customer to develop the blueprint. The blueprint is delivered to the general contractor, who connects with various craftspeople to deliver the blueprint. At Alpha, EDS looked to segment the business into components such as customer relationship management, supply chain management, and workforce management (see Figure 5.1).

Within a functional area, EDS would put together a business model and populate it in a way attractive to Alpha. Take the example of workforce management. EDS would align with an "architect"—a person or firm with credibility with Alpha on intellectual leadership. EDS could then engage Alpha in transforming how workforce management is conducted there. A blueprint for effecting that transformation would be formulated. Then EDS would be the general contractor working to that blueprint.

This work would involve technology and services, with EDS owning the relationship with the craftspeople and delivering the services. For EDS, an obvious "architect" would be A. T. Kearney. The architect would need to be best-of-breed and other than EDS, probably. EDS would need to have prearranged relationships with the craftspeople, so that the sum of the relationships provides a comprehensive solution on workforce management.

The various components would be best-of-breed solutions. For example, relationships with middleware providers could be utilized to prefabricate connections. Craftspeople for web hosting could be from EDS or from Dune Healthcare Claims, say, or from other ISVs. EDS would be responsible for service levels to Alpha. In this scenario EDS could operate as architect perhaps, certainly as the general contractor, and, in parts, as best-of-breed craftspeople. If Alpha accepted this model, one of the advantages to EDS would be a move into non-IT business as well.

One of the challenges of this proposed idea is that Alpha has historically perceived EDS as primarily operational and infrastructure experts but not business experts. To meet the challenge of overcoming Alpha's perceptions of EDS as operational experts, EDS plans to give Alpha exactly what it wants: best-of-breed in every category from architect to craftspeople, who may or may not be EDS employees. For example, EDS will commit to finding architects with Alpha board of directors credibility, be they top consultants from EDS's consulting arm A.T. Kearney or from outside EDS altogether.

Concerning the palpability of the ASP component of the plan, Alpha is clearly committed to outsourcing and packaged solutions but has trouble integrating these systems. EDS's plans build on their strengths as systems integrators—EDS would be held accountable for implementation and integration of the solution.

Another positive aspect is the pricing model. Alpha's commitment to COTS has burdened Alpha with excessive software license fees. Alpha is surprisingly worried about software license costs. It is a large company committed to best-of-breed software, but obviously not immune from such cost concerns. Therefore ASP solutions are attractive even to such companies.

The other side is that software providers may well look at Alpha and assume they can get licenses worldwide, at multiple locations, on a per-seat basis. Their pricing models are not tailored to the size of Alpha. Alpha has even escorted a few of them out the door. EDS would price those costs to Alpha on a monthly basis rather than Alpha spending millions upfront, which will undoubtedly be attractive to Alpha. EDS would also hope to sell solutions to the Alpha extended family of suppliers, enabling them to lower prices by spreading fixed costs over a higher volume of users.

Note, however, that although the EDS ASP *service* is highly customized, this does not mean that the software to support the service always needs to be customized. Certainly, for non-core systems, customization of COTS is less than desirable. Even for mission-critical systems, COTS customization may be unnecessary under the proposed plan. In the past, Alpha has tried to customize COTS significantly for mission-critical applications for scheduling, plant sequencing, and order management. These projects have generally been disasters in terms of cost overruns and integration. Alpha has begun to realize that sometimes it is better to change processes to fit the software. In some cases, ISV software has improved significantly in the last 18 months to accommodate flexibility in templates. For example, Alpha had to write its own timekeeping system to accommodate local union agreements. But EDS has found a Canadian software company that has templated the complexity of local requirements for vacations, approvals, and so on. It proposes to host and offer this application as part of a total workforce automation solution.

CONCLUSIONS

EDS is one of the few giants of information solutions (along with Accenture, CSC, and IBM) which are committed to providing total business solutions to a wide range of customers in terms of size, industry, and location worldwide. Its master plan is to use netsourcing as one of the many delivery channels and pricing models for business application services. For a small or midsized EDS customer, this may be an aggregated ASP solution with minimal or no customization, priced on a per-seat basis. For a large customer such as Alpha, it may be a fully customized business service with perhaps an application hosting component. Unlike startup ASPs, EDS does not have to invest hundreds of millions of dollars in infrastructure, marketing, or hiring. By 2001 it already had excess capacity on its global infrastructure, over 100,000 employees with the necessary skills, established sales channels, and name-brand recognition and trust, particularly in systems integration. So just as the experts have predicted that established players will cannibalize the ASP space as dot.com startups close doors, we already see EDS as the largest—yet unheralded—ASP provider.

In the near future, EDS is also poised to be a heavy hitter in wireless application services. EDS built the Intelligent Network Foundation, which is the infrastructure for wireless applications such as voice-over IP, remote access services, and true mobile services. The next step is to find best-of-breed software that can pass EDS certification and to implement it on the network. But that's a view of EDS's ASP future from a technical perspective. From a business service perspective, EDS probably wants to be the application portfolio manager for its customers. According to one person we interviewed:

> If Y2K did one thing, it highlighted to senior executives in the global 2000 the importance of the application portfolio and what's in the portfolio. What's in those application warehouses? What's running your business both back office and front office? It's highlighted it to senior management to the point where I now visit with CEO and CFOs who ask me questions about looking into the total portfolio. Very rarely has global 2000 done a good job at managing their portfolio. Just like you and I want to manage our financial portfolios so we can retire early and buy the things we want to buy, the global 2000 need to manage their application portfolios.

HOST ANALYTICS

Host Analytics (see Table 5.6) offers application solutions for financial analysis and consolidation, forecasting and budgeting, consumer-packaged goods analysis, and strategic benchmarking for primarily midsized customers through direct sales and to large customers through an information

TABLE 5.6 Host Analytics at a Glance

FOUNDED	May 2000
BUSINESS MODEL	Alternative distribution channel—propriety business intelligence software and services
2001 REVENUES PROJECTED	Approx. $2 million
2001 PROFITS PROJECTED	Approx. $1 million
NUMBER OF EMPLOYEES	12
NUMBER OF CUSTOMERS	3, but will soon triple
NUMBER OF PRODUCTS	4 principal products

builder's partnership. This case is interesting from three perspectives. First, Host Analytics illustrates the concept of mass customization, achieving low cost through standardization for the beginning of the value chain, then customizing the product for each customer during the final stages. Second, the company has a very specific focus on analyzing a customer's specific business data, a highly customized product as opposed to ASPs offering canned solutions. Third, the company has quieted the ASP aspect of its business in favor of marketing itself as a business intelligence provider. Thus ASP has become a complementary delivery option—customers may also load Host Analytics's software directly on a customer's server if they prefer.

Host Analytics used to be promoted as an ASP, but customers kept saying: "IT is our corporate asset. I'm not keen to do this." So Host Analytics switched marketing from ASP to building data warehouses and business intelligence worth $500,000 for $100,000. The result was they began to sell. Clearly, in the beginning, customers were not interested in ASP. But when they worked with Host Analytics for a while, they thought something like, "It would be great not to have to buy hardware or hire network people." So they moved toward trying out an easier alternative—hosting on HA's site.

Host Analytics was founded by current president Jim Eberlin in St. Louis, Missouri, in May 2000. His background was in development and implementation of large-scale customized data warehouses and business intelligence tools for large customers. He implemented these systems while working for several consulting companies, including a business he owned previously and eventually sold. Jim realized that each customer's implementation was customized, costing the customer between $500,000 and $1 million. Jim saw an opportunity to standardize the infrastructure to reduce costs and speed implementation, therefore allowing smaller companies to afford business intelligence.

Ever since his first company, only the largest firms could afford these applications, which cost a minimum of $300,000. More typically it needed up to $1 million for an implementation. Most of the cost was on complete customization, starting at the beginning every time. These were typically large corporations that felt they had to have an entirely custom-built data warehouse to support their unique businesses. In 1999 Jim Eberlin went to the president of his company and suggested the building of a technical framework so they did not have to build from scratch each time. He knew he could get a head start that way and cut out a great deal of costs from customized development.

The president of his previous employer, however, was busy working on the IPO and on providing fully customized solutions for their customers. Jim decided to start his own company using the money he made from the sale of his previous company.

Jim Eberlin decided to take these actions: First, to make things replicable so that customers did not have to pay more than once. Second, he packaged the applications based on business intelligence best practices. The ASP development was based on sharing technical infrastructure, human resources, and anything that could cut costs. By 1999 what he was doing actually had found a name for itself in the marketplace. This was ASP. So Eberlin started up an ASP that focused on business intelligence.

As of first quarter 2001, Host Analytics had 12 employees—four were developers located in India and eight were project managers based in St. Louis. Host Analytics offers proprietary solutions for business intelligence. Host Analytics extracts, transforms, and loads data from a customer's system(s) (typically an ERP) into Host Analytics's products. Host Analytics's project managers work with customers to determine their individual reporting needs, develop the reports, and make them available to users over a browser. Ad hoc capabilities are also available, as customers can slice and dice the data in many ways. Host Analytics offers four main products:

1. The *sales forecasting and budgeting system* is an Internet-architected forecasting and budgeting application. Customers can select from among several forecasting and budgeting methods to do analyses on multiple levels. In addition, the application has reporting and ad hoc analysis capability to help customers understand historical trends and improve forecast accuracy.

2. The *financial analysis and consolidation system* is a complete financial analysis application providing financial consolidations, analysis, and reporting. The system provides currency conversions and allows data to be loaded and viewed in any currency available in the system. Financial reports are provided by individual division, subsidiary, or plant and on a consolidated basis.

3. The *consumer-packaged goods management system* provides business intelligence applications and services that support sales and management personnel of manufacturers and distributors of consumer-packaged goods. Category managers, brokers, and marketing management can manage product categories, brands, and mixes and identify cross-sell and up-sell opportunities. Key business indicators, such as sales growth, product and customer profitability, forecast accuracy, competitive brand information, and effectiveness of trade and market spending, can be viewed easily.

4. The *balanced scorecard system* is a packaged analytical application used to communicate and to manage strategy by linking objectives, initiatives, measures, and reports to an organization's strategy. The system integrates financial measures with other key performance indicators from customers, internal processes, and organizational learning. The practices are based on the balanced scorecard developed by Kaplan and Norton.

All the products provide the ad hoc abilities to analyze multiple levels, including product, time period, customer, scenario, and location. Customers can update information and add parameters on a spreadsheet-like Web interface or by using Excel 2000 live against the databases.

At first, Host Analytics intended to deliver solely through ASP, leasing a server for each customer. Host Analytics subleases servers from a third-party called Onlylink for $10,000 to $15,000 per server. Onlylink provides 24 × 7 technical support, but Host Analytics supports its own customers directly as a first-line help desk. Host Analytics is able to provide round-the-clock support by having the India-based employees man the U.S. nightshift. Thus far, the remote support has not been a problem because users primarily request help with the application, rather than hands-on server tweaking. But as you will see in the following customer vignettes, not all customers chose ASP. For Host Analytics, ASP is an option for customers. They are not forced into it.

Host Analytics's first major customer was a St. Louis–based holding company called Deloro Stellite. Deloro Stellite needed to consolidate and analyze financial data from 15 manufacturing facilities, located in Europe, North America, and Asia. The controller was spending all his time trying to gather data and load them into Excel, leaving little time for analysis before his monthly board meetings. Host Analytics provided a solution by consolidating, cleaning, and loading the data from the 15 plants into a data warehouse.

Host Analytics uses ETL (extraction, translation, load) tools. Their business partners, called Information Builders (IB), have the most complete suite of tools. Most companies that compete with IB actually use their tools. Host Analytics has Java products that sit on top to fill in the gaps. Host Analytics extracts from the source, transforms it, cleans it up, and loads it up into HA's data warehouse. That way a customer can have anything.

To ensure data integrity, Host Analytics and Deloro Stellite each have a designated quality-of-data assurance person. These employees clean the data, such as eliminating double entries. Once data are cleaned and loaded in the data warehouse, any of Host Analytics's four products can be implemented. Deloro Stellite first selected the financial analysis and consolidation system. Host Analytics determined Deloro Stellite's standard reporting needs and developed these reports, available over the Internet. Today, over 50 Deloro Stellite users worldwide access the system to develop ad hoc reports or to use the interface to select among many levels of analyses. At first, Deloro Stellite planned to buy its own server but eventually went with an ASP delivery.

HA's first customer wanted an application for planning, financial analysis, and sales analysis. The original focus was on the business problem. HA told the client about the ASP option. At first the client had no intention of doing this. But HA proved their applications worked and cost a lot less money than the alternatives.

The cost to Deloro Stellite was about $70,000 for implementation, plus $2000 a month for application hosting. Deloro Stellite's controller describes some of the benefits: "We know if one plant is not keeping up with its sales goals by looking at its production and inventory turns. It was hard with the manual system to see problems like this and understand why they were happening."[5]

Host Analytics's second major customer is a beverage distributor located in Washington, Missouri. It had needs similar to those of Deloro Stellite—to consolidate and analyze financial data from various locations. It also needed a general ledger, so Host Analytics helped it select a midrange ERP system. From this system, Host Analytics can extract and load into the company's data warehouse. The distributor first implemented Host Analytics's financial analysis and consolidation tool and is in the process of implementing the balanced scorecard product. The initial implementation cost is about $100,000. Subsequent Host Analytics products cost considerably less because the data are already available. This customer decided not to use ASP for delivery. One respondent reported that the distributor did not do the hosting. Instead they copied HA software on to their machines. In other words, they did not go "ASP" at this point. In fact, because of their location, the connection is not really there, yet, to do Internet.

Host Analytics's third major customer is a pest control subsidiary for a large consumer products company. In addition to the Host Analytics budgeting and forecasting tool, the company intends to host an exterminator support application with Host Analytics. Hosting is ideal for this application because users will be geographically dispersed and mobile.

Currently, the Host Analytics contract does not specify detailed service levels for application availability, application response time, server performance, or network performance. In prior implementations, response time has been under 3 seconds, but excessive activity could slow the application.

Of course, response time is perceptual. At first users think, "Oh, it's a few seconds, that's a ton of time saving. It used to take me days to get this information, then put it into a spreadsheet." However, invariably, a couple of months down the road, the initial response time of 2–3 seconds slows. Users may fill up the database and exceed capacity. What they then need to do is contact HA to come in and tune the database to get it back to a 2–3 second response time.

The help desk, however, is guaranteed to be open 24 × 7. Customers get immediate response. Someone always answers the phone. The majority of support is on the application. HA has network engineers and support people. If human intervention is required at the server room, HA has a pager and cell phone at Onlylink. But most troubleshooting can be done remotely. HA finds that the most frequent end user question is, "How do I do X?" So the help desk is particularly set up to deal with this sort of question.

During mid-2001, Host Analytics believed that it would triple in size over a three-month period, based on its current interactions with potential customers. The sales process can be long because customers have to build a financial justification. The interest HA gets is in their products. Then clients have an initial shock at the cost to support the products. HA makes sure they understand what they need to support the products. There's software, implementation, ongoing management, and support. Clients take all this and go compare the ROI with it if they did it internally. There are immense advantages to the customers to keep Host Analytics's people in place because they intimately know the product. It's there at the end of the day for the clients when they need it over a browser. There are immense advantages to the customers to use HA people in addition to their own support; for instance, since HA only supports its own products and the technology is built in, HA is a simple and inexpensive solution for additional customizations and support.

Host Analytics has been able to woo potential customers based on recommendations from Information Builders and through CFO breakfast meetings. Unlike many other ASPs, the company is not worried about cash burn rates because it has used customer revenues to cover its moderate fixed costs (about $75,000 per month).

CONCLUSIONS

Host Analytics is an excellent example of a company using ASP as a complementary delivery channel for its proprietary software. The company is positioning itself in the marketspace as best-of-breed business intelligence solutions for SMEs, with very little focus on marketing ASP per se. According to the company, it is important for an ASP to have a real focus. It is not enough to claim to be an ASP and offer a client the ability to outsource a network. What clients actually want is applications and support for these applications. In other words, in Host Analytics's view, a client needs to find a company that really knows the applications. For Host Analytics, it is not enough just to have a technical infrastructure.

Although there is a five-year plan to go public, Host Analytics intends to survive the near term by selling, licensing, and/or partnering with larger companies interested in its products. For example, Jim Eberlin is talking with companies in Europe, Asia, and South America about the balanced scorecard product. Much as you will see in the Zland case, Host Analytics needs to expand their sales and distribution channels.

MainPass

MainPass Technologies, Inc., based in Los Angeles, California, and incorporated in the state of Delaware, is an applications service provider (ASP) offering an Internet-based information technology (IT) service to small and medium-sized enterprises (SMEs). The corporation was formed in 2000 in response to the perception widely held by U.S. and European analysts that ASPs may well be the optimal method of delivering software applications for the future.

Throughout 2000 and 2001, MainPass was forming strategic alliances with suppliers and manufacturers and developed and provided value-added suites of software for the Los Angeles legal community, its initially chosen SME market. Subsequently, it plans to move into a number of professional and service business segments (accountants, doctors) across a range of industries, including European clients. By 2001 it was able to provide a fully integrated Web-based business solution along with on-site service and consulting service to this market, with an emphasis on collaborating to develop and market its services and products into handheld wireless devices for remote operation. Funded initially by its prime investors, MainPass looked for a further investment of $5 million to form further joint ventures and alliances with Internet service providers, data center colocation companies, and ISVs. Further funding would also be used to complete the implementation of its wireless solution and form partnerships with major telecom operators and mobile operators.

SERVICE ESSENTIALS

By early 2001 the MainPass service entailed the provision of remote access to and use of the following, via the Internet or other suitable network:

- Computer software, processing power, and data storage
- Automatic software and hardware upgrading
- Applications support
- Software and hardware maintenance
- Training for customers' in-house IT staff
- Business-to-business services providing an electronic brokerage platform
- Hardware leasing and on-site services

MainPass operates as a primary (in terms of its in-house software engineering capability) and intermediary principal agent, designing and assembling the IT service components, which comprise the service outlined above. MainPass hosts and manages these components, including software applications and databases, installation, and wiring of customers' premises. Customers access the service using a Web browser. MainPass assumes responsibility for all these components and their delivery.

Customers can also have mobile access to the service using portable, dataless, wireless devices such as shell laptops and pocket PCs. This creates a mobile virtual office without the accompanying risks of data loss or data insecurity.

The ASP is delivered at a thin client or PC workstation via the *MainPass Virtual Desktop* (MVD), enabling customers to access their applications, files, and data via the Internet. The MVD comprises these fundamental features:

- *Intranet/extranet.* When an authorized user accesses the service, a personalized portal will be presented. The user will be able to suit his or her individual needs and functions by customizing the portal's content. It will contain applications, links, and data specific to the user's role within the business of the SME.
- *Best-of-breed software.* This software provides front- and back-office solutions (e.g., word processing, spreadsheets, accounting, payroll, and stock control). If these

functions have already been implemented, MainPass can also act like a typical outsourcing company.

- *Communication services.* These integrated services range from encrypted e-mail to a virtual meetingplace, network fax and telephony, a calendar, and live chat.
- *Business-to-business services.* An electronic brokerage platform will provide a convenient, cost-effective online research and marketplace for the sale and purchase of, for example, office supplies, courier services, travel facilities, and employment and marketing consultancy services.

OPERATIONAL BENEFITS

For customers, the benefits of using the MainPass service for hosting business critical applications includes avoidance of the need to incur the costs of owning an IT system and staffing an IT department to manage the system. MainPass also offers the following features to help customers achieve operational benefits:

- Immediate implementation of software applications allows customers to save on deployment costs.
- Applications are upgraded continually without costly disruptions to customers.
- Customers enjoy economical access to the latest hardware technology.
- The customer's efficiency of their residual IT staff is improved because they are freed to concentrate on core tasks instead of mundane problem solving.
- Enhanced data center functions such as instantaneous multilocation backup, electronic security as near absolute as current technology permits, server-vault hosting, and disaster recovery provide customers with security and peace of mind.
- The customer's business is less likely to be interrupted because MainPass's system performance and reliability is ensured by a multitier redundant architecture.
- An increase in customer productivity is available to traveling employees due to the mobile virtual office.
- The waste of customer time and money is prevented by blocking general access to the Web and to built-in software diversions.

COMPANY STRATEGY

The MainPass strategy has been to form strategic alliances, partnerships, and/or joint ventures with branded software companies (ISVs) such as *Amicus* and *CompuLaw,* who have an existing customer base and are serving the legal professional market. MainPass comarkets its ASP solution with ISVs and system integrators, who assist in providing local and regional sales channels. The company further targets and acquires subscribers to its services by direct sales, attending legal trade shows and bar conventions, and through print advertisements in legal journals and premiere legal technology periodicals. It also actively forms partnerships, joint ventures, and strategic alliances/acquisitions with Internet service providers (ISP), telecom providers, and other independent software vendors (ISV) in order to assemble these services and components and integrate them with its solution.

MainPass intends to remain on the forefront of technological development and to replicate and expand its business model in several other professional service markets. Set up initially in the legal professional market based in Los Angeles, in 2001 the company sought to expand its target market into the accounting and insurance industries as well as into Europe. Expanding MainPass's presence in these markets is planned to accelerate the company's revenue growth and diversify its customer base.

MARKETING

MainPass's marketing program has consisted of an ongoing advertising campaign as well as attendance and participation in legal industry trade shows and state bar conventions. The company has also further targeted and acquired prospective customers by direct sales, and through print advertisements in legal technology trade publications and journals such as *Law Technology News, AmLaw Tech, Law Office Computing, Legal Management, The Daily Journal, California Lawyer, American Bar Association Journal,* and *Young Lawyers.*

In addition to targeted advertising and trade show participation, MainPass has been working with Los Angeles–based public relations firms that are highly knowledgeable about the specific markets the company chooses to enter. Local public relations firms were also identified as the most qualified advisors to consult the company on its specific niche markets.

TOWARD A COMPETITIVE EDGE

Typically, ASP is a process rather than a piece of proprietary technology and as such, does not lend itself to any form of patenting. The process consists of assembling existing business applications and communication services and integrating them with "Net-centric" software,[6] which enables remote hosting and access. However, the process is itself technical and requires in-house software engineering skills—skills that MainPass possesses. By virtue of these skills and internal management practice, MainPass has sought to create wider choice and better value for its customers. The wider choice derives from:

- A broader range of software packages than that offered by most other ASPs. The range includes most standard and customized applications that can reside on almost any platform without any reengineering.
- The creation from scratch by IT professionals of a service that focuses on providing a multichoice ASP solution, delivering not only the cost savings and operational benefits named above but also solving any preexisting IT-related business problem.

The Mainpass better-value claims derive from the following:

- Its Net-centric software does not require installation or management of any applications software by the customer, whereas most other types do.
- MainPass offers a choice of Net-centric software, whereas most ASPs do not.
- It provides thin-client workstations, whereas most ASPs do not.

- It provides client implementation services.
- The company is endeavoring to be one of the first ASPs to provide mobile access to applications, data, communication services, and its business-to-business center.

CONCLUSIONS

The market for MainPass types of services is competitive but was at an embryonic stage in mid-2001. There are a handful of ASP companies competing directly against MainPass, not the least of which are USinternetworking, Corio, and FutureLink Distribution as general ASP pure plays. However, the majority of companies that have added ASP capabilities to their products and services have really done so only from 2000 at the earliest. Current ASP participants have assumed many different strategies with regard to the type of hosted applications, the structure of the key ASP components, and their targeted markets. No one predominant business model has emerged as the standard, and even in late 2001 it was too early to determine which business model would emerge as the most applicable. In this context, during 2001 many ASPs were still designing their models, spreading risk across several possibilities while still working on implementing their systems.

By early 2001, MainPass had already designed its system, offering a business model. Moreover, against many more generic enterprise ASPs, MainPass had carefully delineated its market niche and had customized its systems and service to suit. We found in our research that this has been one of the key customer requirements from an ASP, in addition to cost efficiency, security, and guarantees of service delivery. From this perspective, MainPass would seem to have taken a lower-risk approach to entry into the ASP marketplace, pursuing a niche strategy in the target markets of professional and service businesses. The objective here would seem to be to gain a stronghold and secure profitability by focusing on enhanced relative customer satisfaction (RCS) against possible competition from more generic application service providers.

In their empirical study of over 300 companies, *Benchmarking Organizational and IT Performance,*[7] Gus Nievelt and Leslie Willcocks show clearly that RCS is a primary driver of organizational economic performance, and that such a strategy, if implemented, delivers relatively higher profitability and market growth in the market segment. This strategy would generate reputation effects and a track record that can then be utilized to expand into serving complementary market segments. As with many ASPs, MainPass's capability to partner with infrastructure providers and software vendors will be critical for any expansion program. However, its focus on vertical service provision, the customer value proposition, and establishing a robust and secure technical and service platform would seem to be key critical success factors for succeeding if a niche strategy is pursued in the post-2001 ASP marketplace.

ZLAND

Zland.com (see Table 5.7) is a very interesting case study because it illustrates how a company continually reinvents itself to try to survive in the competitive application provision environment. In essence, Zland's core capabilities are its proprietary, e-marketing, e-commerce, and e-operations applications for small to midsized customers. Its products are impressive—we witnessed a Zland franchise owner build the major components of an e-marketing site using Zland's advanced templates in less than half an hour. These products are built, improved, and maintained by over 200 product developers headquartered in Aliso Viejo, California. More challenging for Zland—and other startup ASPs with great products—have been the financing, technical infrastructure for delivery, and sales and marketing channels.

On the financing side, the company was financed by private investors. Like most companies operating in the ASP space, Zland saw a steady growth in revenues but in 2001 was still operating at a loss (see Table 5.7). Zland's plans to go public were thwarted by the technology stock market crash. On March 29, 2000, Zland submitted forms for an initial public offering (IPO) to the Securities and Exchange Commission

TABLE 5.7 Zland at a Glance

FOUNDED	1995
BUSINESS MODEL	Franchise: proprietary e-marketing, e-commerce, and e-operations capabilities rented to small to midsized customers via more than 44 franchises
1999 REVENUES	$6.5 million
1999 LOSSES	$13.6 million
NUMBER OF EMPLOYEES	More than 240
NUMBER OF CUSTOMERS	More than 700
NUMBER OF PRODUCTS	More than 160 applications

(SEC), but pulled the request in May when the stock market did not recover. The company went through a rough time in the summer of 2000 trying to raise more cash to keep the company running. Zland considered selling out to a German company. Eventually, the initial investors infused additional funding to keep the company afloat. Long-term survival is still in question.

On the infrastructure side, Zland initially outsourced data center operations to a Seattle-based firm. But as Zland has continued to grow, the need to control service levels and to expand the infrastructure became increasingly more important. But given the immense financial pressures, building its own network operating center was a suboptimal choice. In May 2001, Zland partnered with Sprint E-Solutions to build a state-of-the art network operations center to host Zland's suite of applications. The site will provide Zland customers with access, transport, and colocation services, backed by Sprint's high levels of network availability and performance.[8]

On the sales side, sales initially occurred only through a franchise business model. There are currently over 400 franchise territories worldwide. Franchise operators only need to invest $150,000 to become a licensed franchiser. The added value of this business model is to offer decentralized sales to small and midsized companies while centrally developing excellent products at a reasonable price. But sales were hindered by the local franchise owner's ability to educate, sell, and support local businesses. To help these local franchises, in 2001 Zland started a two-way referral program between the referral partner and the local Zland franchise. But clearly, Zland also needed to develop aggressive and complementary channels for a broader audience. In 2001, Zland opened up another channel for sales through its valued-added reseller program. The idea is that other ASP aggregators, such as IDC Solutions, could add Zland products to their portfolio suite.

The story that Zland tells is really one repeated throughout the chapter: Survival is based on understanding your core capabilities and finding partners to help bolster your weaknesses. In the case of Zland, its strength is clearly its suite of applications. In many ways, assuming survival, we may eventually view Zland more as an ISV than an ASP.

EVOLUTION OF PRODUCTS

The founder, John Veenstra, is the current chairman and CEO. Veenstra's early management experience was in the automotive industry. In the 1990s, he started a company called First Electronic Forms and served as vice-president when First Forms was sold to Wallace Computer Services. He began to look at the Internet as the vision of the future. One of his early online businesses was a community portal for nonprofit agencies. But it was not financially viable. He then turned to the for-profit sector, focusing on common e-business processes. He assembled a team of investors and developers and began coding the Zland suite of applications.

In the early days of the company, Zland's customers did not understand the power of the Internet, let alone the concept of hosted applications. Thus it was difficult to sell many of the applications. In 1998, Zland decided to bundle their applications in a product suite called PowerSuite Express, released in March 1998. The idea was based on the Microsoft Office model of providing more functionality than the customer may initially use.

Eventually, Zland had to repackage again because customers were beginning to understand that they were renting a powerful portfolio of applications, but may only be using a small portion of the functionality. Zland found that the customers were not ready for all the applications. They did not understand the power of the Internet. People weren't buying. Zland came out with PowerSuites Express, the base package. It included applications from every module. They had e-marketing, e-commerce, human resource functionality for a low introductory price. The next phase was customers saying, "well I only want e-marketing, so why do I have to pay for e-commerce capability?" So Zland repackaged again.

As of 2000, Zland had 160 proprietary applications, bundled in three base packages: e-marketing, e-commerce, and e-operations. Zland is striving to add functionality, including the addition of more languages. The products currently support English, German, and Spanish.

To keep customer costs low, ASPs rely on a one-to-many model that requires standard offerings. Zland, however, does offer customization. If the functionality requested is seen as valuable for many customers, headquarters will build the functionality at a reduced cost to the originating customer, then release the functionality in subsequent versions. If the functionality requested is highly idiosyncratic, customers will be charged a premium. In some cases, customers request changes that are unnecessary, so franchise operators try to convince customers to use the practices available in the templates.

Zland found that most customers say they want "real time"—in inventory control, for example. But they don't even have real-time inventory control systems. Zland has a product that integrates orders to back-order inventory systems. It's batch, but it updates every five minutes. Zland shows them how much money they can save with a five-minute batch update. Zland tries to fight against preconceived notions of what customers need. The sales process tends to be long, but Zland does have a record of trying to get a customer's cost as low as possible.

Zland did not initially own a data center but instead used a third-party data center. Zland, however, managed the servers and applications via a network operating center. The Net Operating Center consisted of a "bunker" of dual Cisco 70 routers. Zland looked to outsource to the best operating facility possible. Zland could never match that outsourcer on costs. The operating center is backed up by battery and generators and is state-of-the-art. Zland's strategy is to do what they do best and outsource to the best hosting site. The NOC would become regional as Zland grows, with a Mid-West and a European one, for example.

In this fledgling market, ASP contracts are still immature. Like all the other contracts we've seen, Zland's contract is a few pages long, containing license agreement and payment schedules. The contracts do not include a service-level agreement because corporate lawyers feared that Zland would be exposed to excess liability for services they cannot control over the Internet. This is actually a wise position to take, because many experts have criticized ASPs for promising beyond their domain of control. (One informant told us that most ASPs promise 5 • 99999s and then just hope for the best!)

Given the small size of the current customers, contract service-level agreements have not been a big issue. Zland commits to providing 24 × 7 and delivers industry-standard service. Historically, that has been 99 percent. Zland does not offer remuneration for downtime, mainly because, at this date, it was not an issue in the market they served. The distribution channels, via franchises, also have certain advantages, in getting closer and more familiar with customers on a localized level.

CUSTOMER PERSPECTIVE

In 2000, Zland already had over 700 customers. This is quite an impressive number since more visible ASPs, such as Corio, had only 25 customers at the time of their IPO. Current customers are typically small businesses with less than 100 employees. On Zland's Web site, 11 of their 29 customer success stories were from customers with under 20 employees. In a few days, for as little as $1395, customers can have their own Web site with a full suite of e-commerce capabilities, such as a product catalog, frequently asked questions, press releases, shopping cart, and customer returns. Franchise operators sit down with local customers to select options in the Zland development environment to set parameters for the look and feel of the Web site as well as selecting functionality. The goal is to train customers to support their own Web site through the Zland user-friendly customer maintenance environment. Zland's product and service excellence from a customer perspective is best illustrated through an example.

In St. Louis, Missouri, A.E. Schmidt is a 147-year-old family-owned company that builds custom pool tables. Although this company may not be widely recognized outside St. Louis, St. Louisians covet the artistry of this company's products. If you've "made it" in St. Louis, you own a house in Ladue, drive a Lexus, and own an A.E. Schmidt pool table. A.E. Schmidt customers are extremely loyal and long-lasting. Pool table maintenance and accessories are purchased through A.E. Schmidt during the life of the pool table (which is longer than the life of the customer). A.E. Schmidt was finding that many existing customers were moving from the St. Louis area. The company maintained customer relationships via direct mail but was looking increasingly for a way to better communicate with existing customers, to reach new customers, and to develop better relationships with their authorized dealers. Enter Don Veenstra, general manager (and the founder's brother), and Kevin Davis, sales and marketing manager of Zland's St. Louis franchise.

Don and Kevin worked with A.E. Schmidt to develop a Web-based solution to meet the company's business goals. Beginning with e-marketing (i.e., no transactions) they sat down with Pat Spangler, an A.E. Schmidt employee, to design the Web site. By logging on to the development environment, Kevin and Pat moved through the parameter-driven options. The look and feel of the Web site is selected through a series of templates in much the same way that a user selects a PowerPoint design by clicking on a design option. For example, A.E.

Schmidt chose to have option buttons on the home page to be placed on the left and the logo on the top. Option buttons are numbered sequentially with billiard balls, giving the page a personalized touch. Functionality is added to the Web pages in the same manner—franchise operators point-and-click on application functionality such as "frequently asked questions." While the look and feel and functionality of the site are selected using the development environment, the data content for the site is managed through a user-friendly customer support environment designed to be maintained by the end customer. Kevin trained Pat to use the customer support environment, such as adding a product to the product catalog, including uploading a picture, item number, size, pull-down menu for finishing options, and click buttons for additional product features. Thus one of the ways that Zland keeps customer costs low is to have customers maintain their own data content.

A.E. Schmidt's initial Web-site functionality included an online catalog of pool tables and products, customer support such as locating a dealer for pool table repairs, and interactive dealer support such as price quotes. The dealer support functionality has restricted access, and dealers must sign in using a logon ID and password. Additional functionality was added later, such as online ordering. Visit A.E. Schmidt's Web site at *www.schmidtpool.com*.

> There are several things that impress me about Zland.com. They have great problem-solving abilities. I am a relative novice in the field of Web sites and my earlier experiences with other companies were filled with great quantities of technical babble but little or no training and support for lay people such as myself. My Zland.com representative and his staff were patient and thorough in their explanations and support. They are training me to be self-sufficient in my editing style.
> —*Pat Spangler, A.E. Schmidt*

A.E. Schmidt is representative of Zland's target customers: small to midsized businesses. These customers require a significant amount of handholding and thus the sales effort requires personalized face-to-face support. In the second quarter of 1998, Zland began to franchise actively to rent its products more effectively. The local franchise owner courts, educates, sells, and implements Zland's suite of products for small to midsized customers.

Zland saw the SME market as the best sales opportunity. The downside, of course, is the tremendous transaction costs associated with servicing many small customers in contrast to servicing fewer large-sized customers. Zland did not target large companies because these customers already have e-marketing, e-commerce, and e-operations, plus a large in-house support staff and infrastructure in place.

CONCLUSIONS

When reading the five cases, many similarities emerge: challenges in educating customers about netsourcing while selling netsourcing services, convincing investors to stay onboard during the technology stock market crash, and adapting business models to the evolving demands of both customers and investors.

Corio, MainPass, and Zland, for example, are representative of the struggles that startup ASPs face in this emerging market. These companies have impressive products or services and talented executive teams. Funding these startups has been tremendously challenging because investors worry that companies are not generating profits fast enough (keep in mind that Federal Express took nearly five years to show a profit after startup). Investors also fear that the companies may not be sustainable in the long run, particularly with software giants such as SAP, PeopleSoft, and Oracle developing their own netsourcing offerings or when the big players such as EDS and IBM enter the space in a big way.

Senior management teams often spend their time chasing additional funding when they would much prefer to focus on product development and customer care. Some startups seem prime for acquisition by cash-heavy traditional players. Assuming that they can continue to attract new customers, align themselves with strong partners, and sway investor worries, these suppliers will be challenged to develop the next likely demands on netsourcers: customization, industry specialization, more sophisticated pricing mechanisms, and better service-level agreements. In Chapter 6, you will see the European-based startups face the same challenges as those of U.S.-based startups.

EDS stood among the initial five cases as an exemplar of the quiet strength that a traditional provider has to conquer the netsourcing space. EDS is not plagued by startup problems such as seeking investors, building infrastructure, securing customers, and attracting employees. Their primary challenges are those of repackaging, niche marketing, and helping customers select the best channel for service delivery. In Chapter 6, SAP will stand out among the European-based companies in the same way that the EDS case stood out among U.S.-based companies.

ENDNOTES

1. See *www.itaa.org/asp/aspwc9tran.htm* for entire transcript of Gary Dean's October 24, 2000 Webcast.

2. See E. B. Flanagan's interview transcript of George Kadifa on April 19, 2001 on *www.crn.com*.

3. For a full discussion of EDS's one-to-one business model, see M. Lacity and L. Willcocks, *Global Information Technology Outsourcing*, Wiley, Chichester, West Sussex, England, 2001.

4. Prices are illustrative only.

5. Alan Joch, "Buying Biz Smarts," *eWeek*, December 31, 2000.

6. Such as Citrix and Tarantella.

7. Templeton College, Oxford University, Oxford, 1997.

8. For more information, see *www.zland.com* for 2001 press releases.

6

EUROPEAN-BASED NETSOURCING CASE STUDIES

In Chapter 5 we presented five U.S.-based cases studies. In this chapter we examine five European-based suppliers and their customers: the Lodge, marviQ, SAP, Siennax, and Vistorm. The executive summaries highlight the customer and supplier lessons of these five cases, followed by the in-depth cases themselves. In the summary at the end of this chapter we analyze all 10 cases by comparing suppliers' strategies for offering netsourcing as a sole or complementary delivery channel, targeting customers, and providing infrastructure.

INTRODUCTION TO THE CASE STUDIES

LODGE OVERVIEW

SME customers interested in enterprise-wide application solutions are presented with powerful arguments for selecting a netsourcing solution. Customers looking to harness the advances of SAP solutions that include maintenance, consulting, and integration will find suppliers such as the Lodge a very interesting option. The benefits are especially profound in the financial arrangements that underpin such a solution. However, attention needs to be drawn to the licensing limitations that still exist, which may imply long-term lock-in. Also, careful experiences need to be gathered by customers, emphasizing the need for an incremental sourcing approach.

Suppliers get an insight into the financial arrangements that may underpin complex application solutions such as ERP. A necessary prerequisite is to recover initial customer acquisition and setup costs. In particular, the financial complexities and what these imply in terms of maintaining and keeping existing customers for a longer term are covered in this case.

marviQ OVERVIEW

A full-service provider to customers, marviQ offers applications solutions that encapsulate the complete customer value chain. Developed on the basis of Java programming language, it seamlessly integrates with all types of operating systems, software, and hardware that customers may be using or looking to use. In terms of total information and communication technology (ICT) management, this innovation allows customers to pick and choose what best suits their current needs and then expand their IT services as they grow. Startups as well as large organizations have bought into this solution, as the deployment simplicity, connectivity advantages, and resulting cost benefits outweigh those of developing or hosting application solutions in-house. Customers get an insight into a novel netsourcing solution that offers advantages beyond what even large ICT groups and departments of global Fortune 500 firms can achieve.

For suppliers, marviQ is of particular interest as it displays a customer value chain approach to netsourcing. This becomes possible by extracting application functionality and then integrating it into a full-service netsourcing solution by use of a novel Java approach.

SAP OVERVIEW

The largest enterprise resource planning (ERP) software company worldwide entered the netsourcing market to attract small to medium-sized firms to their otherwise prohibitively expensive solution. The solution offered integrates industry best practice by offering 22 different industry templates. In essence, it spans a collaborative horizontal and vertical e-business software solution. The complexities of an ERP package, though, were not exactly simplified by structuring it into a netsourcing solution. The high system integration and consulting costs associated with such an organization-spanning solution remain. However, the simplicity of accessing the solution and the prohibitively high investment costs have been restructured into monthly payment arrangements. In addition, the licensing arrangements have been simplified, giving customers greater flexibility.

For suppliers, the case is of interest as SAP is in the market themselves with a netsourcing solution, while in parallel it also allows other IT service providers to resell their solution. As a result, netsourcing providers such as the Lodge have established themselves as an SAP application service provider.

SIENNAX OVERVIEW

Customers will get a clear understanding of the options that a specialist application service provider such as Siennax can offer to medium-sized firms. It also highlights the complexities that innovative startups face when entering into company situations where they are confronted with legacy systems and contracts and where they consequently have to offer additional services for which they have little to no in-house experience. Customers will realize when reading through the case that netsourcing practice is rigorously structured and follows a decision process very similar to classical IT outsourcing. The case illustrates clearly the underlying customers' decision process, the subsequent evaluation and netsourcing selection process, and describes the transition, migration, and integration experiences. Attention is drawn here to the novelty of the solutions and the necessity to be patient to achieve customers' expectations. Careful expectation management becomes an essential ingredient.

For suppliers, the case illustrates the difficulties of customer requests that extend into the realm of legacy system outsourcing. Taking over long-term service contracts presents suppliers with the added complexity of slotting in services that exceed existing or previous service levels. In particular, where no experience exists, added services may need to be catered for.

VISTORM OVERVIEW

From a customer perspective, Vistorm represents an attractive supplier on several fronts. It has a 10-year plus pedigree of consistent market performance. It has a core capability in security and VPNs, one of the perennial concerns we identified among potential customers. It has a strong and growing customer base. It allies with recognized brands. Its niche strategy makes clear who its best customers are going to be and how it is customizing its products and services. It clearly provides for its existing customers what so many ASPs promise: scalability, predictable lower costs, speed to application adoption, secure and responsive infrastructure, and ability to integrate applications.

There are learning points for an ASP. Be precise in identifying the profitable market segment you sell into unless you aim at dominating several (compare Oracle and EDS). Develop a core capability that customers respect and that gives you a distinctive competitive advantage—don't just be an intermediary. In Vistorm's case the security/VPN focus gives them a solid base and track record to expand from. Application integration is a core capability that all ASP aspirants need to develop. Control the forward technology trajectory for the client, not least by investing in the core skills and technologies needed to make applications and systems run over the Internet. These characteristics mean that Vistorm is positioned well to ride out any downturn and take advantage of improvements in the business climate.

After the Vistorm case, the summary at the end of this chapter analyzes all 10 case studies by comparing suppliers' strategies for using netsourcing as a sole or complementary delivery channel, targeting customers, and providing infrastructure.

LODGE[1]

The Lodge was founded in January 2000 by Hans Vets as a separate company within the Dutch Vision Web group. Vision Web currently combines 10 different businesses that focus on change management, consultancy, interim management, information and communication technology (ICT) implementation, system integration, application hosting, and ASP solutions. Headquartered in the Netherlands, the group as a whole doubled its turnover in 1999 to 29 million Euros (€)—approximately $28 million.

As a company, the Lodge manages, operates, and facilitates ICT. Its focus is on two core service solutions: (1) single source of services (SSS), which caters for every IT functionality from integration to support, and (2) accelerated business solutions (ABS), which outlines an ASP solution based primarily on SAP's ERP suite. Hans Vets, CEO and founder, explains: "We deliver SAP centric business solutions. ASP is just a way of delivering it. In a year from now there might be an even smarter way."

Since its start, the Lodge has seen solid growth. The company by 2001 had 13 fully paid-up customers. Among them are firms such as Interbrew, the second-largest brewery in the world; Vleesmeesters, meat producers of Dutch Ahold supermarkets; and De Brandt, a large dairy producer in the Netherlands. These and others have contributed to the Lodge's revenue of €3.7 million (approximately $3.5 million) in its first year of operating. The Lodge employed 38 people in late 2000: 28 worked in the Netherlands and 10 in Belgium. In addition, the Lodge had access to over 80 SAP experts who were part of the Vision Web group.

LODGE'S SAP-CENTRIC ASP SOLUTION

The Lodge's ASP solution (i.e., the accelerated business solution) evolved from how fast you can possibly implement and make operational an application for a customer, as Michel Demmenie, cofounder of the Vision Web explained. Since the speed of deployment is often critical to firms, and even more so when thinking about an ERP solution, the Lodge is able to complete a template-driven implementation of SAP within four months. In 2001 this solution focused on companies with a turnover ranging from €45 million to €225 million. The key underlying customer driver, according to Hans Vets, is:

> A way of bringing down the Total Cost of Ownership of a solution for a customer by having shared service centres....We want to bring down the cost of ownership of an application package, which means to us a back office system and a front office system, which includes CRM functionality, B2B, e-procurement and so on. We want to bring that down to a level where everyone can afford it. That means you have to sell it in a shared mode, so customers are sharing the infrastructure cost, to bring down the price per user.

According to the Lodge's market understanding, their ABS type of solution is geared not so much toward larger organizations, since these will usually not change their ERP systems arrangement to an ASP model, but toward small and medium-sized firms.

> In big organizations there is no person who would take on the responsibility, the risk to take the decision to switch to the ASP model, as far as it concerns ERP solutions. Except for maybe the CEO, but the CEO is often not interested at all in

this stuff....If you look at the ASP model for applications like Word and Excel: that's a different story.

—Hans Vets, CEO and founder, the Lodge

To facilitate the key driver of reducing the total cost of ownership (TCO) of an SAP solution, the Lodge uses a creative refinancing model, which in many ways is very different from other ASPs offering SAP applications. For example, unlike KPN ESN's customers, the Lodge's customers own their SAP software licenses while paying monthly fees. Hans Vets explains in more detail how it works:

> The way we do it is through creative refinancing of the cost to the customer. The customer will sign a contract with us, which includes a contract with SAP. Legally he will still sign a contract with SAP, so the customer owns the license, but we pay it for him. We refinance it. This way the customer pays only 111% over three years....We do the same with the service. Depending on the package, there is between 80 and 120 days of consulting, implementation and development services needed. That's included in the price....What we actually do is we say to the customer: "It will cost you so and so much over three years. How you pay for it, you can decide yourself." But most of the customers decide to pay a fixed price per month....The customer can even pay it as a percentage of its revenue, if they want. So if you are a dot.com and you say: "Sorry, the first six months I don't want to pay anything." That's fine. Of course, the price will go up because the percentage for financing it will be higher. The only thing we demand is, that we want the money for the package within three years.
>
> *—Hans Vets, CEO and founder, the Lodge*

So a customer is charged a monthly fee of approximately €754 (i.e., $660) per month per user for a complete and integrated end-to-end ERP solution. That is roughly €25 ($21) per user per day. Of particular importance to the Lodge's operations is being open-book about its pricing arrangements with its customers. By outlining its price arrangements and costs clearly, it generates transparency and confidence with its customers. There is nothing to hide:

If we know a customer's requirements [after talking to the customer]...we have automated the way we calculate the proposal. So in two days the customer gets a full proposal, and we play open book. That's very important. A lot of competitors have a fixed price per user, but there is no transparency about how the price is built up, so actually I make it my goal to show them the full specifications. The customer knows exactly how much I charge for the hardware, for the connectivity, for the license for the service, for the development, etc. I show them everything. This way they feel confident that no one is trying to cheat on them.

—*Hans Vets, CEO and founder, the Lodge*

Another important difference from other ASPs offering SAP or comparable ERP products is the degree of customization that the Lodge allows within its ASP model. The Lodge argues that its customers should have the same options for customization using the ASP model as they would have if they buy the software solution directly from a system integrator or SAP. Most ASPs, especially those offering complex applications such as ERP, often do not cater for extensive customization without raising significant extra charges: the reason being that the more solutions are customized, the less it will be possible to offer it to other customers. Hence, if customers' configuration requirements go beyond the scope of the packaged ASP solution, a more specific solution can be implemented via the application hosting solution. This means high up-front investments since the customer has to buy the software license.

This is another mistake some other companies make. What they do is, they take a big box, Sun Solaris or something similar, and put an SAP system on it. They create multiple clients; every customer has its own clients within the system and its own user-ids. But there are a number of common settings, common tables, in SAP. Technically you cannot prevent that from happening. This means there is a problem, because when one customer has an additional requirement, all others have to do it as well. So it means you have to have a really standardized system. For the price a customer pays, it is commercially impossible to sell a system like that....If I am a customer I want to have access to the system in the way that I would if I had bought it. I need to be able to customize my

SAP system to my needs. That is the strength of SAP; you can parameterize it, customize it the way you want. For example, if you block that [HRM components], you block a large part of the added value of buying an SAP package. Still SAP offers that flexibility.

—Hans Vets, CEO and founder, the Lodge

To solve the paradox between sharing and customization in an ASP solution, the Lodge offers a configuration that combines an optimal mix of dedicated and shared components, to avoid constraints on customization. The solution is not fully dedicated or shared. Currently, this results in an optimal balance between lowering the TCO and keeping unlimited customization options. In the future it is expected that fully shared configurations can accompany unrestricted customization. At least that is where the Lodge wants to go in the future with its ABS ERP solution.

Ideally, in the ASP model you share everything: hardware, infrastructure, applications and databases—except for the data, which is customer specific. I think we are still two years from that situation, at least two years, in the ERP world. No one has it yet; also SAP cannot do this at the moment. A year ago, it was pure dedicated hosting with SAP. Nothing was shared, except for the data center itself. Today, we already have a model where a lot of the components are shared...You can already share a large percentage of the hardware for different customers, without having any constraints in using the SAP system....Today the back office system is still dedicated, but the front; the Workplace, the e-procurement components, the B2B components, and the CRM components can all be shared in a very transparent way. The next step is going to go even further; really sharing the complete application. To get there it will take another two to three years.

—Hans Vets, CEO and founder, the Lodge

CUSTOMER CASE STUDY 1:
PUNCH INTERNATIONAL

Punch International provides electronics manufacturing solutions, which integrate manufacturing services, from product and process engineering to the delivery of finished products. Activities at Punch International focus on combining the system supply of mechanical components with the assembly of printed circuit boards and final assembly services in both the consumer and professional electronics industry. Punch International's range of products includes audio and video equipment, multimedia products, office and industrial printing equipment, pay terminals, and controller boxes. The company's list of customers is comprised of leading original equipment manufacturers (OEMs):

> Simply put, Punch is a part supplier to companies like Philips, Sanyo, and Sony. The parts we provide these companies with can be made from metal or plastics or a combination of both, for videos, car radios, etc. But more and more there is a trend toward subassembly and complete assembly because there is more added value in that.
> —*Wouter Cortebeeck, Global ICT manager, Punch International*

Geographically dispersed, Punch operates 11 facilities in seven countries: Belgium, United Kingdom, France, Slovakia, Hungary, United States, and Mexico. The group's headquarters is based in Ghent, Belgium. Listed on the Belgian stock market, Punch employed approximately 1800 people with a turnover of approximately $97 million.

Punch decided early on that it needed a full-blown ERP system to integrate and manage the local efforts. Due to its rapid international growth, the resulting need for improved coordination and logistics, and the demand for company pervasiveness, ERP was to offer the necessary integrated solution.

> We had different systems in different plants. Our strategy was to be ready, in terms of IT systems, to have 20 to 25 plants. When you have five plants, and for example you need to consolidate your book keeping, you can use Excel; it will be suffi-

cient. When you have 10 plants this is getting difficult; when you have 20 plants this is crazy. So, firstly, the idea was to be prepared for growth. We needed a global system, also to be able to check what is in stock in a certain plant.

—*Wouter Cortebeeck, Global ICT manager, Punch International*

Although the growth was also a reason to choose an ERP package by SAP, the most important reason was an external one: It was a demand from customers. The trend toward sub-assembly and complete assembly, mentioned earlier, is the result of a strong tendency toward outsourcing in the electronics industry. In its report, Punch referred to outsourcing as "the logical solution for the producers of electronics." It indicates a number of developments that foster this tendency toward outsourcing: most important, as illustrated in Figure 6.1, shortening the life cycle and the development time of electronic products.

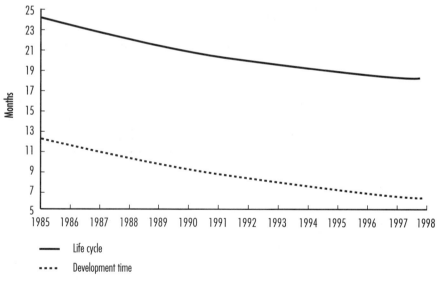

FIGURE 6.1 Product Development Time and Product Life Cycle in the Electronics Market (Data from Punch International. Reprinted by permission of Punch International.)

OEMs seek, in turn, flexibility and reductions in their investments in fixed assets such as manufacturing systems. Outsourcing of the needed manufacturing processes turns these fixed costs into variable costs. As a consequence, the production process has shortened and become more demand driven: Products are produced and delivered to order rather than from stock.

Additionally, many of its key customers increasingly demanded direct access to subassembly products, like theirs, to better coordinate production and sales. SAP, in turn, became a natural choice for interfacing with customers and business partners:

> Quite rapidly we chose SAP. We did have a close look at Navision, Scala, and Remax....More than half of all our customers work with SAP. In fact customers used it as selection criterion. They asked us: "Do you have SAP, because we want to interface?"....We have everything except for project management and advanced production scheduling. So the SAP solution we chose is quite complete.
>
> —*Wouter Cortebeeck, Global ICT manager, Punch International*

Moreover, since outsourcing is a core business practice for Punch International, it was only a small step to source an SAP solution externally. Since the company had no focus on IT and did not have the necessary capabilities to run a complex ERP solution internally—nor did it want to—an IT service supplier was sought:

> Because we have no SAP expertise in-house, the decision to source the solution externally was quickly made. For us this is very interesting because IT is not our core business. We do not have a big IT department, only about five persons centrally and a power user at every plant. For the same reason we source the maintenance of the desktop systems externally.
>
> —*Wouter Cortebeeck, Global ICT manager, Punch International*

Being geographically spread out, Punch decided that it needed greater control through centrally managed systems. Yet it wanted the flexibility to move the central location of its servers, as the company sold and acquired new plants internationally. In turn, it wanted the system to run somewhere remotely, independent of the location of the plants and at the same time accessible from all locations and at all times. The ASP model was thus a perfect match.

The IT partner selected would then take care of the complete process of implementing the solution, including rapid future implementations at new plants and running the system internationally. Following a supplier evaluation period, the Lodge was identified as the preferred choice due to its dynamic character and its SAP expertise:

> We chose the Vision Web. A relatively small company, but very dynamic and flexible. That's what we like; we think like that too. We didn't opt for one of the BIG five, because of experiences in the past. Firstly, these big companies are very expensive, and secondly, they are not flexible and not dynamic. It is more important to have the right people on the project than the name of the company. The philosophy of the Vision Web, the atmosphere was right. We also evaluated Arthur Andersen. We chose the Vision Web. They understood what we wanted very rapidly, and reacted on it very fast. After we decided for the Vision Web, we did a feasibility study, a mini blueprint, on which the contracts were based.
>
> —*Wouter Cortebeeck, Global ICT manager, Punch International*

Because all of Punch International's plants are different, it was decided that the solution was to be implemented in the plants sequentially rather than simultaneously. To ensure that the solution would fit and is likely to complement future processes, an extensive evaluation was undertaken. This *blueprinting* resulted in a master solution entailing all the needed functionality to handle the different scenarios at the different plants within Punch International.

The SAP solution we chose is quite complete: it entails everything except for project management and advanced production scheduling. We had two project managers: one from Solvision, also part of the Vision Web, and one from within Punch International. Together they developed the blueprint on which the SAP solution is based. They visited the plants, talked with the key users, and went through all the key processes. Then they made the blueprint, it was tested, and after some revisions it was approved. So the first contacts with the Vision Web were about one-and-a-half years ago; the creation of the blueprint took about nine months. However, before the completion of the blueprint, we had already implemented the solution in our French plant, although it was a partial solution, only the financial modules. We needed the solution quickly in France. France did go live 1st of November; blueprinting was finished beginning 2001.

—*Wouter Cortebeeck, Global ICT manager, Punch International*

The nine months of blueprinting accounted for a large sum of the overall costs. Under normal conditions, this phase would have entailed a substantial one-time investment. Yet Vision Web largely took care of the evaluation and resulting implementations. Punch partially pays for the individual implementations through its monthly fixed fee. The necessary training is also done by Vision Web; it trains the power users, who in turn then train the other users. The first SAP was rolled out in France:

At the moment there are 10 users in France. In the UK another 20 will be added. In France, implementing the solution was no problem. But there were no legacy systems over there, so it was relatively easy. On the other hand, it meant we had to build it from scratch. In the UK it's different. It's a very mature plant, very well organized. Now the Vision Web will begin installing the system in the UK the first of April; it will be live this summer. It's also the first full implementation, but it will be no problem. For us the UK implementation is a very important benchmark.

—*Wouter Cortebeeck, Global ICT manager, Punch International*

When asked about the experiences so far with the ASP SAP model, it was described by the responsible IT manager as generally very positive. As expected, it allowed the company to focus on its own business instead of worrying about the ERP application solution. So far, the experiences match the expectations, as Wouter Cortebeeck, the Global ICT manager for Punch International, explained:

> The first experiences are very good. No fuss, no hassle. We do our job and they do theirs, that's it. We don't want and we don't need to worry about routers, firewalls, and servers. That's their business. We have an SLA. Every month we review the performance. If they do not meet the SLA standards, we will get a payback. What is important to me, is the response time and the uptime, how they do it, that's not my problem. This is all settled in the SLA. When there is a crash, it should be resolved within eight hours. If it's with a backup server or something else, that's not my problem. The agreed upon uptime is like 99.9 and something percent. The downtime is something like half a day per year. We have one point of contact: the Vision Web. For example, we do not have a contract with PSINet; the Lodge deals with PSINet. For us that is what the ASP concept is about: one point of contact….Another application we are considering to source via this type of arrangement is MS Exchange, among others. MS Exchange is actually in the pipeline already, also via the Vision Web.

CUSTOMER CASE STUDY 2: REALSCALE TECHNOLOGIES

RealScale Technologies (formerly known as Advanced Communication Research) is a startup founded in 1997 by Serge Dujardin and Jean-Christophe Pari. Headquartered in Zaventem, Belgium, RealScale Technologies also has offices in Sophia Antipolis, France. The company has developed an innovative scalable platform that enables Service Providers to offer Internet applications to a high number of users. The underlying architecture has benefited from the founders' experiences gained in the telecom industry. Olav Claassen, vice-president of information services Europe at RealScale Technologies, explains:

> If you've got a 19-inch rack, normally you can only fit in 20 to 40 servers at the most. We designed a server which enables the client to fit 240 servers in the same rack. The idea originates from the telecom servers. We also developed the entire management system. You have to manage a rack of 240 servers, so you need special software to do it. It's like an administrative software layer on top of it. Our system can significantly cut the cost of Service Provision, because our architecture allows ISPs to save on energy, maintenance, and the hardware takes up less space. At the moment we are talking to the big players in the market. It is quite a revolutionary product, so acceptance will take some time. When we tell it to potential clients, there is a lot of disbelief: If you can do it, why can't the big guys do it?

The company, in cooperation with its newly appointed IT services manager, Olav Claassen, decided that the company needed an ERP solution that integrates finance, cost control, enterprise consolidation, and purchasing functionality. Given his experience with SAP, the decision to opt for an SAP solution was not a surprise. However, the decision was still the result of an evaluation of ERP offerings from three independent software vendors.

> I started with package selection. I had a detailed look at three established broad-scoped ERP packages. A broad scope, because for us the financial and cost controlling functionality is just the beginning. Sales and distribution, and production planning are to follow. Most of the packages did not qualify at all because of this scope and the integration aspects. We quickly decided for mySAP.com for its functionality; it has the broadest scope, but also because of pricing reasons. SAP has positioned mySAP.com at a very competitive price in comparison to a lot of other packages. We evaluated some other ERP packages from other ISVs, like Navision and IFS, both Scandinavian products. IFS was very sexy and very promising. The major downside, however, was the fact that there was too little expertise around, and hardly any comparable references.

Because of this, there would have been a certain amount of risk associated with a choice of either of them. Navision is a good product, but was perceived to be too slim. Their market approach and implementation partner strategy results in a high number of tailor-made solutions. We wanted standard....This project was a consultant's dream; it's a Greenfield implementation. We have no legacy systems, no data to convert, no bad habits. We can adopt our processes to the system.
  —*Olav Claassen, vice-president of information services Europe, RealScale Technologies*

For a company the size of RealScale Technologies, it is quite unusual to implement a high-end ERP system such as SAP. However, RealScale Technologies in early 2001 was expecting to grow rapidly in the next twelve months as its products gained exposure. Therefore, the ERP package would eventually fit the expected size of the company rather than its current size.

RealScale Technologies has about 40 employees at the moment. Hardly the size for a full-blown SAP solution. The philosophy of this company is: "We have a new product, and we expect this product to become a huge success." We are now in the phase of preparing for that success. We are penetrating the market and we are in contact with potential clients, but it is in an early stage. However, we want to be totally ready for this success. We expect radical growth: at the end of the year we expect to have at least 80 people. If an ERP solution has to be implemented during such a growth period, it will cost considerably more time and money, because everybody will be tied up in operational issues. That's why we wanted an ERP system implemented that would support us in our growth. Not the current state of the company, but the future state of the company made us decide for SAP. Currently we have 10 users, in time this will grow.
  —*Olav Claassen, vice-president of information services Europe, RealScale Technologies*

Traditionally, SAP packages are beyond the financial reach of smaller companies. First, the traditional pricing model requires paying for the licenses upfront, an investment that often poses a barrier for smaller companies, especially startups and high-growth firms. Second, the implementation of such solutions requires special expertise and, more important, involves high costs. Finally, to run these applications in-house requires specialized skills, which again involves high costs. Smaller companies often lack both the needed money and skills. Nonetheless, the ASP model, in this case, opens up an opportunity for smaller companies to seriously consider high-end ERP packages. Vision Web's model allows customers to spread the cost of software licenses and hardware over three years, making the high upfront investments superfluous.

> I got speaking to Hans Vets from the Vision Web. Here was a guy that understood what I wanted, who listened to me as a client. He came back with a proposal within two days. The proposal included a guaranteed live system on the 2nd of January for a fixed price. This was a company who committed themselves to my requests. That's an easy decision, because that's what you want: commitment.... If I would have had to hire the needed experts to run the SAP systems in-house, that would have cost me over €200,000, because these experts would have had to be extremely knowledgeable. (These costs include salaries and benefits but also the technical infrastructure to run SAP.) That's a lot of money. Especially since we are a startup, we need our cash; we don't want to invest this purely in software. In the current scenario, I don't have to spend that money, because I am paying the ASP to run the systems for me, to help me with technical problems and to help me with functional problems. For me that was an easy decision.
>
> —*Olav Claassen, vice-president of information services Europe, RealScale Technologies*

Vision Web was the only company that could guarantee RealScale Technologies to be up and running with a SAP system within the restricted time frame. In addition, the Vision Web enabled RealScale Technologies to source the SAP solution via a hosting arrangement, combined with a leasing agreement, including licenses, infrastructure, hardware, connectivity, and implementation services. Moreover, the Vision Web enabled the company to focus on its core business and its growth, instead of having to worry about its IT systems.

> So, for cost reasons and for quality reasons I chose the Vision Web. For me that was an easy decision at that time. Of course, we had some discussions about security, and reliability issues. For example, the Vision Web uses PSINet as a connectivity partner. I wanted to be guaranteed that in case PSINet would go bankrupt, they would have a backup partner that could immediately take over and ensure that we can still run our business. The Vision Web has arrangements with backup partners, and that was good enough for me. In the end it's their problem not ours. I buy the service; they have to deliver. How they do it and with whom, I don't care.
> —*Olav Claassen, vice-president of information services Europe, RealScale Technologies*

The deadline demanded implied a challenging time frame of two to three months. This is an unusual time frame for a complete SAP implementation, which is illustrated by the fact that the Vision Web was the only company to commit to the proposed time frame beforehand. The Vision Web managed to implement the system right on schedule. This was made possible in part through the low degree of customization that RealScale Technologies demanded. The process of customization in RealScale took less than a month compared to the nine months of blueprinting in the Punch International firm. The difference can be explained through the complexity of the organization structures to which the solution had to be adapted and the lack of a legacy system.

> We started customizing the system in November, and early December we started testing and training. During the implementation there were two full-time consultants assigned and a project manager from the Vision Web. I had a meeting with the project manager twice a week about the progress. The ERP solution went live on the 2nd of January, right on schedule. It all went unbelievably fast. Especially since it was a multicountry implementation (France and Belgium) and financial reporting according to US-GAAP.
> —*Olav Claassen, vice-president of information services Europe, RealScale Technologies*

So far, RealScale Technologies' experiences with the ASP SAP solution from the Lodge have been very positive. Both the offered functionality and the technical performance of the Internet delivery method are good. The only downside was attributed to RealScale Technologies internally. The adoption of the solution by its users is not yet optimal. The lack of commitment internally is a problem and will determine the success of the solution in the long run. It proves that sourcing arrangements never completely take away the need for management.

RealScale Technologies was especially happy with the efforts of the Vision Web. Its dynamic approach to RealScale Technologies' needs, its speed and efficiency in dealing with issues, and its down-to-earth business approach resulted in higher customer satisfaction.

> I met Hans Vets from the Vision Web for the first time on Tuesday; the deal was closed on Friday. By that time he had presented me with a full-blown proposal. As mentioned before, we were live on time, on budget within three months....It surprised me; the contract with the Vision Web is very clear and very pragmatic. It covers the essential things. It's not the lengthy U.S. type of contract. That was exactly what I wanted and I understand it: I know what I am buying, I know what I am getting for my money, I know what I can expect, and I know what happens in case they cannot live up to the service levels agreed upon.
>
> —*Olav Claassen, vice-president of information services Europe, RealScale Technologies*

MARVIQ[2]

> It was back in October 1998....I remember clearly the early days of our Internet startup. Four guys, a girl, and a refrigerator, packed into one small office room, working like crazy to fulfill our vision of a software solution as a service.
>
> —*Onno Schellekens, CEO[3] and cofounder, marviQ*

At their recent renaming and new logo launch (from Grad-delt to marviQ), the firm marked its transition from a startup phase to a growth and internationalization stage. Since its formation in 1998 the company grew from five to 60 employees in February 2000, to see it double further, to over 120 employees by November 2000. Today, marviQ combines unique technical and application expertise skills based on Java with the experience of formerly high-ranking sales executives and managers from companies such as PricewaterhouseCoopers, Netscape Communications, Ernst & Young Consulting, Philips, Planet Internet, and WorldAccess. This growth has seen marviQ accumulate one of the largest Java development teams in the Benelux (i.e., Netherlands and Belgium) area. In parallel to its physical growth, marviQ's business value and revenue grew by 1600% to a turnover of 5 million guilders (i.e., approximately $2.1 million).

Privately owned, it secured its second round of venture capital (VC) funding of 8.8 million Dutch guilders (approximately $3.7 million) from Remark Capital, Twinning, and Internet Capital Europe in May 2000. Set for growth, the company planned to exploit its innovation in using Java as an operating system–independent infrastructure and hence application delivery solution. In addition, it planned to expand across Europe, the United States, and Asia. The challenge marviQ faces in the coming months and years is to balance its growth with its resources in terms of skills and financial possibilities. The guiding goal continues to be profitability in the long run.

MARVIQ'S FSP STRATEGY

marviQ started out by offering an online workflow application solution to the legal industry. This application supported and enhanced the flow of information within legal departments, allowing lawyers and legal experts not only to access essential legal databases from their desktops, but also to share information with others internally and externally. Over the years this application solution was enhanced by a broader set of application services, leading marviQ to position itself today as a full service provider (FSP). It is now able to offer solutions that integrate and manage the entire ICT delivery chain for all types of customers (see Figure 6.2).

By managing and integrating a customer's ICT delivery chain, marviQ offers content solutions on the basis of information transactions, services, and so on, to end users such as business partners, employees, and consumers. marviQ has named this infrastructure the corporate Internet service provider (CISP) proposition. This proposition integrates three key components.

Connectivity. According to marviQ, a company's network of business partners, customers, and employees can be seen as a value-creating network as opposed to the traditional value chain. For value creation the actors have to be able to interact. Using the ICT delivery chain model, end users must be able to access, use, modify, and exchange content. MarviQ thus links the various actors within the value-creating network, offering them the best possible connectivity in terms of reliability, security, and speed, and also in terms of interfaces. For this, marviQ uses a number of strategic partners, such as Worldcom and Interxion, to facilitate this connectivity.

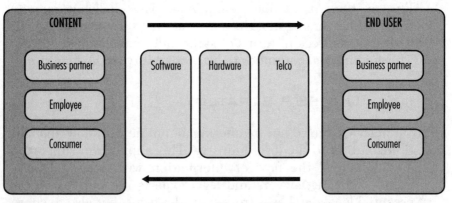

FIGURE 6.2 MarviQ's ICT Delivery Chain (From marviQ brochure, 2001. Reprinted by permission of marviQ.)

Functionality. According to Robert Noteboom, chief marketing officer of marviQ, the ASP model is mostly about efficiency gains, lowering the total cost of ownership, and increasing deployment speed. In contrast, marviQ's FSP model is about effectiveness, providing functionality to end users to empower clients in their interaction with business partners, employees, and consumers. According to Noteboom, marviQ thus does not provide application solutions but instead, offers business functionality, based on high-end applications that support a client's business needs and goals. For example, it offers application functionality to optimize the internal front- and back-end processes of a firm, functionality to optimize external partner relations, functionality to optimize human resources, and functionality to optimize customer relations.

> The idea behind our FSP model is, we deliver functionality according to our own quality standards. In a way, this means that the brand presence of the software components used in our platform becomes less prominent. We break applications up in components, modules, which we then integrate with our other modules to create replicable business functionality that enables us to rapidly deliver custom enterprise solutions.
>
> —*Robert Noteboom, CMO, marviQ*

Using its Java-based infrastructure platform, marviQ is able to combine various functionality modules to offer customers a solution that is optimized to their requirements and accessible on a one-to-many basis by end users.

Integration. Integration, the final value component of the CISP infrastructure, focuses on integrating marviQ's FSP application functionality with that of a client's legacy systems. For this, two interface options are available:

1. *Data migration.* marviQ has established strategic relations with firms that specialize in application protocols that enable the integration of all known

application data output into data formats that fit with marviQ's FSP platform.

2. *Application and data coexistence.* In this arrangement, legacy systems are remotely integrated, provided that these legacy systems consist of data and applications that run on centralized server and storage hardware similar to the technology that marviQ operates.

N-Tier Architecture

marviQ's *n*-tier architecture distinguishes between the access or presentation, business logic, and data (content, functionality, and legacy) layers and its front- and back-end application functionality. This architecture outlines for the customer the likely application functionality accessible through marviQ's FSP platform. Moreover, through this infrastructure marviQ can individualize and offer customers market- or industry-specific business solutions based on a range of application solutions (see Figure 6.3).

The architecture includes the following components:

Tier 1: presentation. The first tier delivers business logic and associated data to end users using Internet technology. Delivery is enabled via standards such as XML, HTML, or WML, over standard protocols such as HTTP and WAP. According to one respondent:

> The interface we use commonly is a browser. For our ERP functionality, we had to overcome a set of difficulties in respect to the web interface. In some cases the customer, for example, needed to download a thin client driver based on Java to access the system. The thin client was then installed and set-up locally. But this is less than desirable and is only a temporary solution. The intention instead was to have a fully browser-enabled interface for all our functionality.

At the core of this presentation layer is IBM's WebSphere application server platform. MarviQ chose WebSphere for its technical facilities, expansion possibilities, its focus on the

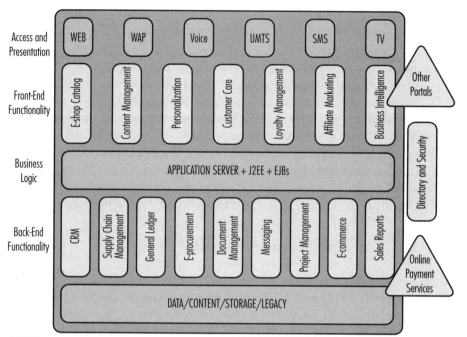

FIGURE 6.3 MarviQ's n-tier Architecture (From company presentation, 2001. Reprinted by permission of marviQ.)

Java 2 Enterprise Edition (essential for marviQ's Java infrastructure), and the availability of an integrated suite of development tools. As a result, all services developed and delivered by marviQ are accessible by various devices, ranging from desktop computers to PDAs and even WAP-enabled mobile phones.

Tier 2: business logic. The second tier consists of the middleware layer. MarviQ uses middleware based primarily on the Java 2 Enterprise Edition (J2EE), a standard that today is used widely by independent software vendors. J2EE services define the middle tier between the user interface and the data/functionality layers. Its core component is Enterprise Java Beans (EJBs), which uses a container layer that provides security. marviQ's middleware platform is used to combine and integrate the various functionality modules with that of the customer's legacy systems. It adds a great deal of flexibility, giving customers the possibility to mix-and-match their application solution.

Tier 3: content, functionality, and legacy. The third tier consists of best-of-breed applications such as Oracle databases, Lawson ERP software, Documentum document management software, Art Technology Group's (ATG) customer management solutions, and iPlanet's e-commerce solutions. All applications are selected for their functionality, scalability, reliability, open standards, and compatibility with the J2EE platform. MarviQ uses specific criteria for selecting software for their services. One of the most important criteria is the fit with marviQ's architecture.

CUSTOMER CASE STUDIES

Major customers of marviQ e-business services include Remark, ING, and Wolters Kluwer. Three specific customer scenarios that outline marviQ's solutions, capabilities, and competencies are described below.

QuoteOnWine. QuoteOnWine (*www.quoteonwine.com*), a multifaceted environment for wine enthusiasts, is the first initiative to explore the business opportunities of the Internet by the Quote Media Group. Quote Media Holding is an independent Dutch publisher of glossy magazines such as *Quote, Elle, Villa d'Arte,* and *Santé.* The objective for QuoteOnWine was to become the most extensive environment for wine enthusiasts. Since wine is an emotional product, it offers opportunities to create value for the Quote brand, as noted by Quote management.

QuoteOnWine offers a clear mix of content, commerce, and community. Apart from selling wine, the site offers extensive information on wine, wine countries, grapes, and harvest years. It is even possible to chat and publish one's own wine opinion on the site.

For this, marviQ built an integrated and highly scalable e-commerce operation which it hosts at its data center. It integrates front- and back-end operations of QuoteOnWine on its *n*-tier FSP platform described above. For this, marviQ developed a solution consisting of three key components:

1. A front-end application that can present the content in a flexible and dynamic way. It offers customers a complete wine shop (information, purchasing wine, virtual wine cellar, and personalization services).

2. A back-end enterprise system that supports Quote's company processes, such as procurement, inventory management, and customer relationship management with application solutions. For this, QuoteOnWine accesses the Lawson modules to conduct these processes via an Internet link using a standard browser and a JAVA plug-in.

3. A middleware layer, which integrates the front-end, the back-end, and payment services into a seamless solution.

All three components are hosted on marviQ's platform, which ensures high security protection, scalability, and reliability.

This e-commerce platform developed initially for Quote-OnWine can easily be adapted and extended for a range of e-commerce solutions to suit future clients' needs and demands, demonstrating the fundamental one-to-many ASP business model that marviQ operates.

Identrus. As a leading global bank, ABN Amro's objective is to be a frontrunner in value-added global network banking. For this it has assertively entered the arena for business-to-business (B2B) e-commerce by becoming a founding member of Identrus LLC, a global alliance formed in 1999 by eight leading international financial institutions to facilitate the growth of B2B e-business between financial institutions and their clients. As the first organization of its kind, Identrus has developed the technical and operational infrastructure to remove the trust and risk barriers impeding the global adoption of B2B transactions over the Internet. The Identrus standard, including digital certificates and a secure transaction environment, guarantees authentication and secure transactions between all types of organizations.

To place itself and the emerging identity trust standard in the market, ABN Amro formalized itself as a trusted agent for online commercial collaboration. To deliver this new functionality and the potential economic opportunities to its clients, it contracted marviQ to develop a secure single sign-on mechanism that incorporates user authentication, secure e-mail, and secure document exchange. Together these define the Identrus Technology components.

marviQ is currently integrating the Identrus trust components into its existing hosted e-mail system as part of its partnership with ABN Amro. This project, the first Identrus implementation in an ASP environment, delivers a Webmail system where users are identified online via a smart card and user rights are validated online, and pending their validation, users are given access to the Webmail system. By incorporating Identrus as a part of its single sign-on mechanism, in the second stage marviQ will offer secure access to all application services in its customer portals.

> Businesses will be able to utilize the identity services regulated by Identrus and delivered by its member banks to obtain guarantees about the validity of the identity of other holders of Identrus compliant digital certificates. As the only Full Service Provider (FSP) participating in and preparing to deliver Identrus-enabled B2B e-services, it has been clear to Graddelt for some time that the success of Identrus and similar TTP [trusted third party] projects is key to the Internet realizing its full potential as a business enabler.
> —*David Edwards, cofounder, marviQ*

CareView. One of marviQ's customer showcases is CareView. This health care information system was commissioned by the Dutch S&L Zorg (National Health Service) and partly subsidized by the Dutch Ministry of Health, Welfare and Sport (VWS). S&L Zorg is a regional health care company offering health care services to mentally handicapped people. CareView, called an e-health solution, connects all stakeholders of the health care chain to the Internet via a portal. CareView then provides people in need of health care and health care institutions with an online communication environment, online access to secured, centrally managed and stored client records, and an online marketplace for health care services and products.

CareView helps make the market for health care services more transparent for people looking for health care services. In addition, clients can access their own records and provide additional information if needed. To health care institutions, CareView offers the means to empower their employees on location and provides health care companies with detailed management information by integrating both front-end solutions and back-end processes. At present, CareView is used only by S&L Zorg. But in the near future marviQ plans to offer this solution on a subscription basis to other health care institutions and companies operating in the industry.

SAP[4]

SAP is the world's third-largest software vendor and is regarded as the leading provider of enterprise resource planning (ERP) solutions. Founded in 1972 by five former IBM systems engineers, SAP employs more than 22,000 people in more than 50 countries worldwide. Headquartered in Walldorf, Germany, it has been quoted publicly since 1988. Its revenues in 2000 exceeded $6 billion, with a reported net income of $634 million. SAP offers industry-specific application solutions for 22 industries and spans a network of more than 900 partners and a customer base of more than 12,000 companies, including more than half of the world's top 500 companies. It had 10 million licensed users for its R/3 ERP solutions around the world in 2001.

MYSAP.COM

In 1999 SAP introduced mySAP.com, a product line defining its Internet strategy. The mySAP.com offering consists in essence of collaborative horizontal and vertical e-business software solutions. Vertical solutions link different horizontal solutions tailored to specific industries. For this, SAP has 22 industry templates, from aerospace and defense to automotive and banking and telecommunications and transportation. These solutions allow organizations not only to fully integrate their operational business processes but also to integrate customers and business partners along the supply and value chain.

The mySAP.com product line consists of four distinguishable building blocks:

1. *Marketplace:* Internet community where companies can transact products and services with others.
2. *Business applications:* role-based application use that links customers, suppliers, partners, and vendors through the Internet. The mySAP.com business applications cover the following areas:

   - Customer relationship management
   - E-commerce
   - Supply chain management
   - Product life-cycle management
   - Knowledge management
   - Business intelligence
   - Strategic enterprise management
   - Financials and cost management
   - Human capital management

3. *Workplace:* an enterprise portal that provides employees in companies with a browser-based personalized working environment from which they access all the functions they need daily in their particular role.
4. *Application hosting:* set of hosting services provided by SAP and partners jointly, including application hosting, application service provision, application management, and hosting of marketplaces.

The last building block (application hosting) contains four different approaches that are seen as new types of outsourcing arrangements: application service provision, application hosting, application management, and hosting of marketplaces.

Application service provision. In our view, an important goal for SAP in adopting the ASP model was a more regular flow of revenues. Licenses generate a one-off income, and maintenance fees create a more steady flow. SAP was interested in increasing the regular flow of revenues over the next few years, and there were advantages in doing this on a large scale.

The SAP ASP offering combines software, implementation, infrastructure, service, and support. It is backed by a rapid implementation philosophy that enables one-stop shopping at the lowest cost of operation and implementation. The ASP model generally is a one-to-many model with little customer configuration and therefore is easily adoptable by many customers. With the one-to-many SAP ASP model, customers can have a standardized full-service package that is accessible via all types of networks, including the Internet.

The difference between SAP's application hosting and .SAP's ASP is ownership of the software license. In the one-to-many model, the software licenses are owned by the ASP: SAP itself or one of SAP's ASP partners. Pricing is per user/ per month. For this the ASP model provides access to a complete SAP ERP solution. Normally, most small and midsize enterprises would not be able to afford SAP's software, but with the ASP model the applications become affordable for almost all firms.

However, SAP is facing a number of challenges for its ASP model. One major challenge has to do with its software architecture in terms of adapting its ERP software to a one-to-many model. As SAP's software was traditionally targeted at large enterprises, it was developed for dedicated scenarios and not for one-to-many scenarios. Another challenge is the architecture integrity of its software. Compared to other ERP software solutions from Lawson, for example, SAP's ERP platform is particularly difficult to integrate with other software and legacy systems. It thus requires complex message brokering or protocol aligners to adapt the ERP output to other applications. Of course, this does not add to the flexibility of the software with respect to integration and implementation simplicity.

Application hosting. If customers' configuration requirements go beyond the scope of a prepackaged ASP solution, a more specific solution can be implemented via a dedicated application hosting solution. Full applications can then be run and maintained on a central processing facility. The basis for pricing for such a solution is either paid up front yearly or in a per user/per month licensing fee. In the application hosting model, the customers eventually own the licenses.

With application hosting customers benefit from substantially lower implementation costs. If in the future the customer decides to buy its own hardware, the solution can be transferred. In the meantime, though, customers have no initial investment costs. Additionally, training efforts are minimized since maintenance and operations are left to SAP.

Application management. The application management service SAP offers covers basically the provision of IT personnel and tools to maintain a customer's application solution. In many ways this part is inherent and integral to the previous two solutions.

Hosting of marketplaces. The hosting of marketplaces refers to a service that offers customized online marketplaces owned by an individual customer, which is then managed according to the specific marketplace or business community requirements. The marketplace will be based on SAP's ERP solution and can be seen as an extension to an ASP service.

SAP Hosting versus Local ASP Strategies

At the moment SAP's ASP activities are spread throughout the company. Although SAP launched a specialized subsidiary (SAPHosting) for application hosting and ASP in March 2000, the ASP efforts have been far from centrally coordinated. The subsidiary, which is based in St. Leon-Rot, Germany, focuses its efforts on offering ASP and hosting services directly and indirectly to customers, as well as providing support and quality benchmarks for its mySAP.com partners.

It seems that SAP is not moving into outsourcing so much as being more directly active in the related areas of application hosting and service provision. But one can see a future where SAP itself hosts or operates some systems as an ASP to gain practical experience and to ensure that all potential for progress is being realized.

SAPHosting is said to operate internationally and target all markets. So far the dedicated ASP/hosting company seems to target mainly Germany, although there are some global initiatives. For example, in November 2000, SAP and SITA (*www.sita.int*), the world's leading providers of integrated telecommunications and information solutions for the air transport industry, decided to join forces to develop an independent ASP for the world's air transport community. With over 400 customers in the aerospace and defense industry, SAP is a leading supplier of enterprise solutions and SITA provides a range of application services to airports, airlines, and airfreight and aerospace companies integrated with its desktop and network infrastructure solutions. The joint venture is to bring together SITA's expertise in Internet technologies and application provision, and its global integrated voice and data network, together with SAP's application solutions for the air transport industry and SAPHosting's experience in providing applications via an ASP model, to deliver mySAP.com e-business solutions over SITA's secure global network.

As explained above, SAPHosting also provides support and quality benchmarks to the expanding network of mySAP.com partners. To become an eligible partner, SAP has an explicit set of criteria for selection and certification:

- *General criteria.* All products and services must be in the language of the country in which they will be used, integrated billing, full responsibility for services performed by the subcontractors, use of SAP templates, and SAP best practices.
- *Infrastructure criteria.* Complete and secure data center, guaranteed security and reliability, and expertise on platform scalability.
- *Implementation and upgrade criteria.* Trained consulting team of sufficient size and coverage, precompiled scenarios for each solution, documented implementation processes for each solution.

- *Solution criteria.* Resources for service and support, including help desk and multiclient capability.
- *Service and support criteria.* Single point of contact, 24 × 7 support availability, service reporting facilities, and regular reviews of performance and use.

ASP and hosting partners range from major hosting companies with proven global outsourcing capabilities to national companies operating in local markets. SAP distinguishes four levels of hosting partnerships:

1. *MySAP.com Partner—Hosting.* This level is designed specifically for smaller companies targeting local markets.
2. *MySap.com Alliance Partner—Hosting.* Alliance partners are able to deliver comprehensive hosting solutions to SAP key accounts in the corresponding markets.
3. *MySAP.com Global Partner—Hosting.* These companies operate in at least two regions, Europe/Americas or Europe/Asia Pacific. Siemens Business Solutions, for example, is a SAP global hosting partner.
4. *MySAP.com Global Alliance Partner—Hosting.* This is the highest level of partnership. These partners are international hosting companies with a dedicated SAP business focus.

In parallel with SAPHosting's efforts, most country-specific subsidiaries are developing their own ASP strategies. In most cases, these local ASP strategies have an indirect channel approach, involving local partners to undertake the true ASP role of hosting the applications, renting them to ASP customers and delivering them via a wide area network. In this indirect channel approach, the local SAP subsidiary provides applications to the ASP partner but has no direct contact with the ASP customer.

At this time SAP was introducing its ASP services worldwide. Guidelines for pricing and conditions for ASP partners were set globally, but the services managed locally per country. It is not intended for the country-specific subsidiaries to become ASPs themselves. Germany has been an exception to this, where SAPHosting is also active as an ASP itself.

In contrast, SAP in the Netherlands has been in the process of teaming up with local ASP partners. SAP Netherlands is a 100% subsidiary of SAP AG, with an annual revenue of about $100 million and over 300 employees. The activities related to the ASP model are coordinated by the product introduction and indirect sales division. SAP Netherlands distinguishes partnerships for horizontal solutions from partnerships for vertical (i.e., industry-specific) solutions. For both horizontal and vertical solutions, in the Netherlands there is only a select group of partners.

In the Netherlands we found SAP still searching for the right formula. Potential ASP partners needed to have marketing power, and should be able to provide a 24 × 7 service. They must also have access to very good data centers and sufficient capacity and expertise to host applications to SAP standards. At this date SAP was talking to a number of parties. Some of them were delivering horizontal solutions, for example, personnel and payroll systems. SAP was also talking to KPN, which had shown interest in focusing on the ASP model. SAP was anxious to combine its branch partners' expertise, KPN's market power, and SAP's market power and expertise. This would then be packaged into branch-specific ASP services.

For example, in partnership with Nationale Nederlanden, the Dutch market leader for integrated financial services, SAP has offered a vertical solution. Nationale Nederlanden is a business unit of the Internationale Nederland Groep (ING Group). Together they are planning to deliver pension insurance solutions to companies across the Benelux area. SAP will supply the applications, and Nationale Nederlanden will provide the specific insurance-related knowledge and will take care of the application services, the application delivery, the customer support, and invoicing for the service.

Another company, SAP Netherlands, has teamed up with KPN Enterprise Solutions Nederland (KPN ESN), a business unit of KPN Telecommunications, to deliver vertical solutions. With four core activities, (1) mobile communication services, (2) Internet, call center, and media (ICM) services, (3) fixed network services, and (4) data/IP services, KPN, together with

SAP, aims to provide ICT solutions to customers for all business processes. KPN ESN wants to be the leading ASP for business applications in the Netherlands within one-and-a-half years and to be among Europe's top three ASPs within three years.

As Figure 6.4 illustrates, in this partnership SAP only delivers the software; KPN ESN is the ASP. A third party (not known at the time of the research) provides the industry-specific expertise to localize the software and customize it to a specific client. In most cases, the latter will be one of SAP's Dutch value-added resellers (VARs), specialized in a particular industry.

With this ASP venture, SAP Netherlands wants to target primarily small and medium-sized companies (SMEs), the reasoning being that KPN has the reach and marketing power in this particular segment. The ASP model in this context will then open up this segment for SAP, giving most firms of this size access to a ERP solution that normally they could not afford.

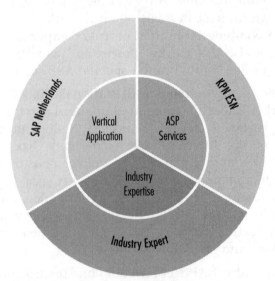

FIGURE 6.4 SAP and KPN's ASP Partnering Model for Vertical Solutions in the Netherlands

With KPN, SAP has been focusing on SMEs to offer these companies a complete, integrated solution using the ASP model. SAP has been seeking the best formula to make use of the expertise of Value Added Resellers and KPN's and SAP's market power. Initial sales would then be done by representatives from a KPN business center and a specific VAR.

Interestingly, to avoid any channel conflicts, SAP will not allow KPN ESN to deliver its applications solutions using an ASP model to companies with annual revenue that exceeds 250 million guilders (about $100 million). Companies exceeding this amount can only be served directly by SAP Netherlands and one of its certified partners. The ASP model will not be made available to companies of this size.

Why this 250 million guilder limit? Our view is that this prevents channel conflicts. SAP needs clarity about who direct sales focuses on and where the VARs put their attention. It is important for SAP to avoid their VARs competing against the SAP direct sales operation—or the other way around.

Since SAP Netherlands is still in the process of teaming up with KPN ESN and has no other ASP partners for its vertical solutions due to the novelty of the solution, there are no ASP customer scenarios available at this time.

In other countries SAP does have a number of ASP scenarios similar to the Dutch SAP/KPN ESN partnership described above. In the United Kingdom, for example, SAP has similar partnerships with Origin, HostLogic, and i-fusion. SAP Belgium signed one of the first ASP contracts with CBSI–BPR. CBSI is a worldwide provider of information technology services to large and midsized companies, which in turn decided to cooperate with PSINet and Hewlett-Packard in order to provide ASP services by use of mySAP.com solutions. Together, SAP and CBSI launched Leasap, targeting in particular medium-sized companies in Belgium and Luxembourg. In the United States, SAPHosting has certified 11 mySAP.com ASPs and hosting partners, each with its own particular industry expertise groups:

- *PriceWaterhouseCoopers:* high tech, automotive, utilities, banking, retail
- *Hunter Group:* human resources
- *FiNetrics:* ASP model for hosting standardized solutions
- *Corio, Inc.:* high tech, dot.com
- *EDS:* consumer products, automotive, utilities, business-to-business
- *eOnline:* service provider, high tech, automotive, human resources, business-to-business
- *Interpath Communications Inc.:* human resources
- *HostLogic, Inc.:* public sector
- *IBM Corp.:* BPO for business-to-business procurement
- *Siemens Business Services:* consumer products, manufacturing
- *Qwest Cyber.Solutions:* service provider, automotive, high tech, human resources, dot.com

Together with SAP USA, these companies mainly target companies, divisions, and subsidiaries with annual revenues of $1 billion, including the public sector. However, smaller clients that traditionally have been locked out of an SAP solution will also be served with a scaled-down solution.

CUSTOMER ADOPTION

In 2000, SAP reached a major milestone when the number of registered licensed users of its mySAP platform reached 1 million. Since then, more than 3 million additional users have licensed the solution (SAP press release, June 2001). The following lists some of the key customers to date: Avaya, Inc.; Bristol-Myers Squibb Co.; The Coca-Cola Company; Colgate-Palmolive Co.; Compaq Computer Corp.; Dow Corning Corp.; Eli Lilly and Company; General Mills, Inc.; Gillette Co.; Hewlett-Packard Co.; Honeywell, Inc.; Kimberly-Clark Corp.; Motorola, Inc.; Palm, Inc.; Philip Morris Companies, Inc.; Procter & Gamble Co.; and Texaco, Inc.

Compaq also announced (2001) that it had chosen mySAP Product Lifecycle Management (mySAP PLM) as its collaborative design and engineering technology. The company installed 10,000 seats of mySAP PLM in plants around the world, the largest SAP product life-cycle management implementation in use anywhere in the world.

SIENNAX[5]

Founded by five former BSO Origin employees, Siennax started out in 1998 as a consulting company headquartered in the Netherlands. Its early objectives were to provide IT consulting services and application solutions on the basis of IT outsourcing to small and medium-sized firms. The idea was to offer application solutions from a centrally managed environment, giving customers access to solutions via a virtual private network and/or Internet. The initial product to be offered was its proprietary solution suite called SX Intranet Suite, comprising e-mail, scheduling, calendars, and document libraries. Together with its hosting partner KPN Dutch Telecom, this defined the first applications solutions that they would rent to customers. Then, in late 1998, Siennax became aware of the application service provision model in the United States:

> Just then we read in magazines and reports like Durlacher that what we were doing had a name: Application Service Provision.
> —*Michiel Steltman, CTO, Siennax*

As a result, in early 1999 Siennax refocused its business toward being an ASP solution provider and in the Benelux became one of the first pure-play ASP startups. Sponsored by venture capitalists, the company reported a 243% revenue growth to €2 million in one year in 1999, which now sees Siennax as one of the leading European ASPs (see Table 6.1).

Since 1999–2000 growth has continued at a rapid pace, seeing Siennax acquire numerous new customers, increasing

TABLE 6.1 Siennax 1998–2000 Financial Figures

	1998		1999		2000	
	x 1000 NLG	x 1000	x 1000 NLG	x 1000	x 1000 NLG	x 1000
REVENUE	1,324.2	600.9	4,545.4	2,062.6	6,661	3,023
PROFIT	– 93.1	–42.2	– 1,046.9	–475.1	–16,959	–7,696

SOURCE: Siennax 1999 annual report.

its end-user base to approximately 15,000. With the general downturn of the technology markets, Siennax still remains on target for a positive cash flow in one-and-a-half years and expects further to become profitable within one year. Siennax employed about 109 people with two main operating markets: Benelux and Germany. In 2001, Siennax secured €14 million (approximately $12 million) venture capital in its second round of funding and was quoted by ASPnews.com in the global top 20 ASPs (being the only non-U.S.-ranked ASP).

SIENNAX'S PURE-PLAY ASP STRATEGY

As Michiel Steltman, the CTO from Siennax, explained, they deliver generic, standard applications on a one-to-many model with a shared service concept and consulting services, the idea being to "install it once and deliver it many times." Through this model Siennax offers a set of Web-based business applications, connectivity services, and implementation and migration services to customers ranging from small to large enterprises. The application solutions offered include an intranet suite, Microsoft Exchange 2000, Lotus Learning Space, electronic document management, and customer relationship management solutions. Prices for these application services are calculated on a per user/per month pricing model, which ranges from 70 NLG (approximately $30) for an intranet seat to about 200 NLG (approx. $87) for an e-learning seat.

Siennax does not, however, provide mission-critical applications such as enterprise resource planning systems, the reason being that the company does not believe that its customers are yet ready to source such applications from an ASP model. Instead, Siennax has long-term plans to focus its services and efforts on broadening its applications solutions, by extending existing services on the application portfolio above. In addition, Siennax offers complex (Web) hosting solutions, which function like a middleware platform upon which customers can base their own application services. This then enables clients to act as an ASP for themselves.

ABZ INSURANCE FACILITATOR: ASP CUSTOMER SCENARIO

Abz is Siennax's largest customer in terms of contract value and potential opportunities. As a customer, Abz can best be characterized as a vertical service supplier of information and application solutions to the insurance industry. As Corné Paalvast, the operational director for Abz, explained:

> The company basically started 16 years ago as a branch initiative in the area of car claims handling. The insurance industry saw that working together to get the process organized and supported by IT was much better handled by all insurers together. So, Abz was the result, and today that means that every damaged car that is being handled by an insurance company in Holland is handled over our IT systems. We provide applications to calculate the damage, to process the damage, to record the damage with photos, etc. So, everybody involved in processing the damage is connected to our system—insurance companies, body repair shops, expertise companies, spare parts companies, etc.

Abz's primary objective, in turn, is to ensure that business processes between insurance firms and insurance takers and providers run efficiently and effectively. For this, Abz's organizational capacity, its unique combination of knowledge of the sector and technology, and its group of strategic partners have enabled it to provide a reliable and standardized information, communication, and transaction-based (ICT) service (Abz Web site 2001). This has allowed Abz to grow to a sizable 66.8 million Dutch guilders (approximately $30 million) in revenues. The company now provides its ICT services to over 3000 companies, serving more than 6000 end users.

In the beginning, Abz was owned by a select number of insurance firms, a number that has grown over the years to 53 companies that now span the complete insurance value chain (e.g., Achmea, Aegon, Amev, and ING Verzekeringen). Today, all shareholders are also Abz's key customers.

Since Abz provides its customers with access to centrally managed systems on a one-to-many basis, using subscription- and transaction-based pricing models, the company can also be classified as a service provider similar to an ASP, the key difference being that the centrally managed systems are not run and managed by Abz but are sourced from external providers, such as Siennax. Abz, in turn, rents access to a complex or advanced hosting environment through which it provides services to its key customers.

This service, including the necessary digital signature service that verifies Abz's customers identity, was the initial service for which Siennax was contracted. Over time, Abz planned, though, to use Siennax for all of its intranet and extranet services and business e-mail services via a thin-client outsourcing arrangement. However, following its initial experiences with the intranet services, Abz resolved to be more careful in the next expansion phases, the reason being in part that they were likely to be more complex than the overall transactional services, involving various applications. In addition, Abz was keenly looking for real value added. Expectations included identifying new IT opportunities, faster time to market for new services by using Siennax's economies of scale and expertise, and new products and services for customers that resulted directly from improved IT functionality. These long-term expectations are summed up by Abz's operational director as follows:

What is do-able, what services are supported by the different options, can we change our sales and offer proposition for our customer, for example by introducing online marketplaces? All this considering that we at the moment only provide the customer with a transaction interface....We want improved time to market for new products. With the old systems it took us six months....By using new technology, for example XML customers can then do their own product introduction online. So we are planning to change the proposition and to make the old transaction services much more rich with added functionality.

VISTORM

Vistorm Limited was started in 1991 as Engineering Software (later shortened to ESOFT) by Charles Sharland, an ex-business manager for Sun and Hewlett-Packard who saw a clear market opportunity to make money by implementing pre-mainstream technical software. According to David Sidwell, business development manager at Vistorm: "We first implemented a firewall in 1994. We first connected two businesses together using the Internet in 1995/6. Now, over 65% of Vistorm's business is in managed Internet security, where we enable businesses to develop and implement a secure virtual private network (VPN). In many cases Vistorm manages that VPN remotely, 24 × 7, to a service level unattainable by the users themselves, on a monthly fee basis."

Vistorm was the European leader in the provision of managed Internet services and was voted European ASP of the year in 1999–2000. It offers online delivery of line-of-business applications to companies worldwide. It operates a large ISV alliance program. With these, Vistorm takes ISV software, ASP-enables it, then delivers it to end customers on a managed, rental basis, supplying all the necessary infrastructure. Applications are hosted in managed data centers and delivered by secure Internet connections direct to the user's desktop or laptop. Vistorm's offer is fast access to best-practice IT management of business application software and technology support at affordable prices and to provide world-class IT infrastructure. Vistorm also offers managed Internet security for firewalls and virtual private networks, and solutions for desktop and server security.

Its primary target market are line-of-business applications aimed at the SME and divisional corporate sectors. According to David Sidwell, business development manager, there are three main parameters for selecting an ASP market:

1. *Scale of application:* level of application complexity, integration, and customization
2. *User profile:* size of user population/type of user
3. *Application type:* business function/industry applicability

These options are mapped in Figure 6.5. On this analysis, and given the company's historically developed core capabilities, Vistorm pinpointed the midrange line-of-business/collaborative applications as the most commercially and technically attractive market, because such applications were the most widely adopted by corporate (more than 500 employees) and SME middle-market (between 100 and 500 employees) companies.

Clearly, the key to Vistorm's success is its technical capability, ability to integrate applications, provision of infrastructure, capability in the Internet security arena, partnering with leading applications providers, and ability to be client and end-user focused. Its customer value proposition is faster and more competitive business operations (i.e., access to new applications faster, applications where and when the business requires, affordable best applications, allowing refocus on the business). The second component of the value proposition is better-managed IT costs (minimal up-front costs for technology, pay for users, predictable IT costs, and less IT staff costs). The third hook is greater reliability, scalability, and flexibility; customers obtain predictable service levels backed by SLAs and industry best practices, all scaled as the customers' businesses grow at their own speeds.

One illustrative customer is Redwood Financial Services, which outsources company accounts. It uses Vistorm's Open Accounts and standard Windows packages to network in real time with clients to access and update their accounts. They

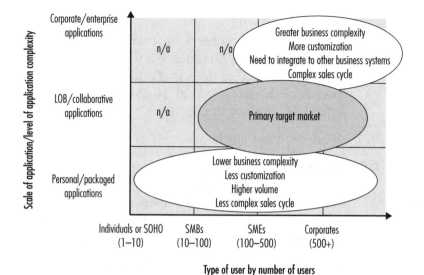

(SOHO, small office, home office; SMB, small business; SME, small/medium enterprise)

FIGURE 6.5 ASP Market Overview According to Vistorm

can also offer the Open Accounts package to clients previously reluctant to pay for superior software. Redwood pays £300 per month per user, as does the client for its users.

CAPABILITIES

The following exchange with David Sidwell gives an idea of the capabilities that an ASP like Vistorm can provide to a desktop:

DS: So I am now just on a desktop and I could be dialing in from home. This works just the same on a 28K line as it does on what we have here. So if I just power up Excel, how fast does Excel load on your machine, your PC?

INT: Not that fast.

DS: Let's use part of the Microsoft Test Suites as a demonstration....Here I'm calculating a random number and I will just create a grid of random numbers and refresh it. As quick as your machine?

INT: Uh, huh.

DS: Now we will do something that looks a little bit more tricky with some graphics. So we will create a graphical package there that does this and we will just go, OK let's just refresh that. So that is Excel running at lightning speed. Where are the servers?

INT: Well, they are not here.

DS: They are in Manchester, connected via the Internet. Now most people cannot believe that a remote service can be faster than locally based servers. However, that's because all I have here is a thin-client device, effectively just a Network card. My whole desktop is remotely delivered over the Internet and it is working quicker than most people's own laptops, without question. Now the first thing to say about ASP is that almost every application currently in use was written to run on a PC. It is written to hog the mouse, the keyboard, the DLLs, the CPU itself, and you put a hundred reentrant users on a single executable and it will not work by accident. It will crash at some time and has no error routines to inform the systems administrator what went wrong and where in the code. One of Vistorm's key skills is making applications that weren't meant to run in a remote environment not only run, but perform faster than when run locally.

Vistorm is set up to make technology fit a customer's business, not by selling products or services, but by creating a platform for other people that can be embedded into their business propositions and infrastructures. MISEC effectively delivers a secure managed Internet connection that people then build as part of their infrastructure moving forward. In itself, it is something of an ASP application because Vistorm maintains it remotely; actual monitoring software for the firewalls run centrally. The firewalls run remotely but the users have commissioned Vistorm to manage the whole thing for them—a piece of application service provision. The next part of the business the company looked at was running applications. Explained David Sidwell:

Right now people are doing things to get connected, which is what MISEC is all about and, in future, they will be connecting to do things, which is what SBC (server-based computing) is all about. One of the dreams of IT has always been to build applications that work independent of its delivery mechanism—on any desktop, over any network, securely. We've been working with Microsoft, Compaq, CheckPoint, and Citrix's product sets for years to achieve this goal and we are now one of their most technically competent partners in Europe, and possibly in the world. As early as 1996, we got thousands of users at Rolls-Royce running Windows applications across a wide range of desktops, all managed centrally. So we were doing ASP back before it was even known as ASP.

The key to delivering applications to any desktop, over any network securely, is in having deep technical skills in the core technologies needed and years of experience in troubleshooting the inevitable teething problems that occur. Day by day, week by week, Vistorm worked at these problems, and made many, many, many incremental changes. But the end result is that we are in a completely different market space now, with a massive step difference between what we can deliver and others, who haven't made the same paradigm shifts.

Up until June 2000 there were only three shareholders in the business: original founder Charles Sharland, Tony Bolland (sales director), and David Sidwell (business development manager). During the late 1990s the company's growth was so rapid (up to 86% compound over five years) that it could not sustain itself financially. The company, in fact, managed to get to sales of £17 million without outside finance, but needed an injection of growth capital to maintain momentum. To that end it raised £25 million in a first round of venture capital through a syndicate led by 3i which included Compaq, Credit Suisse First Boston, and Granville Baird.

By the end of financial year 2001, Vistorm expected to show an increase in revenues of 75% to over £30 million and that rate of growth was projected to be maintained into the next financial year. More important, given the temperature of the financial markets in 2001, all Vistorm's businesses were projected to show a profit during 2002. As one senior manager

commented: "Our business isn't easy, and we're always para-
noid about whether we're doing the right thing or not, but we
must be doing some things right." On our analysis, Vistorm's
long-term development over the 1990s and its recognized core
capabilities in specific areas seen as critical in Internet-
enabled service and application provision, particularly in security, have placed the company in an advantageous position relative to many competitors. Its track record in delivery also
majors on an important customer requirement in a confusing
and immature market.

SUMMARY OF CASE EVALUATIONS

From the customer perspective, a recurring theme in this
book is that netsourcing is merely a delivery option. Customers need business solutions and will select the most economical, reliable, secure, and flexible delivery channel possible.
Global 2000 customers will probably select discrete business
activities for netsourcing, such as document or image management. For them, netsourcing will probably always be viewed
as merely one of the many sourcing options in their application portfolio. For SME customers, netsourcing will also be
viewed as one option among many, but a larger percentage of
an SME's application portfolio will be hosted compared to
larger organizations.

From the perspective of suppliers, netsourcing may either
be core to their business model (i.e., xSP is the only way to
access the products and services they offer) or xSP may be a
complementary delivery channel (see Table 6.2).   Nearly all
startup companies we studied use netsourcing as their sole
delivery channel. For Zland and Siennax, the Internet provided an economical means to sell their proprietary applications to the SME market. In Zland's case, however, the sole
delivery channel proved insufficient to meet their goals for
growth and they have since opened up other channels to let
other ASPs resell their software. For the ISV resellers we studied, their value added is to offer best-of-breed applications to

TABLE 6.2 Netsourcing as a Delivery Channel

	NETSOURCING IS THE ONLY DELIVERY CHANNEL FOR THIS SUPPLIER	NETSOURCING IS A COMPLEMENTARY DELIVERY CHANNEL FOR THIS SUPPLIER
PROPRIETARY SOFTWARE	Zland Siennax (Internet Suite)	Host Analytics SAP
ISV RESELLER	Corio MainPass Siennax Lodge marviQ Vistorm	EDS

SMEs that could not afford infrastructure, personnel, and software licenses through an outright purchase. Host Analytics is the only startup we studied that started off as an ASP but allowed customers to copy the software on the customer's servers when customers were worried about the reliability and security of the Internet. In the case of SAP, netsourcing is obviously one of many delivery options. The majority of its customers still hold SAP licenses and house the software on the customers' servers. EDS is essentially a service company, of which ASP will just be one of the many solutions offered.

As evidenced by the 10 cases presented, suppliers must position themselves in the new marketspace by deciding which products/services to offer to which target customers. Table 6.3 maps our 10 cases along these dimensions. Two overall supplier strategies for the selection of which products and services to offer are emerging: Be the best-in-breed for a *narrow* set of netsource-enabled products/services or provide a *broad* suite of netsourcing services. Three of the suppliers from our case studies are focusing on a narrow product/service line: MainPass, Host Analytics, and Zland. Seven of the suppliers are seeking to add value by providing a portfolio of solutions: Corio, EDS, SAP, Siennax, marviQ, Lodge, and Vistorm.

In addition to which products and services to offer, suppliers are also identifying their target customers: SMEs within a vertical market, SMEs across many industries, or large organizations such as global 2000 and large government agencies. Considering both dimensions of products and customers, typically an xSP with narrow product/service focus attracts SMEs for customers. For example, U.S.-based Host Analytics provides proprietary business intelligence applications for SMEs. Its mission is to offer global 2000 business intelligence capability to SMEs through repeatable, templated software. Its products are targeted horizontally for any SME that needs to extract intelligence from its enterprise system. Some xSPs focusing on the SME market initially target a vertical market (we called these VSPs in Chapter 1). For MainPass, its entrée into application service provision is targeted at the legal profession based on a match between an identified need in this space and its internal expertise and contacts. But although both MainPass and marviQ initially targeted/are targeting the legal industry, both plan to expand services to other industries. On the other end of the spectrum are Corio, EDS, Lodge, Siennax, and SAP. All three offer a broad application portfolio, targeted at small to large enterprises. Although their first hosting customers are SMEs, they are actively pursuing larger clients.

Table 6.3 can also be used to map other service providers discussed in this book. Portera, for example, provides another example of a supplier operating in the broad product/vertical SME niche. Portera offers applications to the professional services market such as business development, resource management, knowledge management, project collaboration, time and expense tracking, project accounting and billing, employee development, and management reporting tools. Easylink provides an example of a narrow product line targeted at customers of all sizes, including global 2000 firms.

For startup suppliers, the direction of targeted customer growth is generally from SME to global 2000. These startups simply do not have the clout, reputation, or credibility to have global 2000 as their initial customers. Typically, only SMEs are willing to give them a try. But early successes with the SME

TABLE 6.3 Supplier Offerings and Their Target Customers

PRODUCT/ SERVICE FOCUS	TARGET CUSTOMER		
	SME: VERTICAL	SME: HORIZONTAL	LARGE CUSTOMERS (GLOBAL 2000)
NARROW	MainPass (communication)	Host Analytics (business intelligence) Zland (e-business)	Siennax
BROAD	SAP	EDS Corio Lodge Siennax marviQ Vistorm SAP	EDS Corio Lodge SAP

customer base can catapult suppliers into the big league, as you can see, for example, with the Lodge and Siennax. For established suppliers such as EDS and SAP, their primary customers were initially large private- and public-sector organizations. Netsourcing merely provides an economical means to infiltrate the SME market after saturating the larger market.

One very important business decision for the suppliers—but often inconsequential to customers—was data center ownership. Does an xSP need to own its own data center, or can a third party provide the technical infrastructure, reliability, and security on behalf of the xSP? The issue is particularly important to the startup service providers studied because many did not want to use their venture capital to build and operate data centers (see Table 6.4). From the suppliers studied, only EDS and SAP have their own data centers (although Zland is planning to build one). EDS and SAP have the critical mass to operate world-class data centers and networks, and position this as an immense strength to customers, particularly large custom-

TABLE 6.4 Data Center Strategies

	Corio	EDS	Host Analytics	Main-Pass	ZLand	Lodge	mySAP	MarviQ	Siennax	Vistorm
Own Data Center		×			(plans to build)		×			
Use Another Data Center	×		×	×	×	×		×	×	×

ers. The remaining eight suppliers rely on third parties. Most of these lease or buy servers, which are housed in locked cages. According to suppliers interviewed for the cases, the xSPs rarely need to visit the data centers but can rely on the on-site data center staff when needed. No incidents of hacking were reported, but server performance has been an issue, especially when customers begin to overpopulate their data warehouses. Exodus is the most frequently used third-party data center, but one questions its long-term health given its excessive capital investment costs poised against negative earnings.

Exodus is certainly not the only supplier under question for survival. Other than EDS and SAP, which can leverage their immense resources to fund and grow their netsourcing space, the remaining suppliers are struggling. We strongly believe that netsourcing is here to stay, but the suppliers operating in this space will radically change through failures, mergers, acquisitions, and partnerships. At this stage, potential customers may feel reticent about adopting xSP despite the value proposition because of the instability of suppliers, as well as other risks, including the reliability and security of netsourcing. In Chapter 7, we provide help to customers who wish not only to assess the risks associated with netsourcing but to mitigate these risks as well.

ENDNOTES

1. *Case sources:* interviews with Hans Vets (founder, the Lodge), Wouter Cortebeeck (Global ICT manager, Punch International), and Olav Claassen (vice-president of information services, RealScale Technologies), transcript of interview with Michel Demmenie (director, Vision Web), the Lodge case study by Jeroen Kreijger, director of corporate presentations, corporate press releases, and corporate Web sites: *www.thevisionweb.com, www.thevisionweb.be, www.thelodge.nl, www.thelodge.be, www.punchinternational.com, www.acresearch.com*

2. *Case sources:* interviews with Robert Noteboom (CMO, marviQ) and Chris Boulle (head of product management, marviQ), marviQ Web site and Web sites of partners, corporate presentation at the launch of the new name marviQ on November 9, 2000, press releases, and company brochures.

3. As of January 1, 2001, Frank Kales succeeded Onno Schellekens as the CEO of marviQ and Onno Schellekens became president of marviQ.

4. *Case sources:* interviews, SAP case study by Jeroen Kreijger, SAP corporate presentations, SAP company brochures, SAP 1999 annual report, SAP Web site, SAPinfo.net Web site, and magazine and press releases.

5. *Case sources:* interviews with Michiel Steltman (cofounder and CTO, Siennax), Pieter Bokelaar (account manager at Siennax dedicated to Abz), and Corné Paalvast (operational director, Abz), Siennax case study by Jeroen Kreijger, Siennax Web site and Web sites of partners, Siennax 1999 annual report, press releases, Siennax press clippings, and Siennax white papers.

7 MITIGATING AND MANAGING RISKS IN NETSOURCING DEALS

Risks in the eyes of customers are those issues that could adversely affect their company and/or operations as a direct result of having entered into a netsourcing deal. From the outset, netsourcing ventures bear a set of risks that need careful assessment and mitigation to avoid surprises. In practice, our experiences from investigating all uses of the IT services market demonstrate unfailingly that a customer cannot step aside from an IT outsourcing/netsourcing arrangement and merely monitor and reward or punish outcomes. Risk management enables problems to be anticipated and mitigated and as such should be a critical ongoing activity across the lifetime of any netsourcing deal.

In the first instance the issue is to enhance awareness of the most common risks associated with a netsourcing venture. For this we asked existing and potential customers from 400 companies in 28 countries to rate such risks (see Appendix A). The resulting list of risks/concerns gives an early set of warning signals by which to assess the degree of risk you might encounter and your state of readiness when opting for a netsourcing option.

But risks will also emerge throughout a deal. Therefore, in the second part of this chapter we detail how risks evolved for a specific netsourcing customer. The case scenario, together with our extensive research into IT outsourcing, allows us to show in detail the different stages of risk evolution and provide a framework of generic risks. This offers any customer an essential tool by which the services and contract on offer from a particular provider can be checked against the reality of other customers' actual experiences in using the rapidly developing netsourcing marketplace. The guiding issue in customers' minds has to be: What risks arise for me when using a netsourcing solution, and how can these risks be mitigated?

THE CUSTOMER PERSPECTIVE: PRIMARY NETSOURCING RISKS

Our recent study of approximately 400 international customers in a netsourcing deal or contemplating one, emphasized that there are real recurring concerns over the potential and inherent risks of a netsourcing solution. Undoubtedly, this receives particular emphasis because of the newness of the netsourcing market and many of its players and because of the rapid downturn in the IT and the ASP market from the end of 2000 into 2001, when we carried out the survey. At the same time we have been studying the risks emerging from using the broader IT services market for many years. As we shall see later, it is clear that the netsourcing market has some distinctive risks, but for customers, most netsourcing risks that emerge are not so different from any use of the IT services market. Not surprisingly, therefore, the same rule applies: Do not expect too much from the supplier or too little from yourselves. A starting point for mitigating netsourcing risks has been spelt out in an earlier chapter: Develop an IT sourcing strategy; understand the market and the suppliers' strategies and capabilities; know how to contract for a netsourcing arrangement to ensure that you get what you need; and build in-house capability that ensures not just delivery of the service performance but also control over your IT destiny. But let us look at netsourcing risks in more detail.

Of the risks that might come into play when looking at a netsourcing solution, potential customers have grave concerns for all issues rated 3 to 4 on a 5-point scale (see Table 7.1). The primary risks for these customers, in order of impact, are:

1. A netsourcing service provider's service and business stability
2. Security issues
3. Reliability issues
4. Netsourcing's longevity and existence
5. Netsourcing's dependency on other parties

This is quite a considerable worry list. How do we explain this? Remember that this is a list from potential customers. Customers with no experience of a netsourcing solution are likely to be more concerned, due to the surrounding uncertainty and perceived immaturity of the market. Developments in 2001 in particular, where netsourcing service providers were struggling to survive the sudden downfall of the technology stock market and the resulting drying up of investment funds, did little to assuage these perceptions.

However, the rising number of netsourcing service providers with track records, growing customer bases, profitability, and sufficient investment capital offer some reassurance as to how these potential risks can be offset. Moreover, the big IT service, software, and telecom firms are much less likely to be confounded by issues of longevity, funding, and stability. Furthermore, referring to Table 7.1, it is noticeable that those customers actually in a netsourcing deal rate the risks identified by potential customers as up to 30% lower (see, for example, ASP dependency on other parties). In other words, fear of these risks is a third higher than the actual experiences of customers indicate that such fear needs to be. This is actually a

TABLE 7.1 Netsourcing Risks (%) Cited by Potential and Existing Customers

Drawback	Rating					Average Rating (1–5)	
	1 No Risk	2	3	4	5 Major Risk		
Higher initial capital outlay	4.2	19.0	53.6	17.9	5.4	3.01	
	10.5	26.3	47.4	15.8	0.0	2.68	
Unproven business model	6.0	16.1	38.1	28.6	11.3	3.23	
	18.4	26.3	28.9	21.1	5.3	2.68	
Company size too small/ large for ASP use	16.7	21.4	41.1	11.3	9.5	2.76	
	26.3	13.2	36.8	10.5	13.2	2.71	
Loss of control	9.5	19.0	28.0	29.8	13.7	3.19	
	10.5	31.6	39.5	10.5	7.9	2.74	
Unclear on ASP concept and practice	16.1	16.1	38.7	19.6	9.5	2.90	
	26.3	15.8	28.9	15.8	13.2	2.74	
Not enough service and application choices	4.8	20.2	41.1	22.6	11.3	3.15	
	5.3	31.6	39.5	21.1	2.6	2.84	
Reduced flexibility	8.9	28.6	31.5	23.2	7.7	2.92	
	13.2	28.9	26.3	18.4	13.2	2.89	
Contract lock-in	2.4	14.3	40.5	29.8	13.1	3.37	
	10.5	18.4	42.1	23.7	5.3	2.95	
Higher IT costs over time	5.4	19.6	42.9	23.8	8.3	3.10	
	15.8	15.8	31.6	31.6	5.3	2.95	
ASP's dependency on other parties	4.8	7.1	26.2	37.5	24.4	3.70	
	5.3	26.3	42.1	13.2	13.2	3.03	
Scalability	7.7	22.6	35.1	25.6	8.9	3.05	
	7.9	13.2	44.7	31.6	2.6	3.08	
Integrating ASP with existing applications	3.6	11.3	30.4	33.3	21.4	3.58	
	13.2	13.2	34.2	26.3	13.2	3.13	
Security	1.8	9.5	22.0	26.2	40.5	3.94	
	0.0	28.9	23.7	26.3	21.1	3.39	
ASP's service and business stability	2.4	5.4	20.8	35.1	36.3	3.98	
	2.6	21.1	23.7	34.2	18.4	3.45	
Reliability	2.4	6.0	24.4	36.3	31.0	3.88	
	0.0	21.1	26.3	28.9	23.7	3.55	
ASP's longevity and existence	2.4	7.7	28.6	34.5	26.8	3.76	
	2.6	7.9	39.5	28.9	21.1	3.58	

■ Potential customers
□ Actual customers

Note: Risks are sorted (ascending) on the average of the response of the respondents that come from companies currently sourcing from an ASP. For each rating, the first row is the percentage of potential customers; the second row, in *italics*, is the percentage of actual customers.

common finding across our research and indicates that netsourcing service providers need to invest a lot of time in customer education, especially while the market is immature, so much is volatile and not well understood.

Nevertheless, if potential customers tend to rate netsourcing risks as more serious than do existing customers, both worry about the same types of risk (see Table 7.1). Although experienced netsourcing customers suggest that many of the issues cited are less problematic than envisaged, they still on average, across the issues, regularly rate the risks as between 2 and 3 on a scale of 1 through 5. Moreover, none of the risks we investigated were actually rated by the existing customers as of no/little risk at all (i.e., 1 to 2). So it is apparent that even when in a netsourcing deal, customers still have many considerable uncertainties and concerns—ranging from technical factors such as security, reliability, and scalability to the managerial issues of lock-in, unproven business model, and dependency on others. All these issues remain, in fact, as attendant, characteristic netsourcing risks.

The gravest concerns for existing customers were:

1. Netsourcing's longevity and existence
2. Reliability issues
3. Netsourcing service provider's service and business stability
4. Security issues
5. Integrating the netsourcing solution with existing applications

All of these will also inform and often shape customers' ongoing management issues in any netsourcing deal. For example, many of the technical issues will be monitored through service-level agreements, while contractual issues will be handled through carefully developed contracts.

The longevity and stability issue poses a significant risk to both potential and existing customers. There remains substantial uncertainty regarding future developments in the general marketplace (e.g., the speed and extent of supplier consolidation, levels of customer demand) but also for specific netsourcing service providers, even those with many customers. For those providers yet to make a profit, much depends on the continuing availability of investment capital and ability to manage cash flow and the financial position. In turn, it seems sensible for those customers already signed up with startups to ensure that they keep themselves informed about their service provider's financial situation and be prepared on short notice to switch their services to a comparable provider. We suggest for those unsure about their service provider's future that they need to prepare a preliminary transition and migration plan that will simplify the process if need be.

Those about to sign netsourcing contracts will now be much more aware of the need to include clauses that cover exit terms such as termination and guarantees and methods of providing continuity of service in the event of a failure. Neglect of these can prove very costly indeed. Thus one large 10-year IT outsourcing deal with a poor termination clause cost the client nearly $50 million to get out of after 17 months.

Security and reliability of service are risk issues that run pretty much throughout any netsourcing venture. A sound policy of monitoring and ensuring that protocols are followed will assist customers in stopping these concerns turning into real threats. Much depends on the detailed attention given to constructing service performance measures before the netsourcing contract was signed. If these are sound and are reviewed and updated regularly, much then depends on the quality of the client's and supplier's monitoring policies and their ability to work together on uncovering and fixing any reliability and security problems. Close ongoing attention to a netsourcing deal's workings on these issues provides one approach to mitigating risks.

The primary risks listed by potential and existing customers form a close match on most issues, although the order of importance varies. Let us comment on the divergence of opinion on two issues. First, a service provider's dependency on other parties is perceived as a much greater source of risk by potential customers. Second, existing customers experience integrating a netsourcing solution with existing applications as a much greater problem than potential customers perceive that it would be. One conclusion for potential customers is that experience shows that a service provider's dependence on third parties, in practice, is less a problem than the more pragmatic, technical problem of integrating systems. However, this disparity in perception between potential and existing customers probably also reflects the fact that for a potential customer, the uppermost worry is the more immediate one of dependency on a third party and their associates. For potential customers the more obvious concern is to minimize this risk and enforce control as much as possible. However, for those customers already in a netsourcing venture, this issue may well have been dealt with already. For them, therefore, the integration of the netsourcing solution with the existing IT services is of greater concern as the parties move to operationalizing the netsourcing service.

Finally, a more overarching point needs to be made regarding the disparity between some of the existing and potential customer ratings. It is evident that potential and existing customers differ the most in their concerns on the following three issues: (1) netsourcing provider's dependency on other parties, (2) security, and (3) netsourcing provider's service and business stability. What are the probable reasons for this wide divergence? The simple answer is experience. Existing customers are much better informed than potential customers; their experiences are different from what is often anticipated; and potential customers are not as well informed as they might be of what using the netsourcing market actually entails. Lack of information may well contribute to raising the fear quotient. Another reason for the differences might be that existing customers had more urgent needs and were therefore willing to bear or ignore more risks than potential customers who could afford to "wait and see."

At the same time, in anticipating higher risks than actually experienced, potential customers do reflect some wider uncertainties. In particular, security, the most often discussed issue of concern in the media, lacks any clear standards on best practice. This also holds for service and business stability of a netsourcing service provider. Specific providers may well be addressing these issues in their contracts with clients, but potential customers will not have experienced this. In view of the 2001 closures and bankruptcies, concern over netsourcing stability is justifiable, and this could only be downrated once a greater sense of continuity is introduced (e.g., through more providers operating profitably, larger IT service firms also operating in the netsourcing market, more deals signed, completion of a shakedown, and consolidation of netsourcing providers).

Finally, the issue of dependency is clearly regarded as less of a risk for existing than for potential customers, due to their better understanding of whom they actually are dependent on, and the specific safeguards they have built into the arrangement. At the same time, the degree of subcontracting that goes on between IT service providers themselves does raise important and often neglected questions: Is it cost-effective to have a netsourcing provider manage the other contractor, or is it better to do it yourself? Who is responsible if the subcontractor is negligent or things go wrong? What are the remedies if things go wrong? Are there additional intellectual copyright issues as a result of subcontracting? All clients of netsourcing need to be much more aware of these sorts of issues, not least because models tend to be very dependent on allies, partners, and subcontractors.

Clearly, netsourcing providers have their work cut out in ensuring that none of the risks truly result in major drawbacks. Given the misperceptions and lack of knowledge among would-be customers, providers also have a big educational task in communicating the real nature of their netsourcing offerings and the attendant risks. As one example, in the MainPass case we found legal firms citing security as one of their primary anxieties with adopting a netsourcing model. However, the MainPass analysis showed that clients' existing security was poor and that the ASP offering would strengthen data security and alleviate privacy concerns considerably.

It will be up to individual managers and the specific application service provider firm to alleviate and mitigate such concerns. Remembering here that all these factors have actually been perceived as genuine, sometimes serious risks in the eyes of customers. According to both existing and potential customers, the four core risks that need to be mitigated throughout any netsourcing venture are security, service and business stability, reliability, and netsourcing longevity. However, all the risks cited in Table 7.1 are felt, real risks associated with applying netsourcing models to client firms. As such, they all need to be addressed in any risk management strategy. From this review of customer and would-be customer perceptions, we now need to build toward a more comprehensive way of analyzing and managing risks. We do this in the next section by developing a risk-profiling framework.

Preliminary Risk-Profiling Framework

It is clear from the discussion above that netsourcing remains a risky business. Risk is here taken to be a negative outcome that has a known or estimated probability of occurrence based on experience or theory.[1] In practice, a detailed review of the last decade finds that there are all too few systematic studies of types of IT outsourcing risks, their salience, and their mitigation. The main studies have been anecdotal or theoretical in character.[2] There are also many studies that deal with IT outsourcing but do not choose to focus on providing a comprehensive analysis of salient risks and/or risk mitigation approaches.

Although there is a limited literature on which to draw for the identification of salient risks, we have distilled an exploratory framework from our previous work. Drawing on this work, the main reasons for failure/negative outcomes in IT outsourcing deals generally have been various combinations of the factors shown in Figure 7.1.

Apart from being built on prior research findings, an earlier version of the framework was also productively utilized and developed further for present use in earlier case work.[3] A finding there was that the framework provided sufficient generic coverage of salient risks to allow complementary detail to be explored in an insightful, qualitative manner.

Figure 7.1 shows that IT outsourcing studies generally have consistently found risks materializing in three areas. The first is classified in Figure 7.1 as *context*. Here the client's distinctive competitive context can determine which IT is likely to be core and differentiating, and what speed of systems development and levels of service are required. Strategic intent can determine its objectives for outsourcing: Should customers go for cost reduction, allow the in-house team to refocus on higher value develop-

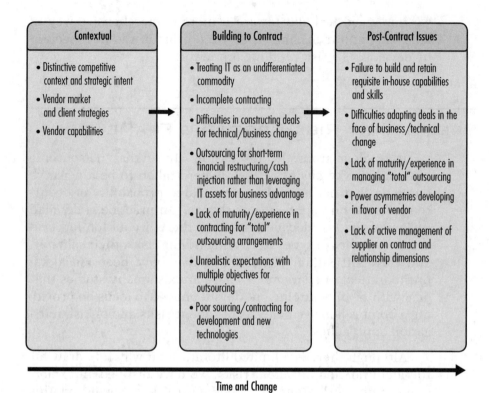

Contextual	Building to Contract	Post-Contract Issues
• Distinctive competitive context and strategic intent • Vendor market and client strategies • Vendor capabilities	• Treating IT as an undifferentiated commodity • Incomplete contracting • Difficulties in constructing deals for technical/business change • Outsourcing for short-term financial restructuring/cash injection rather than leveraging IT assets for business advantage • Lack of maturity/experience in contracting for "total" outsourcing arrangements • Unrealistic expectations with multiple objectives for outsourcing • Poor sourcing/contracting for development and new technologies	• Failure to build and retain requisite in-house capabilities and skills • Difficulties adapting deals in the face of business/technical change • Lack of maturity/experience in managing "total" outsourcing • Power asymmetries developing in favor of vendor • Lack of active management of supplier on contract and relationship dimensions

Time and Change

FIGURE 7.1 Risk Analysis Framework for IT Outsourcing (From Willcocks, Lacity, and Kern, 2000)

ment work, or hire a supplier to achieve global standardization in certain aspects of IT? It is also important to be very clear as to the strategies that prospective suppliers are pursuing in the marketplace and the ramifications of those for the client company over the lifetime of the contract. The supplier's core capabilities also need very careful analysis. The second area is *building to contract*. Figure 7.1 delineates seven major practices that regularly materialize in negative outcomes. The framework actually puts a great deal of weight on risk factors that occur before the contract is operationalized. However, the third grouping defines five major risk factors as *postcontract issues*.

An inherent weakness of the framework is the lack of quantified measures that could be used for the degree of the risk encountered within outsourcing contexts. It is common practice during the risk evaluation period to rate risks on a simple scale of low, medium, and high.[4] A further limitation is that it sees risk primarily from a client, not a supplier perspective, although risk can be studied most usefully from multiple perspectives. Another weakness of the framework is its generalizability, the degree of applicability to most or all outsourcing ventures. Due to the insufficient set of samples used to date, little can be said about its overarching applicability to IT outsourcing. As such, Figure 7.1 retains its status as an exploratory framework, with application service provision presenting yet another opportunity to investigate how the risk profiling it represents can be developed further. We will seek to extend the framework by using the qualitative measure of low, medium, and high to indicate the risks experienced by Abz in its relationship with Siennax in the case study below.

Risky ASP Practice: Siennax and Abz Case

Risks are best visualized in a particular case scenario. A rich case study can examine evolution and origin, context, and history. Such richness of data allows more insight into how risks arise and why they take the form and intensity they do. For our purposes here we found the Siennax–Abz case discussed at length in Chapter 6 to be particularly insightful. The context and the process of implementing the ASP solution in this customer case help to illustrate for potential and existing customers, the major likely risk areas they will encounter. Before we can actually discuss and highlight the risks encountered by Abz, we recapitulate the case briefly.

Siennax–Abz Case Background

As of June 2001, Abz was Siennax's largest customer in contract value and potential opportunities. As a customer, Abz can be best characterized as a vertical service supplier of information and application solutions to the insurance industry. Abz's primary objective was to ensure that business processes between insurance firms and insurance takers and providers ran efficiently and effectively. For this, Abz's organizational capacity, its combination of knowledge of the sector and technology, and its group of strategic partners have enabled it to provide a reliable and standardized information, communication, and transaction-based (ICT) service. This has allowed Abz to grow to a sizable 66.8 million Dutch guilders (approximately $30 million) in revenues. By 2001 the company was providing its ICT services to over 3000 companies, serving more than 6000 end users.

Abz provided its customers with access to centrally managed systems on a one-to-many basis, using subscription- and transaction-based pricing models. As a result, the company could also be classified as a service provider similar to an ASP. The key difference was that the centrally managed systems were not run and managed by Abz but were sourced from external providers, one of which was Siennax. In practice, Abz rented access to a complex or advanced hosting environment through which it provided services to its key customers. As described above, this middleware-type hosting platform allowed Abz's customers not only to access essential applications but also to host their own solutions, which they could then make available to their customers:

> They [Abz] deliver services to the insurance market and we [Siennax] deliver them ASP services to enable them to be a branch organization for the insurance market. In fact, in the vertical group, we [Siennax] are an ASP enabler. We allow companies to become an ASP to their market by selling them the necessary core services.
> —*Michiel Steltman, CTO, Siennax*

This service, including the necessary digital signature service that verifies Abz's customers' identity, was the initial service for which Siennax was contracted. However, over time, Siennax was also chosen to supply Abz with all of its intranet and extranet services and business e-mail services via a thin-client outsourcing arrangement. As of June 2001, the current and expected data traffic was handled via a T1 leased line, which was part of the overall package. It gave end-user clients access to Abz's service via the Internet. The data storage and processing part of solution was handled by Siennax's systems, which were hosted by KPN's cyber center in Amsterdam. However, at the time of the research most of Abz's systems were still run by Getronics IT services. Interestingly, though, one of the possible future scenarios discussed in the former context was that ASP services may replace all of Abz's traditional outsourcing arrangements for these services.

THE ASP DECISION

The actual decision to go for an ASP solution evolved in light of a number of changes and long-term objectives. As Corné Paalvast, the operational director from Abz, explained:

> We have had an outsourcing arrangement with Getronics now for about six years. They provided us with most of our IT services for marketing and selling our services to the insurance industry. Their services covered our complete intranet and extranet environment, which included our transaction services. Yet for our current and long-term development we were looking for an IT partner rather than a commodity type service supplier like Getronics. We sought an IT partner that could help us define new products, services, and generally would be more proactive in its interactions with our customers. Yet all discussions concerning technological opportunities with our existing suppliers lead to the same response: "Tell us what you need and we will provide you with it." However, we were looking for a partner who could tell us what was available and help us identify new opportunities.

The underlying argument for the decision was that IT was not central to Abz's business. Moreover, as they had been in an IT outsourcing contract, over the years they never found it necessary to develop the competencies to handle their own IT infrastructure. Instead, they looked toward their IT suppliers to keep them abreast of innovations and possible opportunities on the back of new IT developments. As a result, in November 1999, when the contract with Getronics was nearing its end, Abz began exploring the market for new solutions, and more important, for an IT supplier. At the time the ASP business model was being widely discussed and covered by media, and Abz found it to be a good fit with their requirement. In fact, what they had envisaged was a solution that would give them flexibility, a means to keep on top of innovations, and give access to benefits from new and ongoing application developments. By February 2000 the company had decided internally to opt for an ASP-driven solution. In the words of the decision maker:

> Back then we did not know much about ASPs. Yet we were convinced that this was a way to help us innovate and develop new services faster than we could think of at the time. The in-depth discussions and negotiations with Graddelt [ASP competitor] and Siennax confirmed this assumption. Yet when we scanned the market, everybody seemed to be claiming they were an ASP—even our existing service provider Getronics. But most of them did not provide the kind of service we sought, the scalability and the necessary "Internet hotel"— the environment where we could run our own business applications from, and the infrastructure to plug in our own business applications.
> —*Corné Paalvast, operational director, Abz*

SELECTING AN APPLICATION SERVICE PROVIDER

Abz was also looking for a new type of service infrastructure, which would allow them to integrate additional functionality with their existing business logic and offer services such as Web-enabled address systems, news systems, mail systems, and application services. The objective here was to increase customer loyalty by offering greater functionality. A further objective was to use Siennax's application services such as the intranet suite or MS office applications as an additional sales channel to its customers. This was in line with Abz's goal of identifying new opportunities and sales channels. The final, long-term objective was to sell Abz's expertise in a repackaged form through an ASP, to the ASP's other customers. As Corné

Paalvast elaborated, that could imply that "… sometimes they resell our products or they take over a service and sell it back to us and to their customers. For example, Siennax could take over our news services and make it into a commodity product and then sell it back to Abz."

Two additional strategic factors played a role in Abz's selection. One was that the larger IT service firms Abz evaluated, CMG and Getronics, were perceived as a strategic sourcing risk since they could become potential competitors. These firms could easily copy Abz's services and activities and then offer them in the same market, either directly or indirectly, through partnerships. Within alliance theory this has been referred to as a *spillover effect*. With ASP startups, like Graddelt (now called marviQ) and Siennax, their resource base is relatively small and thus they are unlikely to go down that track—a minor risk. The second factor was the dependency relationship that may evolve due to size differences. Abz wanted a partnership with a company that was smaller in size, had potentially fewer customers, and was not as well known in the industry. The intention here was to keep focus and attention on their needs, and maintain a balanced relationship that was slightly in Abz's favor. Underlying this was Abz's experience, which had shown that such partnerships led to faster response times, improved communication, and decreased hierarchical interface levels.

The final choice of an ASP boiled down to marviQ or Siennax. The driving selection criteria were the objectives above and whether the ASP could deliver them. Important criteria considered were threefold: the track record of the ASP, the track records of the persons involved, and the degree of trust the persons evoked:

> We chose Siennax because of proven results, that was one of the selection criteria. But most important, the ASP market being an immature market you need to have trust in people and individual relationships. That was one of the most important triggers for choosing Siennax.
>
> —*Corné Paalvast, operational director, Abz*

TRANSITIONING TO AN APPLICATION
SERVICE

In March 2000, Abz and Siennax signed an agreement of intent. Following a due diligence process, a contract and service-level agreement (SLA) was formalized and signed in August 2000. It detailed escalation procedures, responsible managers, uptime guarantees, reaction times, reaction procedures, and change request procedures. At this point, Siennax and Abz had already established a project team responsible for transitioning the services and then managing the operations of the deal. On a higher level, a steering group was formed of executives from both Abz and Siennax, responsible for monitoring the contract, the service performance, resolving escalated problems, and identifying new business opportunities.

It was decided early on to transition the legacy services incrementally from Getronics to the Siennax platform. The migration began with relatively easy parts, such as the HTML front-end applications. It was then expanded over time to cover the entire Abz extranet. Abz desired an incremental approach because it gave them the possibility to retrench if problems became serious and recontract with easily identifiable alternative suppliers or, if necessary, even go back with Getronics. Although complex in nature, the transition was rolled out as planned.

Siennax first discussed the transition of the Abz extranet from Abz's servers to the Siennax environment. Such a transition had never been done before, so it was something new to both organizations. A good project working team was established, which helped in migrating the services smoothly. However, there was one exception to this general level of success: the implementation of the Verisign certification. On that issue both firms faced a number of problems.

The inherent problem was that Abz also acts as a trusted third-party agent to its customers, providing them with a crucial digital signature/passport functionality. In the old Getronics scenario, Abz was delivering this service conjointly on the basis of a Netscape certificate server. However, they had decided to source externally and update this—in their view it was a commodity service. Abz was now looking for a Verisign certification service, the industry-acknowledged market standard. Having done a market sweep, Abz identified Roccade (a large European IT service firm) as a potential provider for this service, which Siennax now only needed to subcontract and integrate into Abz's existing service package:

> We wanted Verisign, which in Holland is re-sold primarily through Roccade. They [Siennax] however could not really live with Roccade because of the competition worries. So Siennax decided to go into business with somebody else which I hadn't heard of before—called BlueX. They said they could arrange the Verisign service before the first of October and it took them till the 22nd of December to do so. Which put us, as a Trusted Third Party, out of business for seven weeks. During this time I don't think we lost any customers, but we have had to pay back money for services not available and we have had to say sorry for a lot of things. But the image loss is probably the worst thing about it.
> —*Corné Paalvast, operational director, Abz*

Of course, the difficulties were in part already planned for. The migration of such a complex service solution was not only a novelty for Siennax and BlueX, but also for Abz, and all parties anticipated some difficulties. However, many were also unanticipated. Some of the resultant problems were apportioned to BlueX, a young startup firm in the Netherlands with little experience in implementing Digital Signature services in an ASP model.

Along with Abz and Siennax, BlueX was doing the job for the first time too. In the very complex migration already in progress, the Verisign Certificate migration was an extra complexity, which cost a lot of time. The Verisign Certificates were in fact delivered just before Christmas 2000. By February 2001 the service was running well, but in many ways this was far too late.

The difficulties with the migration of this service point to an essential issue: how services and performance are to be monitored in such ventures. As both parties from the start had formalized an SLA, it was now a matter of enforcing this agreement. However, measurement of Siennax's performance was not so much done to the letter of the technical measures, but handled more on the feedback from the operational level. Of course, all technical failures and problems were reported, and in practice, the technical performance fell within service-level parameters. However, performance as perceived by the internal end users and its customers have regularly been regarded as providing the more important set of indicators. Here performance measures focused on how problems were being addressed, whether charges were raised for minor issues, whether logs of problems were kept, and whether they could have been planned for and hence prevented. Some serious difficulties arose in this area. Critically, after Abz's difficult experiences with the migration, Abz was subsequently waiting for Siennax's proposal on how to resolve amicably an argument over responsibility for a seven-week revenue loss by Abz and loss of customer confidence in Abz.

Although there were financial penalty arrangements specified in the contract, it was in neither party's interest at this stage to enforce them, not least because both wished to perpetuate the relationship. The operational director emphasized that "financially we have made agreements in the contract. There is a penalty in the contract, which covers damage. But I say to the ASP—keep the money and help me reestablish my image, because that is much more important."

RISK MITIGATION ACROSS A NETSOURCING DEAL

We will use this Siennax-Abz case as an example to highlight the risks likely to arise in a particular netsourcing venture. Based on the case, it is possible to outline a number of risk areas that were not anticipated and planned for. The case emphasizes the criticality of ongoing risk mitigation. By use of the risk profiling framework in Figure 7.1—already applied in the past to various IT outsourcing ventures—a careful analysis of the risks in a netsourcing deal can be performed.

The netsourcing risk framework is used to outline the macro risks that are likely to be encountered during a netsourcing deal. We emphasize, though, that the risk framework is merely an analytical tool summarizing generic risks. As such, it structures and informs analysis, but every deal is different and additional risks may and do arise that will be specific to your netsourcing venture. We have found that use of the framework makes it easier to identify such risks because it gives a detailed point of comparison and contrast otherwise lacking.

Our analysis of the risks in the case draws initially on the Figure 7.1 risk profiling tool. The results are summarized in Table 7.2, where we have extended the analysis by qualitatively rating each of the risks that arose for Abz. The point of departure for the analysis was the customer's perspective.

It can be seen that the risk profiling tool continues to provide a highly useful way of analyzing risks and classifying rich findings in an IT outsourcing context. However, we found the risk-profiling tool requiring a number of amendments and possible additions to make it particularly relevant for netsourcing deals. First, at an overarching level, it seems important to introduce a further phase, the migration, implementation, and/or transition period. Second, we found in the case that during this stage a number of risks became evident. These included whether the supplier:

- Had sufficient skills, capabilities, and technical resources
- Was able to operationalize the service levels
- Introduced the necessary management processes for interacting with the customer and for reporting back on service and technical performance
- Established the necessary management infrastructure
- Was able to integrate the subcontracted services from third parties into a seamless service for the customer

The rationale for making the transition phase explicit derived from the level of difficulty experienced by the client firm, traceable back to the level of uncertainty arising from buying services from a relatively immature marketplace.

As a result, we propose the framework in Figure 7.2 as a more useful tool for analyzing risks in netsourcing and electronic IT sourcing arrangements. We recognize, of course, that this framework needs more thorough empirical validation in a larger-sample setting.

TABLE 7.2 Case Analysis Using the IT Outsourcing Risk Profiling Framework

STAGE	RISK ISSUE	ANALYSIS	RISK
Contextual	Distinctive competitive context and strategic intent	The distinct competitive context that Abz was faced with was that it did not have the in-house competencies to operate its own IT services, as IT did not define its core business. It therefore needed a strategic IT partner who facilitated its business and identified additional technological innovations that it could offer to customers. IT outsourcing, be it with a traditional IT service provider or an ASP, was identified as a necessity to compete. Not to outsource posed a high-risk strategy, with considerable costs to develop the IT competencies required.	High
		Its strategic intent was, in turn, not only about accessing innovation but also about wanting to transfer its outsourcing services to a strategic IT partner that could be more proactive than its existing provider, Getronics, with identifying technological advances and benefits. The goal was one of accessing and harnessing these technological opportunities touted to generate growth and differentiate services through new and additional IT services that others could then not duplicate so easily.	Medium
	Vendor market and client strategies	Siennax, being a startup desperate to procure business, jumped at the opportunity to offer its services. Its market strategy is one of customer numbers to generate size, growth, and turnover. Aggressive in its approach, the danger is one of overpromising on solutions, capabilities, and competencies, while in parallel not having a lengthy track record of experiences, customers, and success stories. Siennax, in turn, may have been a high-risk option. Still, Abz was aware of this potential danger and decided early on to mitigate these risks by sourcing incrementally a function that it could easily insource, procure in the market in the short term, or even outsource with another provider. In addition, Abz undertook some of the work of identifying necessary IT services providers that Siennax needed to subcontract to offer, for example, the required digital signature service.	Medium

TABLE 7.2 Case Analysis Using the IT Outsourcing Risk Profiling Framework (continued)

STAGE	RISK ISSUE	ANALYSIS	RISK
	Vendor capabilities	Siennax had experience with offering and running ASP solutions in contexts where legacy systems were operated in-house, and customers were looking for additional application services. In other words, they were offering a one-to-many application sourcing solution in a primarily "greenfield" environment. Thus they were not really in the business of outsourcing existing customer applications, technology, and whole functions and then providing an IT service in return. The situation was further complicated by the fact that they had to take over outsourced services from an existing IT service provider (i.e., competitor), revamp these by adding additional and new functionality, and then host the service on their own servers. Siennax, in turn, had some of the technical and application capabilities but did not have the experience with outsourcing services in general, and more specifically, with implementing digital signature solutions.	High
Building to contract	Treating IT as an undifferentiated commodity	Clearly, IT to Abz is far more than a commodity, as its revenue streams and hence whole business offering is dependent on the underlying IT services. Being thus prevented and hindered in offering to existing customers services that previously they had expected as a given (e.g., the digital signature service) not only curtails revenues but also causes customer and end-user dissatisfaction, leading potentially to customer loss.	High
	Incomplete contracting	Due to the fact that the service had previously been contracted out to another IT service provider, Abz had significant in-house expertise and experience at defining a comprehensive overarching contract and, more important, service levels. However, for many of the services that Siennax was contracted to deliver, some of the specific detail of the actual services and levels still had to be formalised as they became available to Abz. This was due in part to the long delay in implementing and migrating the digital signature service.	Medium

233

TABLE 7.2 Case Analysis Using the IT Outsourcing Risk Profiling Framework (continued)

STAGE	RISK ISSUE	ANALYSIS	RISK
	Difficulties in constructing deals for technical/ business change	Abz had in some ways catered for this risk by planning to implement the sourcing arrangement in an incremental phase, starting with the extranet, then the intranet, and finally, the critical application operations in-house. In this sense the deal allowed for greater flexibility in terms of responding to change, but it seemed that any changes to what had been agreed with Siennax would be at cost, and Siennax was preparing to identify new opportunities for Abz to expand its services. So change, in many ways, was inherent, but the procedures for change did not seem explicit.	Medium
	Outsourcing for short-term financial restructuring/ cash injection rather than leveraging IT assets for business advantage	In this instance Abz was clearly not focusing on financial restructuring or cash injection. The service it needed had already been outsourced with Getronics, so it was recontracting the service with another supplier. This would see switching costs arise but also introduce extra costs as it was planning to change its service requirements and procure additional services. In turn, the deal was focused more on leveraging IT assets as a means to access business and customer advantages.	Low
	Lack of maturity/ experience in contracting for total outsourcing arrangements	Abz did have experience with contracting for outsourcing solutions. However, it was not willing nor planning to use the power of the contract to enforce its service demands. Instead, it was intent on developing the relationship with Siennax, as it planned to take advantage of Siennax's innovativeness and access to new technology solutions that Abz could then resell to its customers. The issue here, then, is to mitigate risk by knowing when and when not to assert the formal contract, so that the relationship can function properly together with the supplier's ability to develop added value.	Low

TABLE 7.2 Case Analysis Using the IT Outsourcing Risk Profiling Framework (continued)

STAGE	RISK ISSUE	ANALYSIS	RISK
	Unrealistic expectations with multiple objectives for outsourcing	In part we do find some support for arguing that Abz had placed high expectations on Siennax's ability to deliver on its IT service requirements. Yet it seemed clear to both parties that delivering the envisaged service would be something that Siennax had never done before and thus had no experience with. The expectation remained, though, that Siennax could respond to service demands, roll-out the solution, and cover the necessary capabilities to offer the solution. There seems to be some evidence of overpromising and overexpectation, considering, for example, the seven-week implementation delay.	Medium
	Poor sourcing/ contracting for development and new technologies	Although Abz had prior contracting experience for outsourcing deals, in this ASP scenario it was clear that the service levels were plagued by uncertainty about how the entire solution was going to be provided by Siennax. In turn, the detail of the services had not been finalized, even though the migration had already been initiated. To this extent, there was a lot of uncertainty inherent in the contract and the specifics of the deal, which later became an issue as Siennax encountered problems with implementing the key service of digital signatures. In turn, the additional complexity that Abz was facing related to how to contract for new and novel service and technology solutions. This was a matter of defining close strategic relations to ensure that services are eventually operational, but could be at significant costs to Abz. For the long term this clearly poses a major risk, as Siennax increases its penetration into Abz's service and identifies new technical opportunities, solutions, and benefits.	High
Post-contract issues	Failure to build and retain requisite in-house capabilities	Abz did not have to build or retain the requisite in-house skills, as it had already outsourced most of its IT to Getronics, so that it merely continued with the existing management structure to handle Siennax. It is likely, though, that in the long term, as the degree of outsourcing and the increase in planned IT services matures with Siennax, additional in-house capabilities will need to be developed to avoid an overly high dependency on Siennax's management. A fundamental risk for Abz lay in handing over too much responsibility for technical architecture and nonroutine technical fixing tasks, even though the ASP model suggests that this would not be problematic. It was also clear that Abz needed to strengthen its contract monitoring and contract facilitation core capability, together with its ability to elicit and deliver on business requirements.	Low (long-term increase to medium)

TABLE 7.2 Case Analysis Using the IT Outsourcing Risk Profiling Framework (continued)

Stage	Risk Issue	Analysis	Risk
	Difficulties adapting deals in face of business/ technical change	At this point of the deal's development there was insufficient insight to be able to predict the long-term difficulties of adapting to change. The real complexities of the migration were still to come, with the larger service portfolio encapsulated in the intranet. Again this would suggest that Abz needs to be careful to build up more of its internal capability in the business, technical, and managing external supply fronts.	N/A
	Lack of maturity/ experience in managing total outsourcing	Abz certainly has the experience of managing outsourcing deals and in fact itself operates as an outsourcing service provider. To judge from its past and current operations and experiences, this poses a small risk. The danger, rather, lies with Siennax, which has had little experience with outsourcing. It may thus require Abz to enforce process, structures, and service performance demands on Siennax and in the long run also necessitates a rather more active management involvement in the deal. Considering this potential threat, risks may evolve unexpectedly as the service portfolio increases, and so with Abz's dependency.	Medium
	Power asymmetries developing in favor of vendor	Abz had purposely chosen a smaller supplier this time around to ensure that it can maintain a greater degree of influence and possible power over the supplier. Recall that Abz has significant size and prestige within the insurance industry. To this extent, a bad experience and potential breakdown of relations could have equally adverse effects, but more so for Siennax in terms of being able to deliver services to established firms such as Abz. The long-term development may look different, though, as Siennax increasingly takes hold of services and the dependency IT services increase.	Low (long-term increase to medium)
	Lack of active management of supplier on contract and relationship dimensions	Again, experience and management interface structures have been put in place, but it is too early to tell whether there are any risks at this point. However, the ability of Abz to manage actively will depend on the extent to which it strengthens its internal capability as described above.	N/A

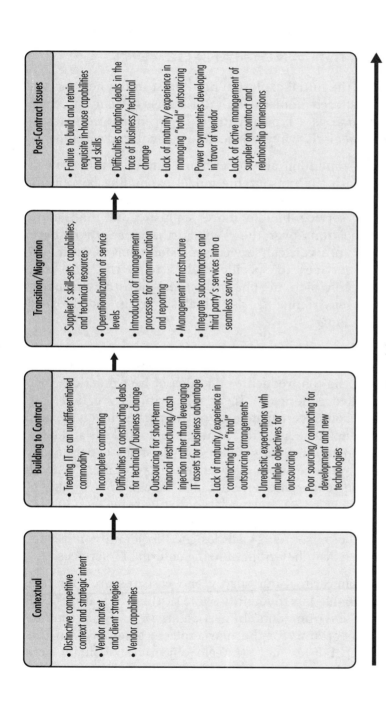

Contextual

- Distinctive competitive context and strategic intent
- Vendor market and client strategies
- Vendor capabilities

Building to Contract

- Treating IT as an undifferentiated commodity
- Incomplete contracting
- Difficulties in constructing deals for technical/business change
- Outsourcing for short-term financial restructuring/cash injection rather than leveraging IT assets for business advantage
- Lack of maturity/experience in contracting for "total" outsourcing arrangements
- Unrealistic expectations with multiple objectives for outsourcing
- Poor sourcing/contracting for development and new technologies

Transition/Migration

- Supplier's skill-sets, capabilities, and technical resources
- Operationalization of service levels
- Introduction of management processes for communication and reporting
- Management infrastructure
- Integrate subcontractors and third party's services into a seamless service

Post-Contract Issues

- Failure to build and retain requisite in-house capabilities and skills
- Difficulties adapting deals in the face of business/technical change
- Lack of maturity/experience in managing "total" outsourcing
- Power asymmetries developing in favor of vendor
- Lack of active management of supplier on contract and relationship dimensions

Time and Change

FIGURE 7.2 Risk Analysis Framework for Electronic/Netsourcing Deals (From Kern and Willcocks, 2001)

237

BETTER PRACTICES FOR NETSOURCING RISK MITIGATION AND MANAGEMENT

By 2001 the initial explosion in interest in the netsourcing model had faltered, not least with the demise of many startups. This, of course, is a typical pattern in an immature marketplace, and precisely why risks need to be analyzed carefully.

In fact, something altogether more interesting has been occurring, with the netsourcing model expanding beyond its boundaries into business or managed service provision, reflecting a service bundle more sophisticated than mere rented applications over the Web. Furthermore, there have been moves into vertical service provision, that is, trying to offer more services to specific niches (e.g., the legal and accounting profession, the pharmaceutical industry). In such a fast-moving environment, risk analysis again needs very detailed handling.

The analysis and management of risk in netsourcing environments are also immature but fast developing. As such, it is dangerous to be too wedded to the idea of best practices that can be applied generically. Invariably, with IT we find that competitive contexts, capabilities of the parties involved, and types of technology being utilized are specific to deals and have big effects on the distinctive nature of the risks experienced. Fortunately, we have at our disposal a bedrock of more general IT outsourcing experiences from which we can draw innumerable lessons. Figure 7.1 encapsulated that learning, and in earlier chapters we have spelled out the detail of best practice in the field of IT outsourcing—all designed to identify, mitigate, and manage risks inherent in utilizing external IT services.

At the same time, our survey and case research for this book have enabled us to identify some distinctive features and risks in ASP environments. In particular, we find that the fluidity and uncertainty of the marketplace, together with the changing capabilities and strategic objectives of many netsourcing suppliers and the lack of knowledge of these matters on the part of many clients, make us emphasize that detailed netsourcing risk analysis is an utterly essential prerequisite for would-be customers. Support for this statement can be found by looking again at the Siennax–Abz case study. The thrust of Figure 7.2, including the additional set of transition/migration risks, is to argue that the netsourcing customer needs to be alive to risks from the first moment netsourcing is contemplated to the last moment of any deal that is actually operationalized. It is also clear that our review of netsourcing risks pulls would-be customers into being much more active and detailed in their analysis of risk and in developing risk-mitigation capabilities and processes than many would believe necessary at the front end of any deal. However, the devil *is* in the details, and salvation *is* in investigating and detailing risk and in persisting in active daily management of the supplier and its performance.

CONCLUSIONS

In the fast-moving netsourcing environment, risk analysis needs very detailed handling. Looking at the multiple risks that exist in netsourcing deals according to customers and the severity of some of the risk issues, it is of importance to any customer to mitigate risks carefully and manage them throughout the deal. By drawing attention to the key risks, as we do in Table 7.1, and commenting on how these arise and are perceived, we make an important step in eliciting a list of factors to include in any netsourcing risk-mitigation portfolio.

We have also shown in this chapter that much can be gained from looking at risks in IT outsourcing more generally, but that there are a number of distinctive risks that arose in the case of Siennax–Abz which suggest that the Figure 7.2 framework is a more refined and useful one to use in netsourcing risk profiling from a customer perspective. This framework can be applied against other netsourcing arrangements to highlight and identify further risks, through the process of analysis that it demands and structures.

ENDNOTES

1. R. Charette, *Application Strategies for Risk Analysis*, McGraw-Hill, New York, 1991; L. Willcocks and H. Margetts, "Risk Assessment in Information Systems," *European Journal of Information Systems*, 4 (1), 1–12, 1994.

2. M. J. Earl, "The Risks of Outsourcing IT," *Sloan Management Review*, 37(3), 26–32, 1996; R. W. Klepper and W. Jones, *Outsourcing Information Technology, Systems and Services*, Prentice Hall, Upper Saddle River, N.J., 1998; S. Ang and S. K. Toh, "Failure in Software Outsourcing: A Case Analysis," in L. Willcocks and M. Lacity (eds.), *Strategic Sourcing of Information Systems*, Wiley, Chichester, West Sussex, England, 1998; J. Jurison, "The Role of Risk and Return in Information Technology Outsourcing Decisions," *Journal of Information Technology*, 10 (4), 239–247, 1995.

3. L. Willcocks and M. Lacity, "IT Outsourcing in Insurance Services: Risk, Creative Contracting and Business Advantage," *Information Systems Journal*, 9, 163–180, 1999; L. Willcocks, M. Lacity, and T. Kern, "Risk Mitigation in IT Outsourcing Strategy Revisited: Longitudinal Case Research at LISA," *Journal of Strategic Information Systems*, 8, 285–314, 1999.

4. Jurison (1995), op. cit.

8 NETSOURCING DRIVERS: CUSTOMER DECISION CHECKLIST

What do potential customers look for in a netsourcing solution? What are their key expectations? Moreover, what do customers anticipate as the downsides that explain their wariness of netsourcing? Consider five key *drivers*—in essence, those factors that make netsourcing a compelling solution for customer organizations to consider. Taken together, the drivers serve many purposes:

1. They describe the business logic of the netsourcing business model for customers.
2. They highlight customers' primary decision and selection criteria when considering a netsourcing solution.
3. They outline the key areas of customer expectations.

4. For service providers, they define the basis upon which they need to differentiate their service solutions from direct and indirect competitors.

5. They outline the basis against which a netsourcing provider's performance can be assessed, not least by the provider itself.

We classify the netsourcing drivers as business, technical, economic, IT services market, and relational. An intimate understanding of these is an essential foundation for understanding the market, options, and potential of the netsourcing solution.

Bringing these ideas together, we provide a checklist of issues about customer perceptions and use of netsourcing in the United States and Europe. Effectively, we show customers a set of evaluative pointers to guide netsourcing decisions concerning both internal and external providers. We also provide guidelines for providers themselves on how they need to respond to the customer requirements identified.[1]

BUSINESS DRIVERS

For the customer, business drivers define the potential strategic, organizational, and operational advantages and disadvantages from selecting netsourcing as an IT/e-business sourcing option. For the provider, the business drivers focus on making a service offering available that addresses true business needs in a way that gives the provider a competitive advantage.

As discussed in Chapter 1, customers need to consider the total value proposition of netsourcing vis-à-vis other sourcing options. The notion of economies of scale that a netsourcing provider can achieve informs the business logic for netsourcing. Implied here is that providers can achieve an increased efficiency in operations and offer access to a larger skill and knowledge base. However, unlike IT outsourcing, where a customer transfers not only people and assets but also its management to a service provider, the netsourcing model in essence is about renting a business solution. Therefore, the netsourcing solution frees up useful resources and improves organizational flexibility. Adopting a netsourcing solution, in turn, gives client organizations the advantage of focusing on core operations and what they do best while leaving the application management and maintenance concerns to a provider.

Innovation and access to applications that normally are prohibitively expensive, especially for smaller organizations, are noted as additional business reasons for seeking a netsourcing provider. Netsourcing providers supposedly represent the leading edge of application management, since they focus primarily on solving customers' business demands through the applications and services provided. Therefore, they will have a better understanding of applications than will most customers since it defines their core business. As such, innovations in terms of operations and technological improvements can be touted. Recall the market cost and capabilities matrix provided in Chapter 2. What the customer is looking for ranges from delivery of a commodity activity through to the provision of a total business solution. The customer, in turn, needs to take care that critical differentiator assets and activities of his or her own business are not outsourced. A buy-in policy can be adopted, though, where key capabilities are lacking and hence need to be built. Critical and useful commodities, however, are clear targets for netsourcing.

In this search, the netsourcing provider needs to be assessed on cost. Here the focus should be on whether a provider can achieve the requirement at a superior or at least a competitive price compared to in-house and to other external providers. If this is the case, the customer needs to look for a detailed explanation: in particular, in terms of exploring the process for achieving the economies of scale, the existence of any superior IT management practices, and the benefits of learning curve effects in a provider's practices and offerings. The customer also needs to diagnose whether the netsourcing provider does offer superior capability in terms of any or all of: expertise, service, speed, and complementary resources.

The customer also needs to assess the probability and impact of drawbacks in the case of each specific service provider. One major actual drawback with netsourcing centers is the potential loss of customer control and resulting dependency on the supplier. Forty-four percent of existing customers experienced this outcome. Once a firm signs up with a netsourcing provider, there will be a lock-in for the length of the contract. However, lock-in is not just merely to the terms of the contract. It implies, for example, a commitment of intention and resources and an acceptance of the opportunity costs of not doing other things and not servicing IT in other ways. Most companies will not opt to terminate a contract early, due to the costs and the disruption it is likely to cause to operations—remembering that applications will touch most, if not all, organizational processes. Thereafter, hidden costs and lack of delivery on original expectations are the key risk issues to check against and for which to develop mitigation practices. Interestingly, we found that potential customers fear lock-in and loss of control much more than is warranted in the light of actual customer experiences (see Chapter 7 for a full discussion of risk analysis and mitigation).

Our international survey revealed some fundamental insights into customer experiences of business drivers. The eight top business benefits being experienced strongly (scoring between 3 and 4 out of 5) are listed below. The figures indicate the percentage of existing customers recording the benefit.

1. Enable focus on core activities (95%)
2. Significant cost savings (70%)
3. Increased roll-out speed for applications (66%)
4. Enhanced business flexibility due to scalability of applications (74%)
5. Competitive advantage from access to skills, applications, and services not otherwise available (74%)
6. Make IT costs more predictable (77%)
7. Enhance business innovation (55%)
8. Improve IT and service quality (44%)

Clearly, most existing customers are getting some real business benefits from their netsourcing providers. What is particularly interesting is that these benefits exceed the types of benefits emerging from surveys carried out in the more general IT outsourcing markets in Europe, the United States, and Australia. This undoubtedly reflects that the netsourcing market tends to service smaller, less IT-capable enterprises. It certainly argues that netsourcing providers are doing a much better job than their media profile suggests. Interestingly, would-be customers also expect to get these benefits but have lower expectations about the size of the benefits on offer, again suggesting that netsourcing providers need to think a lot more about improving their customer education programs.

NETSOURCING PROVIDERS: MAKING A RESPONSE

For netsourcing providers, the customer value proposition outlines the key features likely to be attractive to customers in terms of added value. Customer value propositions can be met only if the netsourcing provider has the necessary capabilities or can partner effectively to make these available. Netsourcing providers face the challenge of acquiring these capabilities to offer best-in-class services and achieve economies of scale by making these services available on a one-to-many basis. Netsourcing providers can differentiate themselves and attain a competitive advantage only if the combination of the capabilities a netsourcing provider holds is unique and can be deployed in a profitable manner. To achieve this, a netsourcing provider needs to evaluate continually whether or not its capabilities and the way these are deployed allow it to achieve each customer's value expectations, meet customers' detailed requirements, and outclass or differentiate its offerings against competitors. Profitability and cash flow are also fundamental considerations in a netsourcing strategy. Without attention to these, the netsourcing provider is not only likely to do critical (if eventual damage) to its service delivery, it will also dissuade intelligent customers with superior buying capability from signing up in the first place.

BUSINESS DRIVERS:
CHECKLIST QUESTIONS

The business drivers detail the core business reasons for seeking a netsourcing solution. For a customer it is a matter of evaluating and weighing these advantages and the possible value added to its business against potential drawbacks of netsourcing. For the netsourcing provider it entails combining capabilities and resources in such a way that both the netsourcing provider and its customers will compare these services advantageously against competitors' offerings.

Guiding questions for customers:

1. To what degree do the potential business advantages really characterize the model being presented by the netsourcing provider?
2. How do you as a potential netsourcing customer perceive the probable drawbacks of the solution?
3. What are the trade-offs and their likely impacts?
4. How well does the netsourcing provider manage and cater to the potential drawbacks?
5. What risk-mitigation strategies and practices does the customer need to adopt?
6. What are alternative solutions?

TECHNOLOGY DRIVERS

The technical drivers describe the technical characteristics of a netsourcing solution. For customers, a netsourcing provider's performance on these features determines its technical capabilities and whether or not it can truly deliver services and business benefits. The challenge for a netsourcing provider is to deliver high technology standards necessary to gain superior marks from the customer on relative perceived quality and relative customer satisfaction.

A wide range of technical issues taxes customers. Typically, customers look toward netsourcing providers to offer an underlying IT infrastructure and a broad range of applications—beyond what is available to the customer without netsourcing. Customers look to netsourcing providers for a reliable, readily available, and secure service that can either replace, amend, or expand their current application service portfolio. Reliability implies that a service remains constant and consistent and compares favorably against other technical options. Similar assumptions apply to the security and confidentiality of application services, especially with respect to data that netsourcing providers might be storing for customers on their server farms. Responsiveness is another important criterion by which technical services need to be judged, along with quality of technical skills and capabilities. Availability of applications and services matters most to the business at crucial times (e.g., peak periods). The netsourcing provider needs to recognize that 99.9% availability means little to a customer if the 0.1% unavailability causes serious business disruption.

Scalability of services often plays a crucial role in fast-growing businesses but also for firms where service volume increase is likely to occur, for example, during end-of-year accounting periods. Customers seek the possibility of easily increasing the number of terminals and processing volumes. In part, a netsourcing provider's flexibility in responding to these scalability requirements of solutions facilitates a greater operational flexibility for a customer.

Another important issue for clients is application customization. Here the focus needs to be on the degree of customization available, which determines to what extent standard applications can be altered, modularized, or componentized to meet a client's unique business needs. This will influence the extent to which company specific information can and cannot be handled and processed.

Customers are also likely to look toward a netsourcing provider for leading-edge technologies, which could improve their company's technical performance, make innovations available, provide more solution possibilities, and offer new options to customers. These state-of-the-art technologies can enhance a customer's internal business processes, operations, and innovativeness.

Customers are very concerned that netsourcing providers are able to supply Web-oriented applications, that they are able to supply integration of netsourcing offerings and of these offerings with the customer's own systems, that the applications provided are continuously up to date, and that the netsourcing provider supplies sufficient help-desk and technical support.

Finally, it is clear that different customers attribute different levels of importance to individual technical features. Thus a netsourcing provider's portfolio of solutions will be of great interest. How important are these issues to customers? The following nine issues were rated as very important by the percentage of potential customers indicated.

1. Availability (85%)
2. Quality of services (85%)
3. Security (83%)
4. Reliability (80%)
5. Responsiveness (79%)
6. Skills and technical capabilities (75%)
7. SLA and contract management (75%)
8. Scalability of service (66%)
9. Application customization (58%)

Noticeably, potential customers are focused on service issues, with underlying IT infrastructure, IT ownership, and strategic IT advisory services being ascribed much less importance.

On actual netsourcing performance levels, we found some causes for concern that netsourcing providers need to address, especially given the high expectations revealed by potential customers. There are dangers of an expectation–outcome mismatch developing on technical and service issues, as we found existed in the more general experiences of IT outsourcing. On average, out of a maximum score of 1 = poor, 5 = excellent, netsourcing providers are scoring as follows:

1. Availability, 3.4
2. Quality of services, 3.66
3. Security, 3.69

4. Reliability, 3.5

5. Responsiveness, 3.43

6. Skills and technical capabilities, 3.54

7. SLA and contract management, 3.6

8. Scalability of service, 3.51

9. Application customization, 3.51

The averages hide that 25% of suppliers are performing excellently on security, 20% on responsiveness, 17% on skills and capabilities, 17% on quality, and 17% on new technologies and innovations.

By contrast, the top five technical problems, as experienced by the percentage of customers indicated, were:

1. Slow application response time (41%)

2. Application unavailable (25%)

3. Inability to integrate netsourcing with existing applications (16%)

4. Unanticipated technical costs (16%)

5. Lack of qualified netsourcing provider staff (16%)

If these results look quite good, the more general picture is less flattering. Most netsourcing technical and service performance falls between 2 and 4 out of 5. There are no real obvious disasters (although 13% of customers rate their netsourcing service as poor) but too few excellent performances. What remains is plenty of room for improvement, not least to match the high expectations of potential customers.

NETSOURCING PROVIDERS: MAKING A RESPONSE

The full listing of supply-side considerations we uncovered is provided in Table 8.1 at the end of this chapter. You can see that the netsourcing provider needs to make available technical skills and capabilities, required quality and range of services and products, IT infrastructure, customization, responsiveness, customer support, and Web-oriented up-to-date applications.

For netsourcing providers to do justice to customers' requirements, they themselves are invariably dependent to some degree on other partner firms for networks, bandwidth, server farms, systems integration, applications, and consulting services. Thus before contracting with customers it is essential for netsourcing providers to determine whether its partners' technical infrastructure and services are sufficient to cater to a customer's needs or whether additional partners have to be identified. Its own technical prowess will be a key consideration here, together with its own ability to source, using the guidelines provided in Chapter 2.

Because in many instances additional services or products have to be adopted to deliver their service requirements to customers, netsourcing providers need to have the technical capabilities and facilities to easily integrate systems, services, and applications, not least with customer legacy systems and any new systems being developed.

TECHNOLOGY DRIVERS: CHECKLIST QUESTIONS

The technology drivers define the key technical features of a netsourcing solution. Different customers will attribute different levels of importance to technical capabilities and naturally will tend to apply their own criteria as a means to weight netsourcing providers' solutions to address their particular requirements. For some customers the technology drivers will define, in turn, the primary netsourcing selection and evaluation criteria. In contrast, for netsourcing providers these drivers outline the critical range in which their technical, managerial, and service capabilities and offerings need to fall.

Guiding questions for customers:

1. Does the netsourcing provider offer a technical solution, and can it be made easily compatible with existing systems?
2. What are the specific technical measurements in terms of scalability, reliability, quality, security, availability, and degree of customization by which you will assess the netsourcing provider's technical performance?

3. What kind of technology innovations/up-to-dateness does the netsourcing provider offer, and are these likely to provide real technical advantages or benefits?
4. What are the technical fall-back positions should anything go wrong?
5. How well does the netsourcing provider score on Web orientation, customer support, systems integration, and technical partnering capability?

ECONOMIC DRIVERS

For the customer, netsourcing promises considerable economic benefits. Essential to the netsourcing business model are the favorable pricing models, cost benefits, and savings it is likely to provide for customers. The comparison is commonly performed on total cost of ownership as compared against sourcing applications directly from a netsourcing provider. Indeed, netsourcing providers often reinforce this by arguing that customers should perform a total cost of ownership comparison against sourcing applications directly from a netsourcing provider.

Customers looking at the netsourcing model will probably see it as a means to, at a minimum, stabilize costs, improve cost control by changing the variable costs to fixed, and achieve additional cost savings. Additionally, netsourcing offers the opportunity to spread payments and financial risk. Customers are commonly confronted by relatively high up-front investment costs in the applications and underlying server technology, which the netsourcing model can alleviate. Additionally, cost benefits come from the netsourcing providers' economies of scale for implementing applications across the business, which can be much lower, depending on the degree of customization that is required. Netsourcing providers may also claim superior management practices and experience curve effects allowing them to achieve significant cost savings for the customer.

Cost control, which can be further improved by the payment arrangements underpinning the netsourcing model, offers the customer sufficient flexibility to make it work with their internal accounting procedures. At the end of the day, this could imply payment arrangements that would see usage costs for applications calculated on a transaction basis, per user per desk, or a weekly and/or monthly total basis. In any case, determination of the costs will be fixed and clear to the customer, giving greater customer control over expenditures.

The actual experiences of customers on the economics of using a netsourcing provider paints a clear picture. You saw above that 77% are finding that netsourcing is making costs more predictable and that 70% are receiving significant cost savings on the total cost of ownership. More than 70% of customers are paying netsourcing fees of only up to $10,000 a month. This reflects the relatively small size of netsourcing deals to date and the fact that respondents to our survey were procuring mainly standard commodity-type applications. At the same time, some 16% of customers were paying fees in excess of $50,000 a month. On setup fees, some 45% of customers were paying less than $5000, and all were paying less than potential customers themselves were anticipating. In practice, some 85% of existing customers were achieving yearly savings between $3000 and $180,000. Generally, potential customers are overly pessimistic about cost savings. Finally, the top six pricing models in use, in order of frequency, are:

1. Based on number of users (31% of customers)
2. Flat rental fee (25%)
3. Based on data volumes (22%)
4. Based on number of applications (19%)
5. Based on number of desktops (16%)
6. Based on degree of customization (12%)

In contrast, the most popular pricing models among potential customers were:

1. Based on number of users (52%)
2. Based on number of applications (34%)
3. Flat rental fees (33%)
4. Based on degree of customization (28%)

Some of the respondents cited a preference for more than one pricing model. In practice, potential customers were less certain and less knowledgeable about the most appropriate pricing model, and so tended to cite more pricing models. Here, netsourcing providers have to clarify to their clients the appropriateness and disadvantages of different pricing models.

Netsourcing Providers: Making a Response

For a netsourcing provider, the main economic focus will be chiefly on achieving and maintaining its economies of scale to ensure that it retrieves and maintains its often slim profit margins. For most startups this presents a significant challenge, though, since netsourcing service provisions are calculated on a two- to three-year write-off period. This implies that high initial outlays are recovered only after a longer period of operation. For netsourcing startups that are often cash hampered, this will present a short-term survival challenge. In many ways, the netsourcing model is thus dependent on long-term business deals, high initial financing, repeat business, and additional business with existing customers to make it profitable. However, netsourcing providers can be quite creative in their ability to offer finance deals that allow customers maximum flexibility in payment for services, without harming their own long-term financial position.

A netsourcing provider's economic model also depends on ever-greater numbers of customers to whom it can deliver the same service that it is already providing to existing customers. As the contract numbers increase, so will the return on their initial investments. The goal being to have numerous one-to-many relationships that together facilitate large economies of scale. In turn, you need to be sure to consider the learning and experience curve of implementing and delivering netsourcing services, which will help you to determine the economies-of-scale areas of providers.

Finally, netsourcing pricing models not only provide a competitive advantage but also differentiate netsourcing providers. The challenge that netsourcing providers face is one of breaking down their services into units and transactions, allowing customers greater freedom in selecting and hence customizing their particular service provision payment schemes. Specifying services by units or transactions will also give customers an improved means to control and monitor costs for IT services, giving them greater predictability of potential costs for volume increases and subsequent operational costs.

ECONOMIC DRIVERS: CHECKLIST QUESTIONS

Since economic drivers are both a core part of a customer's decision to select netsourcing and essential to making the service provision to customers profitable for netsourcing providers, they require very careful attention. The questions thus need to concentrate on issues such as economies of scale, cost savings, profitability, and pricing arrangements to discover both the supply- and demand-side advantages.

Guiding questions for customers:

1. What are the likely up-front and ongoing costs?
2. What pricing models/arrangements does the netsourcing provider offer?
3. How does a specific netsourcing provider achieve and maintain economies of scale?
4. What is the time frame for achieving return on investments for a netsourcing provider?
5. How robust is the financial model being used by the netsourcing provider?
6. Does the netsourcing provider offer sustainable value for money that compares favorably with the financial impacts of all other sourcing options?

THE IT SERVICES MARKET

The IT services market drivers explore the market context. For netsourcing customers the market conditions influence the perceived value of the netsourcing solution versus the alternatives. For netsourcing providers the IT services market describes the backdrop against which they need to stand out and assert their offering as being differentiated and leading edge. The netsourcing providers who look to compete primarily on price alone will be playing a losing game. Instead, efforts should be focused on differentiating their product/service offerings and seeking opportunities and managing threats.

The scarcity of IT resources and capabilities has put a serious constraint on companies' in-house deployment of IT skills across the developed economies. In the majority of cases, but especially in small and medium-sized enterprises, this drives companies with IT capability shortages to source vital skills from external suppliers. The wide acceptance of the Internet, the usage-based pricing models, lower total cost of ownership (TCO), and a lower initial capital outlay make netsourcing a particularly interesting option for many companies. For small and medium-sized enterprises (SMEs), companies pursuing maximum growth strategies, and Internet-based startups, the netsourcing model makes accessible applications they could normally not afford. For instance, the netsourcing model makes formerly prohibitively expensive ERP applications now affordable for many SMEs. For larger companies, the netsourcing model may reduce the efforts involved in maintaining and managing applications but also makes essential applications accessible at competitive and attractive prices.

Before evaluating specific netsourcing providers, customers have to identify the capabilities they expect from their netsourcing provider. Only then can a customer evaluate specific netsourcing providers' service offerings. Brands, reputation, track records, size, and the netsourcing provider's main suppliers are all things to be taken into account. Also, the immaturity of the netsourcing market and the novelty of the netsourcing solution bring about uncertainty that makes adoption of the netsourcing model risky. For example, uncertainty about the netsourcing model's longevity and business and financial stability are key features to be considered when comparing different netsourcing providers.

In practice, the gravest concerns among existing customers are, in order of importance:

1. Netsourcing provider longevity and existence
2. Reliability

3. Service and business stability

4. Security

5. Integrating netsourcing and host applications

These tend to be rated as medium-risk issues (between 2 and 3 out of 5) by existing customers, while potential customers tend to be much more worried by these and an entire range of other issues (see also Chapter 7 on risks).

Over 60% of both potential and existing customers now expect the netsourcing market to be offering not just applications but hosting, help-desk, and integration skills and services. Between 20 and 60% of potential and existing customers expect to be able to buy from the netsourcing market the following:

- Technology maintenance and service
- Security verification services
- Colocation services
- Application customization
- IT consulting
- Internet service access provision
- IT outsourcing services
- Data warehousing
- Legacy systems outsourcing and management
- WAP-based services

Clearly, there is a widening requirement for the types of service that customers are prepared to contract for from the netsourcing market, raising important questions as to whether netsourcing providers can rise to match the full range of these demands.

However, there is some disparity between existing and potential customer requirements. Thus there is some discrepancy where potential customers rate netsourcing skills in the customization of applications as much more essential than do existing customers. Conversely, existing customers regularly rate legacy systems outsourcing and management, hosting services, WAP-based services, and strategic management consulting as more important than do potential customers.

Netsourcing Providers:
Making a Response

Throughout 2001, the supply side had consisted of a diverse range of established and new startup service firms, experiencing both shakedown and consolidation. The established companies found their core in Internet service provision/access, network infrastructure provision, telecommunications, software developing, reselling, systems integration, and consulting services. Startups often positioned themselves as pure-play ASPs, offering applications from well-known software firms as a netsourcing solution and/or combining various applications into a total solution. Today, the various players in the IT service market cover all necessary application service provision capabilities. With the ongoing consolidation of the netsourcing market, large outsourcing service providers, technology firms, and consultancies will be able to combine the various capabilities into full service provision offerings. For netsourcing startups to flourish, therefore, they have to continue to specialize in particular industries, packages, or service solutions to ensure that they can sufficiently differentiate themselves from those that offer a full-range netsourcing solution. Alliances and partnerships in many cases remain a fundamental means of acquiring essential capabilities, competing, and branding and marketing of services.

Next to market positioning, generating trust is still a crucial driver for the success of individual netsourcing providers. Making use of trusted third parties and security audits through well-known auditing firms helps to generate trust in netsourcing and business. Industry recognition, industry standards, and further segmentation continue to reduce overall uncertainty associated with the netsourcing industry and generate trust in the netsourcing solution in customers' eyes.

IT Services Market:
Checklist Questions

The demand-side considerations concerning the IT services market drivers are to link internal needs to the right netsourcing suppliers. This involves listing internal needs, evaluating different netsourcing providers, and selecting a suitable netsourcing provider. The supply-side questions concerning the IT services market are about positioning, given expected market developments, and how to generate trust in the netsourcing solutions generally and in an individual netsourcing offering.

Guiding questions for customers:

1. What are your primary concerns when looking at the netsourcing market and the netsourcing solution in general?
2. What should netsourcing providers be doing to generate trust in the netsourcing concept?
3. How is the market likely to develop: At what speed will it mature, and in what directions?
4. How does the netsourcing provider's strategy and capabilities fit with your short- and long-term business, financial, and technical requirements?
5. Will this netsourcing provider be able to continue its business to guarantee offering your company the service(s) you need?
6. Do you have the necessary informed buying capability in place to understand, make judgments about, and contract with external netsourcing suppliers?

RELATIONAL DRIVERS

The relational drivers refer, first, to the relationship between a netsourcing supplier and its customers, and second, to the relationships between a netsourcing provider and its business partners. The latter can be either a straightforward buyer–supplier relationship or a preferred/strategic partner relationship.

The drivers regarding the relation between the netsourcing supplier and the netsourcing customer can be classified in terms of stakeholder (i.e., client and provider) interests. On the demand side, client considerations aim at controlling the relationship and ensuring that services are performed according to the SLAs. On the other hand, netsourcing supply-side considerations focus on achieving service performance, customer business goals and satisfaction, and satisfactory profit and revenue.

To control the relation with its supplier, the customer needs continually to monitor and evaluate the netsourcing provider's performance. The technical performance can be monitored relatively easily using periodic performance reviews of service levels, which most netsourcing providers will make readily available to their clients. Penalties for not meeting service-level agreement (SLA) standards can be an effective enforcement instrument when used properly. Based on our findings, the best SLAs will focus on user training programs provided by the netsourcing provider, adequate exit and continuity of service clauses, contingency, security and future flexibility guarantees, and the degree of knowledge sharing and cooperation that surrounds SLA performance.

A client should also monitor and evaluate if the provider's services delivered actually meet their needs. For this, clients will definitely have to develop in-house evaluation procedures. If the netsourcing providers service does not meet the client's business needs, it could very well indicate that the contract needs to be renegotiated, or that the client needs to re-source its applications from a different netsourcing provider.

Control over the relationship with the netsourcing provider will vary according to the strategic importance of the sourced applications for the customer's business. For instance, the e-commerce platforms that some dot.coms have sourced from netsourcing providers are at the heart of their business and enable their core operations. Obviously, the sourced applications and the resulting relationship with a netsourcing provider will be of considerable strategic importance to the dot.com. On the other hand, if the applications sourced can be classified as commodities, the customer–supplier relationship may be of less strategic importance.

Given the sourcing of mission-critical applications, relations are likely to be more long term in nature. Therefore, the netsourcing supplier selection process will be vital. Not only operational, technical, and economic selection criteria but also the longer-term strategic intent of the netsourcing provider will have to be taken into account. In all cases in Chapter 3, however, the customer needed to retain core IT capabilities in the areas of contract facilitation, contract monitoring, informed buying, and vendor development. An important neglect frequently found among customers is a failure to provide adequate point of contact and relationship building processes until mounting problems force the issue.

Trust and confidence remain crucial to relationship building. Both potential and existing customers cite five top sources about how trust and confidence are generated:

1. Industry recognition of the netsourcing provider (e.g., Vistorm has won a number of European awards)
2. Alliances and partnerships with recognized, often large telecom providers, hardware manufacturers, and software vendors
3. Verification services (e.g., Verisign, TRUSTe)
4. Security audits by well-known audit firms
5. Branding and marketing by the netsourcing provider

In contrast, the top nine items that customers indicated they included in their contracts for good client-netsourcing provider relations were:

1. Application availability metrics and guarantees
2. Security of data guarantees
3. Confidentiality of customer data clauses
4. Guaranteed levels of customer service
5. Guaranteed level of application response time
6. Penalty clauses for nonperformance
7. Force major clauses
8. Warranty clauses
9. Liability and indemnity clauses

Customers felt strongly that these clauses gave guarantees and a level of trust and expectation from which the relationship could develop further. Put another way, good detailed contracts were the foundations of good relationships.

Netsourcing Providers:
Making a Response

Achieving and maintaining customer satisfaction is not only about service management and performance by the netsourcing provider but also about customer care and the provision of staffing and processes designed to develop the relationship with the customer. Service management and performance entails the more technical process of delivering what is agreed upon and ensuring quality of services. Customer care, and relationship building, on the other hand, focuses more on managing and delivering on the users' ever-developing requirements and expectations. This involves a much more holistic view of the customer–supplier interaction than only the technical performance.

The service solution and the relationship approach to customers will become one of the main differentiators between suppliers as the netsourcing market starts to mature. The one-to-many nature of the netsourcing model implies that software has a high degree of standardization, and suppliers have to differentiate themselves on the basis of service management, including partnering capabilities rather than just solutions. Basic steps to ensuring customer care will involve, for example, setting up feedback loops, providing a single point of contact and providing training and support for customers. Critical will be a netsourcing provider's ability to develop relationships and skills for establishing interfirm rapport with customers, including knowledge-sharing and mutual learning processes.

As explained in the IT services market driver section above, alliances and partnerships are a fundamental means for netsourcing providers to acquire essential capabilities, to compete, and for branding and marketing of services. This becomes ever more important with the consolidation and maturing of the market. Hence a collaborative approach can provide netsourcing providers with access to information, resources, markets, and technologies. Furthermore, alliances and partnerships can give rise to learning opportunities, to scale and scope economies, and to means to mitigate risks. In

addition, existing interfirm relationships can facilitate exten-
sions of these relationships to other aspects of the business.
The entire network of relationships in which a netsourcing
provider is thus embedded will be decisive for its success.
Given these predicaments there are some elements netsourcing providers have to consider, including the potential challenges of maintaining alliances and partnerships.

Collaborative agreements and strategic partnerships may,
however, lock providers into unproductive relationships resulting in negative "lock-in" effects. On the other hand, existing ties
may constrain future networking opportunities, leading to negative "lock-out" effects. Such effects may seriously limit the
resources that a netsourcing provider can devote to creating new
ties. Yet the exclusivity of relationship may become a potential
competitive advantage by raising the bar to market entry.

RELATIONAL DRIVERS: CHECKLIST QUESTIONS

The demand-side considerations of the relational drivers
are about controlling the customer–supplier relationship; the
supply-side considerations are, first, about managing customer
satisfaction, and second, about using interfirm relationships
for competitive advantage.

Guiding questions for customers:

1. What relationship management infrastructure and
   process are the netsourcing provider planning to put
   in place to handle your account?
2. What controls can your company put in place to
   develop and maintain the relationship with your netsourcing supplier while ensuring that you get what you
   pay for?
3. How does the netsourcing provider manage its customers' rising expectations and deliver satisfaction?
4. How does the netsourcing provider use interfirm ties
   as a source for competitive advantage in offering superior products and services?

5. In what degree of alliance and partner dependency is the netsourcing provider?

6. Is the service underpinned by a comprehensive SLA, surrounded by a degree of cooperation and knowledge sharing that adds significant value?

SUMMARY: DECISION AND SELECTION CHECKLIST

The issues discussed in this chapter are captured in Table 8.1. This decision checklist illustrates both the provider (supply-side) and customer (demand-side) considerations for entering into a netsourcing deal. To date, most understanding of the netsourcing business model is based on supplier practice and offerings. In turn, our understanding of customer selection and decision criteria and resulting expectations are at an early stage.

The checklist framework is structured in terms of four main issues:

1. Drivers underpinning the reason to opt for a netsourcing service/solution

2. Supply-side (i.e., netsourcing provider company) considerations

3. Demand-side (i.e., client/customer company) considerations

4. Central questions that these considerations raise for deciding, evaluating, and selecting netsourcing providers. These will assist customers to develop and formulate their expectations.

Following this structure, we developed an overview table that integrates all the aspects discussed previously that customers may want to reflect on when developing their netsourcing strategy, evaluating the netsourcing business model, and/or selecting a netsourcing provider. More important, these together illustrate our view of the core issues undergirding the drivers of the netsourcing solution.

TABLE 8.1 Customer Driver Checklist for Netsourcing

DRIVER	SUPPLY-SIDE CONSIDERATIONS	CENTRAL QUESTIONS	DEMAND-SIDE CONSIDERATIONS

Business	• Customer value proposition
	• Delivery speed
	• Competition/cooperation
	• Customer centricity
	• Switching policies
		• To what degree do the potential business advantages and drawbacks really characterize the netsourcing model?
		• How do netsourcing customers perceive these potential advantages and drawbacks?
		• How do netsourcing providers manage and cater for these potential advantages and drawbacks?
			• Advantages
			  • Core focus
			  • Effectiveness
			  • Efficiency
			  • Flexibility
			  • Speed/time to market
			  • Innovativeness
			  • Differentiation
			  • Access to skills/knowledge
			• Drawbacks
			  • Loss of control
			  • Dependence
			  • Lock in

Technology	• Skills/technical capabilities
	• IT infrastructure
	• Suppliers
	  • Reliability/track record
	  • Industry leaders
	• Range of services/products
	• Responsiveness
	• Quality of products and services
	• Customization techniques
	• Customer support
	• Systems integration capability
	• Web-oriented, up-to-date applications
		• What are the main technical problems that customers who use the netsourcing solution encounter?
		• What criteria do netsourcing customers use to measure their provider's technical performance?
		• What is their relative importance?
		• How can providers manage their performance on these criteria?
			• Scalability
			• Customization options
			• Availability
			• Reliability
			• Security
			• Innovativeness
			• Quality of products/services/people
			• Infrastructure
			• Best-of-breed applications
			• Technical help desk/support
			• Integration skills/processes

TABLE 8.1 Customer Driver Checklist for Netsourcing (continued)

DRIVER	SUPPLY-SIDE CONSIDERATIONS	CENTRAL QUESTIONS	DEMAND-SIDE CONSIDERATIONS

Economic	• Pricing models made available
	• One-to-many relations
	• Economies of scale
	• Experience curve
		• What are the likely costs for customers?
		• What pricing models/arrangements do customers expect and prefer?
		• How do providers achieve and maintain their economies of scale?
		• What is the average time frame for achieving return on investments?
		• What pricing models can providers offer?
			• Total cost of ownership
			• Implementation costs
			• Pricing models
			• Flat rental fees (subscription)
			• Fee based on:
			  • Number of users
			  • Number of desktops
			  • Number of applications
			  • Volume of data
			  • Degree of customization
			  • Complexity
			  • Size of the firm

IT-services market	• Segmentation and positioning
	• Financial structure and sustainability
	• Security audits
	• Branding and marketing
	• Industry recognition
	• Use of trusted third parties
	• Alliances and partnerships
	• Industry standards
	• Regulations
	  • Privacy
	  • Security
		• What are the main concerns among (potential) customers looking at the netsourcing market and the netsourcing concept?
		• What could be done to generate trust in the netsourcing concept?
		• What do (potential) customers expect from their provider?
		• What selection criteria do they use selecting a netsourcing provider?
		• How does the provider achieve long-term financial viability?
			• Market perception:
			  • Maturity
			  • Trust
			• Concerns
			  • Longevity
			  • Reliability
			  • Security
			  • Scalability
			  • Customization
			  • Lock-in
			• Expectations
			  • Products and services
			  • Skills
			• Selection criteria
			  • Brands and track records
			  • Price
			  • Quality
			  • Range of products and services
			  • References and recommendations

TABLE 8.1 Customer Driver Checklist for Netsourcing (continued)

DRIVER	SUPPLY-SIDE CONSIDERATION	CENTRAL QUESTIONS	DEMAND-SIDE CONSIDERATIONS

Relational	• Service level agreements
	  • Guarantees
	  • Penalties
	  • Clauses
	• Performance reviews
	• Customer satisfaction reviews
	• Degree of cooperation/ integration/ knowledge sharing
	• Relationship staffing and processes
	• Help with implementation/setup
		• How do netsourcing customers control their relationship with their provider supplier to ensure that they get what they pay for?
		• How can providers manage their customers' satisfaction?
		• How do providers use interfirm ties as a source for competitive advantage?
			• Service-level agreements
			  • Guarantees
			  • Penalties
			  • Clauses
			  • Security
			  • Contingency planning
			  • Future flexibility
			• Performance reviews/detailed monitoring
			• Degree of partnering/knowledge sharing
			• Core partnering capabilities in-house
			• User training programs
			• Exit strategy/clauses/continuity guarantees

ENDNOTES

1. In this chapter we draw upon the comprehensive findings of the customer survey (see Appendix A).

9

PAST, PRESENT, AND FUTURE OF NETSOURCING

The emergence of new markets has happened systematically in the past, allowing for reasonable predictions in new markets, such as netsourcing. The *industry life cycle*, first described in 1975 by Harold Fox, is an S-shaped curve that describes unit sales of a product/industry over time. Although there are many tweaks and variations of this model, an adaptation of the industry life cycle in Philip Kotler's book *Marketing Management*[1] is likely to fit the evolution of netsourcing. The curve describes five distinct phases of a new industry: embryonic, growth, shakeout, maturity, and decline (Figure 9.1). In this chapter we adopt some of the ideas of the industry life cycle to describe what is happening in the netsourcing space and to predict what will probably happen in the future.

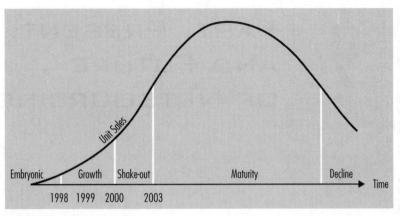

FIGURE 9.1 Industry Life Cycle

LIFE-CYCLE STAGES

EMBRYONIC STAGE

In the embryonic stage, entrepreneurs, having developed a new product or service, typically start their own company because existing companies (1) do not yet accept the vision, (2) choose to wait to respond, or (3) are unable to respond in the short term. During the early years (or in the case of netsourcing, early *months*), founding fathers of a new industry spend much of their time attracting venture capital to launch their new enterprises and educating the marketplace about the new industry. Most early entrants outsource/subcontract many activities to minimize fixed costs. Profits are typically negative, due to heavy expenses in marketing, infrastructure, and operations.

During the embryonic stage, netsourcing was initially called application service provision (ASP). In the ASP context, founding fathers include Traver Gruen-Kennedy of Citrix and past chairman of the ASP Consortium, Christopher R. McCleary of USInternetworking, Jonathan Lee of Corio, Cameron Chell of FutureLink (now CEO of Chell.com), and John Veenstra of Zland. As the model predicts, most early ASP entrants chose to outsource many noncore activities, and much of their time was (and is) spent on marketing not only their own products but also spent aggressively crusading for the entire ASP industry. Traver Gruen-Kennedy, for example, is not only a full-time chief strategist and vice-president of Citrix, but travels the globe giving speeches, press conferences, and interviews for the ASP industry consortium. The messianic efforts have been immensely successful as gauged by the amount of press coverage on ASP. For example, people who subscribe to Searchasp.com's listserve receive a daily e-mail message on the major stories covered on netsourcing around the globe, often 10 stories per day. However, most of the press coverage in 2000 was supplier-driven. Of the customer-driven press, the majority voiced concerns over reliability and security before they would consider adoption. Clearly, more early adopters needed to share their experiences.

According to the industry life cycle, most early adopters (i.e., customers in the embryonic stage) are willing to pay a premium for the new product/service. In the ASP context, it was the reverse, precisely the lower up-front costs that attracted early customers. The majority of early ASP adopters were new startup companies seeking quick-to-market application solutions. But these customers were as inherently risky as ASP ventures—their products and services were untested, rapid cash burn rates led to early demise, or they were acquired by established players. In April 2000, the entire dot.com technology stock market crashed. Thus, although early ASP adopters were in some ways ideal customers because they had no legacy systems or inflexible business practices to hinder standard software solutions, they were not the desired target market to sustain the new netsourcing industry. To put some numbers on the S-curve, total sales in the ASP space during the embryonic stage in 1998–1999 were about $1 billion, according to the Forrester Research Group.

GROWTH STAGE

During the growth stage, there are (1) rapid market acceptance of the new industry, (2) more entrants in the space, and

(3) more demanding customers. Clearly, the ASP industry in 2000 demonstrated all three characteristics of the growth stage. Concerning market acceptance, sales in this space doubled in 2000 to $2 billion. [In 2000, sales were projected to grow to between $7.8 billion (International Data Corporation estimate) and $25 billion (Dataquest estimate) by 2004.] The number of members in the ASP Consortium served as a good estimate of the astounding and rapid growth rate of new entrants. In May 1999, 25 companies joined ASP Consortium. In June 2000, there were 400 ASPs in the ASP Consortium. In November 2000, 700 ASPs in 28 countries were members of the consortium, and nearly 1000 by year end. Another 500 vendors were operating in this space worldwide, bringing the total to an estimated 1500 players in this space in 2000.

In addition to the new entrants, more traditional players entered the ASP space, including consulting firms, telecommunications companies, and independent software vendors (ISVs). Many of the ISVs entered the ASP space two ways: via a strategic partnership with existing ASPs as well as launching their own hosting businesses. PeopleSoft launched their own ASP delivery with PeopleSoft eCenter in 2000 but also licensed to many ASPs.[2] SAP and J.D. Edwards—and eventually even Oracle—had the same strategy. Oracle initially planned to do it all themselves but found that customers don't just want Oracle products but want Oracle ERP integrated with Siebel CRM. In 1999 Larry Ellison seemed very against partnering with other ASPs. However, by late 2000 Oracle was much more sympathetic to partnering.

Thus, many ISVs both competed and cooperated with existing ASPs during the growth stage. Microsoft was and remains, however, more apt to partner primarily with existing ASPs rather than create their own ASP. Microsoft launched Office Online 2000, a hosted version of MS Office, by licensing 20 ASPs through their ASP Microsoft Certified Partner Program. In June 2000, Microsoft announced their .NET strategy, positioning themselves as the technology infrastructure and integrators in the ASP space.

Microsoft.NET intends to shift focus from individual web sites, or individual devices connected to the Internet. Instead the focus will be on large groups of computers, services, and technologies able, in combination, to deliver richer and broader solutions. The vision is one of a content-centric era where people will have a great deal of control over how information is delivered, when, and in what form. The technologies themselves will be much more collaborative, where before the user provided a lot of the integration. Businesses will now be able to offer products and services seamlessly, but also in ways that mean customers can imbed them quickly into their own information and computer configuration. In one view this would be the final delivery on the original intent behind personal computing.

Although the ASP market size was less than anticipated, the expectations and demands of early ASP customers—as well as the demands of potential customers now aware of ASP—certainly increased. Tough ASP customers began forcing innovation and improvements in ASP delivery. But tough customers are precisely the kind of customers that ASPs needed to court to quickly create a competitive advantage. Michael Porter of the Harvard Business School has identified tough local customers as the key to global competitive advantage. Early ASP customers liked the speed of ASP delivery but clearly demanded customized solutions, better pricing mechanisms, and more thorough contracts, including service-level agreements and tighter security. (These trends are discussed more thoroughly below.) The challenges ASPs faced in this stage were simultaneously innovating products and services without further eroding profit margins, retaining current customers, and attracting more traditional customers before exhausting venture capital.

SHAKEOUT STAGE

In 2000, the ASP industry began a tremendous shakeout characterized by failures, mergers, and acquisitions. In addition to the normal shakeout characteristic of all new industries, netsourcing suffered a double whammy with the concurrent technology stock market crash. Another major blow to the entire netsourcing industry was an October 2000 *Fortune* article by Adam Lashinsky. He warned people not to invest in ASPs: "I've definitely had enough of ASP. . . . Watch the ASP bubble carefully before deciding if this is really where you want to plunk down your money. As the life span of Internet fads gets shorter and shorter, ASPs could be the next sector to bite investors."[3]

Was Lashinsky correct? By looking at Table 9.1, the high stock prices listed were all in March 2000 except for Qwest Communications and Corio, the latter of which did not go public until July 2000. Five of the stock prices listed in Table 9.1 plummeted to their 52-week low on the date the stock prices were analyzed—March 16, 2001—indicating that the downward spiral was likely to continue. But the question remained: Weren't many of these companies undervalued given their revenue growth?

There were many reasons why Wall Street analysts were no longer netsourcing believers. Wall Street analysts revived their old rules of finance—they expected companies like xSPs to be profitable within a year. But many xSPs require more time to become profitable because they invested millions in infrastructure and only collect revenues with monthly subscription fees. According to the Cahner's In-Stat Group, ASPs spent $1 billion on infrastructure technology in 2000. In particular, the In-Stat Group found that U.S.-based ASPs spent, on average, 34% on hardware (such as servers and networks), 19% on telecommunications, 19% on personnel, and 13% on software.[4] Such spending will be recovered in years, not months.

Wall Street analysts believed that many ASPs would not survive. Indeed, the Gartner Group predicted 60% of ASPs would close their doors by the end of 2001. ASPs that have already closed shop include Agillion, BlueStar, Hotoffice, iTango, eBaseOne, Red Gorilla, Pandesic, Utility.com, VitaGo, and XS-Media. The Pandesic failure was particularly disappointing because this company had received so much press since it was funded by Intel and SAP and because it had already served over 100 customers.[5] SAP and Intel lost interest because they had set up in parallel their own ASP divisions

TABLE 9.1 Stock Performance of Selected Providers during Shakeout Phase

COMPANY NAME	52-WEEK HIGH	52-WEEK LOW	200-DAY AVERAGE PRICE AS OF FIRST QUARTER 2000	P/E RATIO	REVENUE GROWTH[a] %
CITRIX (MIDDLEWARE)	$108.50 March 14, 2000	$14.25 August 3, 2000	$23.81	40.43	
CORIO (ASP)	$21.75 July 21, 2000	$1.41 Dec. 21, 2001	6.41	n/a	145
BREAKAWAY SOLUTIONS (ASP)	$83.50 March 14, 2000	$0.41 March 16, 2001	11.46	n/a	133
EXODUS (HOSTS)	$89.81 March 23, 2000	$10.13 March 16, 2001	37.14	n/a	
FUTURELINK (HOSTS)	$34.875 March 13, 2000	$.50 Dec. 27, 2000	3.23	n/a	
LOUDCLOUD (ASP)	$6.56 March 9, 2000	$3.88 March 16, 2001	5.63	n/a	
INTERLIANT (ASP)	$44.75 March 20, 2000	$1.65 March 16, 2001	9.83	n/a	149
TRIZETTO GROUP (ASP)	$75.00 March 24, 2000	$8.75 August 24, 2000	15.20	n/a	152
QWEST COMMUNICATIONS (PARENT TO CYBER.SOLUTIONS)	$59.00 July 5, 2000	$32.13 Dec. 20, 2000	45.24	62.73	
USINTERNETWORKING (ASP)	$63.00 March 13, 2000	$1.44 March 16, 2001	7.88	n/a	162

a. Growth figures are from Art Williams, "ASP Revenues Soar, Profits Coming Soon," www.aspnews.com, July 6, 2001.

(i.e., Intel online services and mySAP.com). In addition, Pandesic had not become as profitable in the time frame they had envisaged, so SAP and Intel decided to stop investing and funding the venture altogether. Even J.D. Edwards closed its application service provider division, JDe.sourcing, in 2001. J.D. Edwards decided that they should focus on their core capabilities in software engineering and to partner with ASPs to deliver in that channel, much like Microsoft's strategy. Failures affect not only investor expectations but customer expectations—no customer wants to sign a three-year contact for business applications if the supplier is likely to fail.

If Wall Street analysts were cold on ASP stocks during the shakeout, who are the believers? Certainly, there are a number of other companies—most notably Microsoft—and venture capitalists who still believe in the long-term promise of the netsourcing concept. For example, Microsoft acquired Great Plains Software, an ERP with ASP delivery channel in a deal worth $1.1 billion on January 16, 2001. Microsoft invested $12 million in FirstWorld, an ASP that will deliver Microsoft products in its ASP portfolio. Microsoft also invested $50 million in USInternetworking and $10 million in Corio in 2000. Microsoft's investments show a commitment to the vision of delivering software as a service. Private investors who still believed in the netsourcing vision during the shakeout include Pequot Capital and Chell Merchant Capital Group. The former invested $50 million in FutureLink in October 2000. The latter invested over $1 million in ApplicationStation.com on January 19, 2001. Although Wall Street was bearish on netsourcing stocks in 2001, technology companies and many private investors remained the Zionists of the netsourcing vision.

In addition to the technology stock market crash, dot.com ASPs faced stiff competition not only from their immediate rivals but from the large independent software vendors, telecos, and consulting firms entering the market during the shakeout. ASPs were scrambling to find strategic partners to expand their products, markets, and particularly for their services. Enter the large outsourcing service providers and consulting firms. EDS, CSC, IBM, Anderson, Ernst & Young, KPMG, and PWC have or are poised to snatch-up cash-hampered ASPs. Perot Systems, for example, bought Covation.com, Accenture has invested in Jamcracker, Ernst & Young partnered with Corio, and KPMG partnered with Qwest Communications. The traditional consulting companies offer strategic direction, implementation, and customization for customers, supplementing the ASP's standard fare. However, in January 2001, KPMG sold their 49% equity stake in Qwest Cyber.Solutions back to Qwest Communications after the ASP lost $65 million over a three-month period. This provided an example of continual entry and exit strategies during a shakeout phase.

Another survival mechanism during a shakeout phase is niche marketing to differentiate products and services. This was covered in the netsourcing industry with the explosion of acronyms discussed in Chapter 1. Many ASPs tried to differentiate themselves by focusing on industries (vertical service providers), services (full service providers), or entire management of business processes (business service providers), for example.

Some futurists suggest that the netsourcing shakeout will result in a handful of players, much like the shakeout in automotive manufacturing at the turn of the century. We believe, however, that many players will survive because netsourcing is not about a specific product but an entirely new delivery mechanism for business services.

MATURITY STAGE

Although the netsourcing industry has passed through the first two stages in only a few years and will probably pass through the shakeout stage in the next two to three years, the maturity stage will probably last for five to 10 years. This assessment is based on past innovations in this industry. When client–server computing was first adopted in the early 1990s, the Fortune 500 initially showed little enthusiasm because they had billions of dollars invested in mainframe technology. But as software vendors increasingly moved to client–server platforms, customer demand exploded. Although the mainframe still services many legacy systems, nearly all Fortune 500 companies have bought client–server systems, driven by Y2K and enterprise resource planning. The upfront investment costs were just too compelling, and the newer software products were so much better on client–server than on mainframe technology. And yes, it did take a few years for the client–server security, maintenance, and utilities to catch up to mainframe capabilities, but clearly the client–server market soon reached maturity.

In the netsourcing space, the software most widely delivered is communication and e-commerce capabilities, ideally suited for netsourcing because of customer reach (millions of customers access over the Internet versus limited customers over a private network). As independent software companies rewrite systems for the Internet, more traditional companies will probably become netsourcing customers, adopting innovations slower than desperate small players who are often willing to bear more risk.

We strongly believe that the netsourcing industry will thrive in the coming decade, although the players, products, and services will change significantly. Below we describe the probable trends in the netsourcing market during the next few years.

TRENDS DRIVEN BY THE TOUGH CUSTOMER

Early ASPs use a one-to-many business model. By offering a standard service to many customers, the ASP is able to keep costs low and retain a decent profit margin. This business model was well suited for early customers—primarily new startup companies—because they had no entrenched business practices and instead, needed rapid implementation of business systems. But for the industry to mature, the customer base must surely include more traditional organizations such as global 2000 companies and large government agencies. Although many of these organizations halted spending after the Y2K/ERP splurge at the close of the millennium, these systems will soon need upgrades, enhanced functionality, and even replacement. Before adopting netsourcing, these larger customers will require customization, more sophisticated pricing mechanisms, better service-level agreements, tighter security, better applications, and global delivery, including multilanguage and multicurrency capabilities.

MASS CUSTOMIZATION

Our international survey indicates that 46.8% of existing netsourcing customers want customization, to the degree of template-driven solutions (mass customization) that are specific either to their type of organizational structure or industry.

Slightly different from existing customers, potential customers interested in netsourcing are split between seeking a template-driven (36% of respondents) and a standard solution (38%).

Mass customization is one of the most compelling business ideas of the twentieth century. Mass customization is the idea that a product (or service) should be as standardized as possible through the value chain to keep costs low but allow customers to customize the product during the last stage of production. Although results have not been consistently outstanding in all industries, the strategy makes sense. Mass customization embraces both low costs and product/service excellence, challenging the established notion that companies either compete on low price for standard offerings or high price for differentiated offerings.

Consider how SAP revolutionized business process redesign (BPR) with its products. Before SAP, most companies would redesign business processes from scratch, then custom build expensive software to support the new processes. Nearly 80% of BPR projects failed. SAP inverted the sequence by arguing that SAP software has predefined best business practices and that it is cheaper and better for a company to change their business processes to suit the software. SAP implementation required the customer to select options from predefined templates—thus the realization of mass customization. Although there are many limitations with current templated software (such as many companies still needed to customize ERP packages for their idiosyncratic requirements), there is no denying the benefits. By using templates and by not touching source code, the customer benefits in terms of lower implementation, maintenance, and version upgrade costs. The key is having a discretely defined scope of functionality, something Microsoft has excelled at with their office systems. Mass customization will probably succeed in commodity software (such as e-marketing and e-commerce applications) or in industry-specific solutions.

CUSTOMIZATION

No matter how far the software industry moves toward mass customization, it is very likely that very large organizations will still have idiosyncratic needs requiring changes to underlying source code. Indeed, our international survey found that 26% of potential netsourcing customers would adopt netsourcing only if the solution were fully customized, not mass customized. Although customization erodes the benefits of netsourcing's initial one-to-many business model, large customers will probably be able to get a one-to-one solution because the sheer size of their business will enable providers to customize and still generate a profit. We certainly saw this in the EDS case study in Chapter 5; EDS has the ability to provide total solutions to customers, with a portion of the solution delivered in a one-to-many model and another portion delivered in a one-to-one model, depending on the customer's needs.

INTEGRATION

Although some applications, such as e-mail, may be self-contained, most business applications require significant integration with existing systems and other packages to truly add value. For example, renting an e-commerce application may generate an order, but the company still needs to fill the order, bill the customer, and collect payment. The issue of integration is particularly important for large organizations with an immense portfolio of legacy systems. For these potential customers, the implementation issue alone may be a major impediment to adopting netsourcing.

Throughout this book you have seen a number of ways in which netsourcing suppliers assist customers with integration. In the case study on Corio, you saw that their Orion product is an automatic router that integrates some of their applications, such as Siebel and SAP. This type of integration is ideal for a customer seeking to rent both those applications for a first time. But in most cases, customers have existing systems that must be integrated with any netsourced solution. In these cases, customers typically have to incur a customized solution, requiring systems integration skills. For example, you saw in the case of Host Analytics that the company has first to use an extraction, translator, and load tool to get data from a customer's existing system to a Host Analytics product. Of course, once the customer bears the one-time expense, the customer may purchase additional HA products without integration issues. In the case of EDS, you saw its focus on customization and integration as one of the main ways it can offer total solutions to clients. In other examples, the netsourcing providers partner with third parties to help customers do one-time integration projects, such as Corio's use of implementation partners.

INDUSTRY-SPECIFIC SOLUTIONS

Looking at the Web sites of ASPs in 2001, most were attracting customers from diverse industries rather than targeting a specific industry. For example, the USInternetworking Web site listed 45 customers, including customers from manufacturing, professional services, retail, journalism, pharmaceuticals, and insurance. Certainly during the embryonic stage, ASPs should have taken all newcomers, and for some commodity-type applications such as e-mail, functionality fits a diverse customer base. But for applications such as work orders, assembly, scheduling, inventory, and supply chain management, midsized to large customers require specific functionality suited to their specific industry. As discussed above, the most likely way to meet their requirements and still retain profit margins is through mass customization via template-based functionality targeted at a specific industry.

Some providers are already positioning themselves vertically. Portera specializes in hosting professional services automation applications, TriZetto focuses on health care applications, and LoadSpring offers three product categories for engineering firms. In some cases, the push for vertical integration is spearheaded by independent software vendors that license to ASPs. PeopleSoft, for example, was looking very closely at the ASPs it licenses. In December 2000 Peo-pleSoft looked to swap some of these out in the coming months. One thing the company was doing was looking at all their ASP partners and asking them if they were getting verti-cal strategy.

A word of caution is warranted, however. Many of the hun-dreds of providers claim to focus vertically on specific indus-tries, but indeed do not. For example, the listings on Vendor Central housed by *www.searchasp.techtarget.com* allow potential customers to search for a subset of providers who cater to its industries. But when customers select an industry category such as automotive, education, energy, engineering, financial services, health care, high tech, professional services, real estate, or retail, customers find that many providers cross-list their names on all 10 categories. Looking at the individual provider Web sites for a list of current customers is a better way to access industry capability.

As noted earlier, some large customers within an industry have started their own industry-specific ventures. The most famous is Covisint (see Chapter 2), started by General Motors and other partners for supply chain management within the automotive industry. In another example, Chevron started Upstreaminfo.com, a virtual workspace in which engineers can run seismic analyses. The idea is that the engineers log on to the site and specify which data and which models to run (often 2 terabytes in size!) and the results (not the 2 terabytes) are delivered over the Internet. Such ventures may proliferate for critical commodities discussed in Chapter 2 because they are very expensive for individual players within an industry to maintain. In theory, all parties can reduce their costs via shared industry ventures.

LARGER-SIZED CUSTOMERS

Most people think of netsourcing deals as worth a few thou-sand dollars a month. But when larger customers adopt net-sourcing, the deals will get much bigger. For example, Qwest Cyber.Solutions signed a $22 million, five-year deal with Expanets to provide Oracle ERP and Siebel CRM. Qwest also signed an $18 million, five-year deal with Redback Networks.[6] From the beginning, Qwest Cyber.Solutions has targeted Fortune 1000 companies. In an interview with Qwest's senior vice-president of marketing, Denzil Samuels stated that the Fortune 1000 companies were targeted because they can pay their bills, because most technology innovations come from larger customers, and because these customers request more services than Qwest delivers successfully on initial assignments.[7] As of mid-2001, Qwest Cyber.Solutions had over 60 customers in Fortune 1000 companies (200 customers overall).

MORE DETAILED CONTRACTS

There are many lessons from history about the evolution of service contracts. Back in 1989, when Kodak revolutionized Fortune 500 IT management by outsourcing to IBM, DEC, and BusinessLand, the deals were sealed with contracts a few pages long. Since Kodak, the number of companies outsourcing IT grew astronomically, and today IT outsourcing is a $1 trillion industry worldwide. As customers gained experience with IT outsourcing during the 1990s, they became tougher customers by requiring more accountability from their suppliers. The length of contracts swelled as customers learned to articulate service-level agreements, detailed pricing mechanisms, penalties for nonperformance, contingencies for change, and plans for termination. For example, the contracts between the government of South Australia and EDS, British Aerospace and CSC, and DuPont and CSC/AC had over 500 service-level agreements in each of their contracts. DuPont's contracts contained more than 30,000 lines. There will probably be a similar trend in the netsourcing space. Netsourcing contracts will not be as lengthy as IT outsourcing contracts because netsourcing providers do not provide the on-site management provided by IT outsourcing suppliers. But clearly, reliability, availability, and application, server, and network performance will become standard in netsourcing contracts.

The principles of sound service-level agreements found in traditional IT outsourcing contracts may be a good starting point for advancing netsourcing contracts. Traditional IT outsourcing service-level agreements include 100% accountability, define accuracy as well as timeliness of the service, identify customer and supplier responsibilities, rate criticality of service, establish SLA monitoring and reporting systems, define procedures for escalation, and award penalties for nonperformance.

Consider the following service level for an ASP: "95% of calls to the ASP help desk will be answered by the ASP support staff within six rings." This is not a well-written SLA because it does not require 100% accountability. Literally 5% of calls can never be answered and the supplier has met their service-level agreement. In this context, an auxiliary clause might include: "The ASP will respond to 100% of calls to the ASP help desk within 24 hours." Additional service levels will be needed to define the accuracy of the service—merely answering the phone does not constitute successful customer care. To protect the ASP, customer duties must also be identified because customer behavior can cause service lapses for which the ASP should not be held accountable. Criticality of service prioritizes which services are most important to the customer. The SLA monitoring and reporting system should be understood by the customer. Escalation procedures for missed SLA—even cash penalties for nonperformance—will probably become an industry standard.

Others have argued against detailed ASP service-level agreements, claiming that customers do not understand technical terms: "An SLA [for ASP] can really be one page . . . a common mistake ASPs make is assuming customers understand technical terms, when in reality they would be better served by the use of business terms that cannot be misconstrued."[8] In addition, detailed service-level agreements increase transaction costs. But these SLA principles are precisely the best practices that customers are accustomed to in the IT outsourcing realm. To argue that current netsourcing customers are too naive to understand detailed service-level agreements is to assume that such customers will remain naive. As customers gain experience with netsourcing, they will surely become "tougher" customers, as seen many times over in the industry life cycle.

Other experts believe that netsourcing providers will probably offer more sophisticated service-level agreements and are helping customers catch up to the level of SLA found in IT outsourcing. At Comdex 2000, the ASP Consortium released a white paper on service-level agreements:

> The paper suggests that SLAs detail obligations in these key areas: the network connection between customer and the ASP, the hosting facility, the application itself and customer care, as well as help desk availability.
> —*Sana Siwolop*[9]

The ASP Consortium is doing everything possible to help the entire industry succeed. In addition to advancing contracts, they are working with the World Intellectual Property Organization to establish a global dispute avoidance and settlement standard. In a similar effort, the Information Technology Association of America (ITAA) published the Application Service Provider Service Level Agreement Guidelines. ITAA's guide helps both service providers and customers in the preparation and negotiation of service-level agreements.

Some suppliers are advancing SLAs in the netsourcing space by developing SLA software to deliver SLA management capabilities to providers. For example, Oblicore offers a product that allows ASPs to customize service-level parameters for each of their customers, to monitor compliance, and to warn of impending violations. Oblicore charges providers a setup fee of between $75,000 and $150,000 and charges the provider a monthly fee based on the number of service-level agreements tracked.[10]

Law firms are offering customers help in negotiating SLA agreements in the ASP context, such as the law firm of McKenna & Cuneo in Washington, D.C.: "Beware of any service provider that does not offer its customer a service-level agreement. Service-level agreements are now common place within the service provider industry," says John Bonello, an attorney at McKenna & Cuneo. When representing service providers, Bonello advises them to include the critical provisions their potential customers will be seeking:

> When representing an ASP, as opposed to a customer, you approach the service-level agreement from a different perspective. The purpose of a service-level agreement is twofold. It is both a legal document and a marketing piece. If the service provider does not offer the fundamentals, it will not attract a significant client base. Most quality service providers recognize this and are willing to offer comprehensive service-level agreements.

When representing customers, Bonello provides an example of a customer from a nonprofit organization he recently assisted in obtaining a favorable service-level agreement:

> When we were initially retained by the non-profit, they were considering paying a monthly fee to a service provider for use of a non-profit portal that included a variety of useful applications. However, rather than offering the non-profit a service-level agreement, the service provider offered its potential customer a bare bones contract that would have locked the potential customer into monthly payments for three years with no real ability to opt out if there was dissatisfaction with the service provider. Moreover, the service provider could essentially provide whatever services it felt like. There were no performance or availability standards. At the end of the day, we were able to negotiate a very favorable service-level agreement for the non-profit.

Many smaller customers wonder if such outside expertise is beyond their pocketbooks. John Bonello, for example, usually charges by the hour for his services, and his fees generally fall within the range $500 to $5,000, depending on the complexity of the transaction.

MORE SOPHISTICATED PRICING MECHANISMS

As of 2001, the majority of netsourcing providers offer only two types of pricing, based on number of users and/or transaction-based pricing (number of transactions or percentage of value of the transaction). These monthly pricing models are easy to administer and give the customer a fixed monthly expense, presuming that the number of users and/or number of transactions remains within the contractual range. But setting even these simple pricing mechanisms can be tricky, as you saw in the EDS case in Chapter 5. Another example of pricing difficulties was Microsoft's initial pricing for ASP versions of Office productivity tools; Microsoft essentially took the shrink-wrapped prices and divided them by 24 months. Because many SMEs do not upgrade Microsoft products in two-year time frames, the netsourcing prices were higher than the shrink-wrapped options. Other than the few anomalies, however, simple pricing was ideal for early adopters of the netsourcing model—startup companies that wished to use their venture capital on their core business while outsourcing noncore capabilities such as IT. But we have already noted that as the netsourcing industry matures, more traditional companies and larger customers will demand more sophisticated services and more sophisticated pricing.

The first step is tiered pricing, allowing customers with a large number of employees (i.e., users) a volume discount. As an example, providers may charge $50 per user per month for an ERP application for small customers with fewer than 100 users; $40 per user per month for customers with 100 to 500 employees, or $30 per user per month for customers with more than 500 employees.

Beyond tiered pricing is more resource-based pricing, found in large-scale IT outsourcing contracts: for example, the $4 billion DuPont and CSC/AC deal's unit price over 20 resources in 22 different countries. Resources in the netsourcing space might include a unit price for a megabyte of storage per month, size of server (presuming a dedicated server for larger customers), number of times and length of time that an application is accessed on a server (presuming multitenancy), size of bandwidth, and worker-hours for consulting, maintenance, and support. Customers' monthly bills are based on the volume of each resource times the unit price. The impediments to such sophisticated pricing models in the netsourcing industry have been the licensing agreements between the independent software vendors and the netsourcing provider as well as the need for the netsourcing to implement metering and billing capabilities.

Many other pricing innovations have also been proposed. Jim Geisman, president of Marketshare, suggested a cellular phone model by charging customers a discounted fixed price for a block of time and a premium price for overage.[11] This model assumes that the suppliers in the industry have limited capacity, and thus the customers would be willing to pay a premium for overages. In the netsourcing industry, many entrants have an abundance of capacity and instead, need to focus on gaining customers. This might suggest a reverse strategy for these providers by discounting for more use rather than less, as discussed above.

There are several reports that address netsourcing pricing models more fully. Summit Strategies published "ASP Pricing Strategies: The Push to Profitability" in 2000. Pricing alternatives explored include a per company per month or per annual revenue per month model.[12] Feisal Mosleh, in her article "ASP Pricing: Selling Milk, Not the Cow,"[13] offers guidelines on how ASPs should calculate their prices based on their costs.

One thing is clear: Netsourcing providers will have to add enough value to charge a price that generates a profit. Although bargain basement prices attract early adopters, the idea of capturing a customer base and increasing prices later is not sustainable in the netsourcing space. Unlike traditional IT outsourcing, switching costs in the netsourcing space are generally much lower. Customers become accustomed to low prices and ask such questions as: Why are my prices going up—shouldn't IT price/performance improvements drive prices down over time? They will probably shop elsewhere unless the provider has differentiated on service or customized products to increase customer switching costs. Providers may still be able to attract early customers with slightly higher prices than bargain-basement competitors by showing that their business models are sustainable—the extreme discounters cannot stay in business without eventually raising prices.

GLOBALIZATION

As a trend, globalized netsourcing means several things:

1. New netsourcing providers being founded in countries outside North America and Europe
2. A netsourcing provider's ability to offer services outside their own country to foreign customers
3. A netsourcing provider's ability to service large global customers (i.e., with users in many countries)
4. The ability of a netsourcing provider's products or services to handle multiple languages and multiple currencies

The ASP industry started in California-based startup companies in the United States during the 1998–1999 time frame. The rate of globalization among netsourcing providers has been astounding, with providers based in over 30 countries in mid-2001. InformationWeek estimates that there were 100 European-based ASPs in November 2000. Clearly, tech-savvy entrepreneurs have immediately embraced the notion of netsourcing delivery, but customer awareness worldwide lags behind. For example, Rhetorik surveyed IT directors from large companies (over £100 million) in Germany, France, and the United Kingdom. It found that 39% of respondents did not know what ASP means.[14] Another report by Forrester, entitled *Europe Connects Through ASPs,* postulates that European customers will not be interested in ASP:

> The U.S. mark of success is in terms characterized by cost savings. So [U.S.] companies want to get rid of expensive systems and put them in the ASP environment. We've come to the conclusion that most companies in Europe worry more about e-business initiatives than how to connect in the ASP market space.
>
> —*Charles Homs, Forrester Research European Research Center*[15]

U.S.-based netsourcing providers are clearly intending to expand services. A recent study by the Information Resource Group of 222 U.S.-based ASPs found that 35% of ASPs say that they offer services in Europe and another 36% plan to service Europe within the year. Twenty-two percent of respondents claim to serve the Pacific Rim, and 29% expect to serve by this year.[16] The ability to service foreign markets, however, does not mean that these ASPs have already signed up customers. Again, looking at the ASP's current customer list is the best way to assess global capabilities.

The netsourcing providers most ready to service large global customers are the established independent software vendors with newly opened ASP distribution and established global IT outsourcing firms such as EDS, IBM, and CSC. Oracle Business Online, for example, won Cigna International as a customer because Oracle could deliver ERP in 26 countries, support multiple languages, and bill Cigna in multiple currencies. Furthermore, Oracle has already built a thin-client version of their ERP for better performance.[17]

Based on customer contracts announced in the trade press, customers seem to place more priority on the ability of a netsourcing provider to deliver 24 x 7 customer support. The fact that the applications may be housed thousands of miles from the customer seems less of a concern, and clearly, early adopters are willing to sacrifice multiple language and multiple currency capabilities only in the short term. For example, Mitsubishi and CommodiNet eventually expect their ASPs (Qwest and Corio, respectively) to support multiple languages and currency or they will probably not renew their contracts.[18]

CONCLUSIONS

The future of netsourcing looks bright because, as we have shown throughout this book, the netsourcing industry is based on a solid-value proposition to customers. It is not surprising, however, that the birth of a new industry such as netsourcing experienced an initial unbridled enthusiasm, followed by the discovery of risks and pitfalls and the entry and exit of a staggering number of providers. Compounded on this normal industry life cycle was the technology stock market crash of 2000–2001 and global economic downturn. Throughout this final chapter we have assumed that the future of the netsourcing space can be predicted from the perspective of the "tough customer." Based on our knowledge of customer behavior in past industries, the tough customers have always been a bellwether to how new industries morph. Now, with thousands of netsourcing providers in existence, those that will survive will probably meet the demands of tough customers through customization; integration; vertical focus for business applications; better contracts, including better service-level agreements and more sophisticated pricing mechanisms; and global capabilities. Other service innovations will probably include netsourcing insurance and more strategic, technical, and legal consulting services to reduce customer risks. Product innovations also on the horizon include the explosion of wireless applications, tighter security, better pipelines (particularly for the "last mile"), and faster-performing software, such as thin-client versions of existing business software. Both of these forces—customer demand for service excellence and technology supply to reduce costs and risks—will shape the netsourcing industry in the years to come.

ENDNOTES

1. P. Kotler, *Marketing Management,* Prentice Hall, Upper Saddle River, NJ, 1997.

2. Jennifer Maselli, "PeopleSoft ECenter Launches ASP Services in UK," *InformationWeek*, November 7, 2000.

3. Adam Lashinsky, "Don't Get Bitten by the ASPs," *Fortune*, October 2, 2000. ©Time Inc. All rights reserved.

4. Jennifer Hagendorf, "ASP Pulse: Spending Spree," *www.crn.com*, April 17, 2000.

5. Steven Bird, "The Case for ASPs," *www.aspinsights.com*, December 7, 2000.

6. Fred Aun, "Qwest Cyber.Solutions Makes a Sweet Spot Hit," viewed March 2, 2001 on *www.zdnet.com*.

7. "Executive Q&A: For Qwest, Smaller ASP Users Not Worth Effort," viewed February 21, 2001 on *www.aspstreet.com*.

8. Eric Parizo, "SLA Advice: Keep It Simple," viewed November 16, 2000 on *www.searchebusiness.com*.

9. "The ABCs of SLAs," *www.PlanetIT.com/docs/PIT20001120S0024*.

10. Jennifer Hagendorf Follet, "Oblicore Targets SLA Management," *www.crn.com*, November 13, 2000.

11. Jim Geisman, "Best Pricing Model for Your Outsourcing Needs and Approaches to Setting Prices," *www.searchebusiness.com*, September 12, 2000.

12. Eric Parizo, "Report: ASP Pricing Strategies Must Change," *www.searchebusiness.com*, November 30, 2000.

13. See *www.a-cominteractive.com/articles/0b1sec8.html*.

14. "ASP Services—Are They Working?," *www.it-director.com*, November 3, 2000.

15. Eric Parizo, "Forrester: ASPs Face Long Road to European Success," *www.searchebusiness.com*, December 6, 2000.

16. Jennifer Maselli, "The Great Compromise," *InformationWeek*, November 27, 2000.

17. Ibid.

18. Ibid.

A

INTERNATIONAL SURVEY OF NETSOURCING CUSTOMERS

Throughout this book we have inserted results from an online international survey of current and potential netsourcing customers. The survey was a collaboration between Ramses Zuiderwijk from Erasmus University and ourselves. The survey was sponsored by CMG. In this appendix we describe the research method and survey respondents to help readers understand how our findings were generated.

RESEARCH METHOD

The survey was designed on the basis of a drivers' framework based on the notion that customers' expectations and their netsourcing choices are motivated by five leading drivers:

1. *Business drivers* define the potential strategic, organizational, and operational advantages and disadvantages for selecting netsourcing as an IT sourcing and/or outsourcing option.
2. *Economic drivers* that are essential to netsourcing are the pricing models as well as the total cost benefits and savings.
3. *Technology drivers* describe the technical characteristics of a netsourcing solution. These technical features largely describe the means by which the netsourcing solution will be operationalized.
4. *IT service market drivers* focus on the perceived suitability of the netsourcing solution.
5. *Relational drivers* deal with the postcontract management relationship and those factors that will shape the success of operationalizing the deal.

The responses to the questions associated with the five drivers were discussed fully in Chapter 7.

The respondents to the survey were persons who freely wished to participate in the study. For their time and effort they were offered a free summary of the core findings of the study and instant statistical feedback on 10 of the questions upon completing the entire questionnaire. By structuring the questionnaire as an interactive Web-enabled tool, data were collected and collated centrally in a database, simplifying the resulting analysis process. By using the power of the Internet to enhance the questionnaire's accessibility, customers from around the globe were able to participate.

The questionnaire was structured into three main sections. (1) An entry screen detailing the purpose of the study and our definition of application service provision introduced the study and requested participants to fill in their name, company, country, and e-mail address. Respondents were able to continue to the next set of questions and screen only by entering data into all required fields. Data entry was mandatory throughout the questionnaire. (2) The next screens (i.e., second section) determined the split among potential, terminated, and current netsourcing users. (3) Depending on their ticked response, respondents were directed automatically to a set of screens that then asked them 40 customer-specific questions about the five drivers listed earlier.

However, as a research team, we still had to make companies aware of the survey. For this, a number of international press releases were issued by our sponsoring company, CMG Benelux, highlighting the questionnaire and Web site. In addition, a sample of 2000 IT managers in various European companies were contacted by e-mail to inform them of the survey. Additional international awareness was created by a netsourcing information portal (*www.aspscope.com*) that included a banner on their main Web page with a hyperlink to our survey.

To prevent bias in the results, we carefully counterchecked and verified the respondents to the survey. This became fundamental as we found market research firms and a number of IT suppliers had entered their details into the survey. Since these firms were not our target respondents, they were deleted from the data set. The remaining 400 respondents were verified for correctness by e-mail. Generally, those that were found as fictitious or respondents wishing to bias the survey by giving only negative or all positive answers were eliminated. In all, 83 responses were deleted from the final data set during the data verification phase. This proved an essential step to ensure reliability of results.

RESEARCH RESPONDENTS

In all, respondents from 28 different countries completed the questionnaire. Most respondents were located in the (1)

Netherlands (45%), (2) Great Britain (12.1%), (3) Germany (11.2%), (4) Belgium and France (8%), and (5) the United States (3.8%). The following industry sectors were represented by the customers in this survey study (see Figure A.1). As the figure shows, in our study computer-related (i.e., information technology) firms were the primary group interested in the netsourcing solution. There are a number of plausible reasons why this group is so large. The netsourcing market appeals to startup companies that quickly need to access business software without expending huge up-front costs. Given that most startup companies are in computer-related businesses, it is understandable why so many participants from this industry responded to the survey. Another reason might be that the survey was online and managers from IT firms may spend more time online than do managers from non-IT firms. Managers from IT firms may also be more aware of computer and information technology developments, such as netsourcing, because IT is their business. Additionally, the netsourcing solution intuitively appeals more immediately to the more IT literate sectors, which also may well have fewer political problems gaining support for a netsourcing initiative. Furthermore, the IT sector may well be less put off by security and privacy concerns, feeling that they understand and can control these issues. Overall, it may well be that this overrepresentation also points to the immaturity of the netsourcing marketplace and the need for a lot more customer education.

To get an understanding of which people actually make the decision to go with a netsourcing provider, we asked participants to indicate their position within the company and the positions of those who are either in charge of a netsourcing deal or are thinking about using such a service in the near future. In order of significance, we found (1) CIOs/IT managers; (2) CEOs, owners, or partners; (3) CTOs (chief technical officers); and (4) directors and operational managers to be those most likely to be responsible for selecting a netsourcing solution. This set of job titles in general indicated a high level of authority in the business.

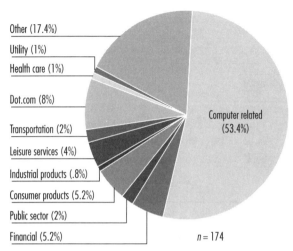

Other (17.4%)

Utility (1%)

Health care (1%)

Dot.com (8%)

Transportation (2%)

Leisure services (4%)

Industrial products (.8%)

Consumer products (5.2%)

Public sector (2%)

Financial (5.2%)

Computer related (53.4%)

$n = 174$

FIGURE A.1 Respondents' Industry Sectors

The types of companies represented in the customer data set varied in size, although it is safe to say that SMEs were the largest contributing group. Figures A.2 to A.5 illustrate the participants' annual revenue and profits, employee numbers, and annual IT expenditure. The picture that the figures paint is of customer groups with an annual revenue of up to $20 million, accounting for 58.5% of the sample. Companies with annual profits of up to $1 million accounted for 51.4%. Over 17.5% of companies sampled operated at a loss. Businesses with employee numbers of up to 500 people made up 69.6%, and those with an annual IT expenditure of less than $500,000 composed 55.7% of the sample. These firms are currently involved and most interested in a netsourcing solution, although there are clear signs that larger firms are seriously evaluating and considering their IT services market options. An additional point to note is that 88% of the respondents are currently outsourcing and procuring up to 40% of their IT infrastructure in the IT marketplace. This means that most of the businesses attracted to considering a netsourcing solution already have a steady history and experience base for using external IT suppliers.

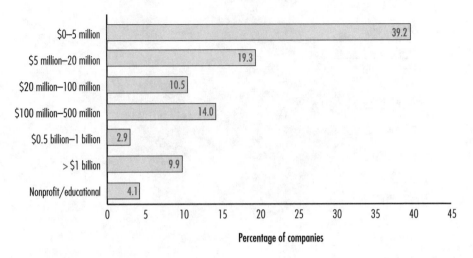

$n = 171$

FIGURE A.2 Respondents' Company Size by Annual Revenue (U.S. Dollars)

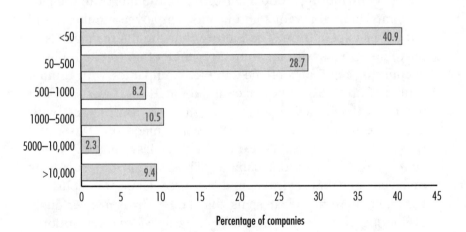

$n = 171$

FIGURE A.3 Respondent Companies' Number of Employees

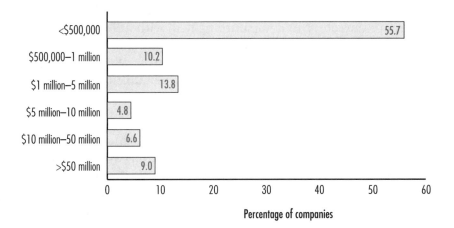

n = 167

FIGURE A.4 Respondent Companies' Annual IT Budget

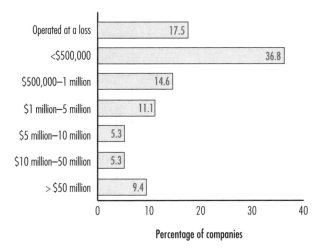

n = 171

FIGURE A.5 Respondent Companies' Annual Profits

Of the overall customer population, 27% of the respondents are currently in a netsourcing deal with at least one service provider, whereas the other 73% are going to evaluate the netsourcing solution in the coming months. We also sought customers who had terminated their netsourcing deal early, but we received no response here.

Below we provide an overview of those customers currently in a netsourcing deal and those likely to evaluate it as an option. The number of customers in our survey currently in a venture are generally consistent with the market figures regularly quoted by netsourcing providers and market research firms. However, insights into those customers' planning to evaluate the netsourcing option, and insights into customer expectations, are far more interesting and of greater use to netsourcing and IT service providers, as they describe the likelihood, detail, and potential of any future netsourcing market. Therefore, what is of particular interest here is to elicit the differences and similarities in, and characteristics of, customers interested in netsourcing solutions.

CURRENT NETSOURCING CUSTOMERS

The majority of customers who responded as being currently in a netsourcing venture signed their contracts within the previous six months (i.e., after September 2000). Thus our learning about customers' perspectives and experience of netsourcing solutions is at best early in the life cycle of two- to five-year deals.

The netsourcing market is clearly immature/embryonic in nature as of mid-2001, as the majority of netsourcing deals have only been operational for less than 12 months at present. This becomes even more apparent when looking at the overall picture, which shows that there is a maximum of up to three years of experience (see Figure A.6). The other issue raised by the figures is the terminology or description

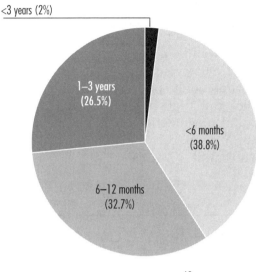

<3 years (2%)

1–3 years
(26.5%)

<6 months
(38.8%)

6–12 months
(32.7%)

n = 49

FIGURE A.6 Operating Period of Current Netsourcing Deals

that customers apply to their application deals. It seems that our understanding of what we term netsourcing today did not emerge until late 1998 and evolved from there. In turn, we can see some early adopters of a netsourcing type of arrangement, emphasizing that what we know and term netsourcing today has been around much longer. In fact, we can safely argue that netsourcing practice is far more established as a sourcing option than initially anticipated and often presented by the media.

The very small set of users who have been in deals that have lasted the entire contract period makes a discussion about success and overall benefits of a netsourcing venture very difficult. At best, our study, and any other, can present results that reflect only a very select group of customers. In turn, the overall experience level regarding the advantages and disadvantages of netsourcing remains limited. In part, this may also be the reason why the majority of netsourcing ventures only span a contract period of less than 12 months.

Uncertainty about the sustainability of these arrangements may still prevent managers from signing long-term deals. One can also point out that a lot of experimentation and test-it-and-see trailing may well be going on. Here comparisons can be drawn with the 1990s evolution of IT outsourcing practice more generally, where only after outsourcing practice had really evolved since the 1960s with time sharing and bureau service solutions did organizations feel sufficiently confident in signing long-term megadeals for a complete IT infrastructure that spans 10 years.[1]

POTENTIAL NETSOURCING CUSTOMERS

The second set of customers are those planning or currently evaluating the netsourcing solution. As Table A.1 shows, the netsourcing solution was revealed to be on the agenda of over 50.2% of the potential customers who responded to our survey. These plan to evaluate the solution over the next 6 to 36 months, as an option to procure, outsource, or amend their current application portfolio. Of equal interest is the high percentage (nearly 50%) of potential customers undecided as to when they might consider a netsourcing solution. Manifestly, there is still a large group needing further insights and success stories to become convinced that this solution offers benefits and opportunities. Here, we will see that ongoing concerns that are outlined later in the report need to be addressed. Particularly noteworthy in Table A.1 is that despite a period of retrenchment in the general economies in Europe and the United States, over 20% of the sample are in the process of evaluating a netsourcing provider for their business over the next six months. One interpretation here is that a netsourcing solution might also be up for consideration from a fresh point of view: namely, how it might assist a customer's business in a downturn. If so, it may well be that some netsourcing providers need to reexamine the basis of their service offerings to reflect a revised set of customer needs from 2001.

TABLE A.1 Potential Customers' Evaluation Period for ASP[a]

	%	CUMULATIVE %
Undecided	50.2	50.2
In the next 6 months	20.1	70.3
In the next 6–12 months	14.6	84.9
In the next 12–18 months	7.8	92.7
In the next 18–24 months	3.2	95.9
In the next 24–36 months	4.1	100.0

a. $n = 219$

We wished to get a feeling for the number of customers who were fully aware of what application service provision actually implies. Were potential customers knowledgeable about the business logic, general operational infrastructure, and possible benefits and drawbacks? Our study showed a generally broad understanding of what a netsourcing solution represents, to the extent that the majority of customers had come across the ASP term—46.6% were somewhat familiar with the ASP term, while a further 32.9% were very familiar with ASP. But we suspect a high degree of nonresponse bias, in that many people may have ignored the survey because they were not familiar with the ASP term or had no interest in ASP. This is certainly a positive development to the degree that it reflects that the marketing undertaken by providers around the world is actually reaching customers. However, we identify a large customer group that is not completely sure what ASP could imply for their specific business, let alone how a netsourcing solution would actually work for them. This low level of awareness is likely to remain for the near future, as the current downturn in the technology stock market, the decrease in available funding, and the push for early profitability in netsourcing startups inherently implies cost cutting where possible. As a result, marketing and customer education expenditure in many providers has been cut significantly. However, this points to a "Catch-22" for providers. Business is dependent on wider customer education, but expenditure on customer education cannot be funded except from more business. This needs to be resolved perhaps not so much by large-scale expenditure as by providers getting much closer to specific market segments and their customers.

SUMMARY OF FINDINGS
FROM THE INTERNATIONAL SURVEY

Findings from this survey of existing and potential netsourcing customers have been inserted throughout the book in the relevant topic areas. Below, we highlight the major findings again.

- The netsourcing market is clearly immature/embryonic in nature as of mid-2001, as the majority of netsourcing deals have been operational for less than 12 months at the time of the survey.
- The majority of netsourcing deals span a contract period of less than 12 months, probably due to the rapid change of customer requirements and application and technology developments.
- In the majority of cases, current netsourcing deal sizes span fewer than 100 users, although there is evidence that a number of larger netsourcing deals have been signed.
- Most common applications procured or sourced from netsourcing providers to date are e-mail and communication solutions.
- 46.8% of netsourcing customers want customization to the degree of template-driven solutions that are specific to either their type of organizational structure or type of industry.
- 50.2% of potential customers are planning to evaluate the netsourcing option over the next 6 to 36 months, whereas 20% are evaluating it over the next 6 months.
- 46.6% are somewhat familiar with the ASP concept, and 32.9% are very familiar with the ASP solution.
- Potential customers seek as their first choice e-mail and communication applications; second choice, B2B e-commerce solutions; and third choice, desktop and personal productivity applications.

- Potential customers are adopting a careful approach by looking for smaller deals. But some larger deals are likely to evolve.

- 49% of current netsourcing customers and 47% of potential customers find that netsourcing providers improve and are likely to improve the overall quality of IT activities in their business.

- 74% of customers in netsourcing deals, and 52% considering such a solution, find that netsourcing offers a clear competitive advantage.

- Providers were indeed found to facilitate customers to focus on their core business.

- 70% of existing customers experienced significant cost savings, whereas only 43% of potential customers expect to be able to achieve savings.

- 77% of existing customers and 66% of potential customers accept that netsourcing ventures will make IT costs more predictable.

- 74% of customers experienced significant business flexibility through access to scalable application solutions, whereas 57% expect to achieve greater flexibility through a netsourcing solution.

- Both potential and existing customers agreed that netsourcing providers offer access to applications that customers could normally not have afforded (particularly true for SMEs).

- 66% of experienced and 62% of potential customers noted the improved application rollout speed of a netsourcing solution.

- 56% of customers do not believe that there is a loss of control, whereas 42% suspect that it is very likely that they will become locked in.

- On average, both existing (55%) and potential customers (51%) expect to receive innovations from a netsourcing deal.

- 85% rated availability and 80% rated reliability as very important, which is likely to lead to an expectation mismatch, especially as customers' experience of netsourcing providers revealed performance on service availability to be only 3.4 out of 5 and reliability to be 3.5 out of 5.

- 54% of potential customers rate quality of services as very important, which according to current customer performance rating of mediocre (31%) to good (43%) seems justified.

- 70% of potential customers rate scalability as important, while actual netsourcing provider performance is again only slightly above average (3.5 out of 5).

- Current customers rate providers as 3.7 out of 5 on security performance; 63% of potential customers rate security as very important.

- Customers rate it important to clarify the ownership of IT, data warehouse, and network infrastructure, yet performance in clarifying these issues for customers is moderate.

- For 55% of current netsourcing customers, the Internet was found to be sufficiently safe, reliable, and efficient to deliver the required application services, whereas the largest group of potential customers (40%) would seek to access their service via a virtual private network.

- Current netsourcing customers rate the technical performance of their netsourcing on average as 7 on a scale of 10, indicating a good performance rating overall.

- Customers noted application availability and service response or uptime as the primary technical problem areas in their netsourcing service.

- The number of users is the most popular netsourcing pricing approach for both current and potential netsourcing customers.

- Nearly 45% of customers expect to pay, and are paying, less than $2500 per month for their netsourcing service.

- Smaller customers tend to expect netsourcing setup costs to be higher—typically, between $5000 and $25,000—than experience actually proves them to be. 45% of customers actually pay less than $5000 in setup costs.

- Some 85% of netsourcing customers are making yearly savings of between $3000 and $180,000, yet 30% of potential customers expect to achieve no savings at all or at most $3000 annually. There is a noticeable discrepancy between results anticipated by potential customers and actual cost savings achieved.

■ The biggest concerns of potential customers are in order of impact: (1) a netsourcing provider's service and business stability, (2) security, (3) reliability, (4) netsourcing provider's longevity and existence, and (5) netsourcing provider's dependence on other parties.

■ The most important concerns for existing customers, which are largely comparable to potential customer lists, were in order of concern: (1) netsourcing provider's longevity and existence, (2) reliability, (3) netsourcing provider's service and business stability, (4) security, and (5) integrating netsourcing with existing applications.

■ Over 60% of both potential and existing customers commonly expect hosting, help desk, and system integration skills and services to be integral to a netsourcing provider's application solution.

■ Compared to 36% of existing customers, 54% of the potential customers think that application customization capabilities and skills are absolutely essential and integral to a netsourcing provider's success.

■ Experienced customers rate as more important than do potential customers, in order of frequency: (1) legacy systems outsourcing, (2) legacy systems management, (3) hosting services and WAP-based services, and (4) strategic management consulting skills.

■ Best practice shows that customers include, in order of importance, the following specifics in their netsourcing contracts: (1) application availability metrics, (2) security guarantees, (3) confidentiality clauses, (4) customer services, and (5) application response times.

■ Some 62% of potential customers see service performance reviews as a daily or weekly task, while actual practice (57%) tends to carry out performance reviews on a monthly or quarterly basis.

■ Both potential and existing customers agreed that the key to confidence and trust in a netsourcing providers service is generated primarily through alliances and partnerships and industry recognition.

The entire survey report, entitled "ASP Marketspace Report: Mastering Customers' Expectations," including detailed data charts, can be ordered for $175 from:

The Department Assistant
Department of Information and Decision Sciences, F1-18
Rotterdam School of Management
Erasmus University Rotterdam
Postbus 1738
3000 DR Rotterdam
The Netherlands
Tel.: (0)10 408 2032
Fax.: (0)10 408 9010
e-mail: cschoof@fbk.eur.nl

ENDNOTES

1. T. Kern and L. Willcocks, *The Relationship Advantage: Information Technologies, Sourcing and Management*, Oxford University Press, Oxford, 2001.

B

GUIDE TO AUTHORS' PUBLICATIONS ON SOURCING IT AND IT-ENABLED BUSINESS SYSTEMS, 1993-2001

BOOKS AND REPORTS

Cullen, S., Seddon, P., Willcocks, L., et al., *Information Technology Outsourcing in Australia,* Deloitte Touche Tohmatsu/University of Melbourne, Melbourne, Australia, 2001.

Graeser, V., and Willcocks, L., *Delivering the Business Value of IT,* Butterwoth-Heinemann, London, 2001.

Kern, T., and Willcocks, L., *The Relationship Advantage: Information Technologies, Sourcing and Management,* Oxford University Press, Oxford, 2001.

Lacity, M., and Willcocks, L., *Global IT Outsourcing: Search for Business Advantage,* Wiley, Chichester, West Sussex, England, 2001.

Lacity, M., and Willcocks, L., "Relationship Management: A Stakeholder Perspective," *Cutter Consortium,* Executive Report, Vol. 2, No. 3, 2001.

Sauer, C., and Willcocks, L., *Building the E-Business Infrastructure,* Business Intelligence, London, 2001.

Willcocks, L., and Sauer, C. (eds.), *Moving to E-Business,* Random House, London, 2001. See especially Chapter 10.

Lacity, M., and Willcocks, L., *Inside IT Outsourcing: A State-of-Art Report,* Templeton Research, Templeton College, Oxford, March 2000.

Willcocks, L., and Lester, S. (eds.), *Beyond the IT Productivity Paradox: Assessment Issues,* Wiley, Chichester, West Sussex, England, 1999. See especially Chapters 9 and 10.

Currie, W., and Willcocks, L., *New Strategies in IT Outsourcing: Major Trends and Global Best Practices,* Business Intelligence, London, 1998.

Graeser, V., and Willcocks, L., *Developing the IT Scorecard: Evaluation and Management Practices,* Business Intelligence, London, 1998.

Willcocks, L., and Lacity, M. (eds.), *Strategic Sourcing of Information Systems,* Wiley, Chichester, West Sussex, England, 1998.

Willcocks, L., Feeny, D., and Islei, G., *Managing Information Technology as a Strategic Resource,* McGraw-Hill, Maidenhead, Berkshire, England, 1997. See especially Chapters 11, 12, and 17.

Lacity, M., and Willcocks, L., *Best Practices in Information Technology Sourcing,* Oxford Executive Research Briefings, No. 2., Templeton College, Oxford, June 1996.

Lacity, M., and Hirschheim, R., *Beyond the Information Systems Outsourcing Bandwagon: The Insourcing Response,* Wiley, Chichester, West Sussex, England, 1995.

Willcocks, L., and Fitzgerald, G., *A Business Guide to Outsourcing Information Technology: A Study of European Best Practice in the Selection, Management and Use of External IT Services,* Business Intelligence, London, 1994.

Lacity, M., and Hirschheim, R., *Information Systems Outsourcing: Myths, Metaphors and Realities,* Wiley, Chichester, West Sussex, England, 1993.

REFEREED PAPERS: JOURNALS

Kern, T., and Willcocks, L., "Exploring Relationships in IT Outsourcing: The Interaction Approach," *European Journal of Information Systems*, Spring 2001.

Kern, T., and Willcocks, L., "Exploring IT Outsourcing Relationships: Theory and Practice," *Journal of Strategic Information Systems,* 9, 321–350, 2001.

Willcocks, L., Lacity, M., and Kern, T., "Risk in IT Outsourcing Strategy Revisited: Longitudinal Case Research at LISA," *Journal of Strategic Information Systems,* April, Vol. 8, 1999, pp. 285–314.

Hirschheim, R., and Lacity, M., "Four Stories of Information Technology Insourcing," *Communications of the ACM,* February 2000.

Kern, T., and Willcocks, L., "Contracts, Control, and Presentiation in IT Outsourcing: Research in Thirteen UK Organizations," *Journal of Global Information Management*, 20–35, October–December 2000.

Lacity, M., and Willcocks, L., "A Survey of IT Outsourcing Experiences in USA and UK," *Journal of Global Information Management*, 8(2), April/June 2000.

Willcocks, L., and Sykes, R., "The Role of the CIO and IT Function in ERP: Asleep at the Wheel?" *Communications of the ACM*, April 2000.

Willcocks, L., and Lacity, M., "IT Outsourcing in Financial Services: Risk, Creative Contracting and Business Advantage," *Information Systems Journal*, September 1999.

Willcocks, L., and Lacity, M., "Information Technology Outsourcing: Practices, Lessons and Prospects," *ASX Perspective*, April 1999.

Willcocks, L., Lacity, M., and Kern, T., "Risk Mitigation in IT Outsourcing Strategy Revisited: Longitudinal Case Research," *Journal of Strategic Information Systems*, 8, 285–314, 1999.

Currie, W., and Willcocks, L., "Analysing IT Outsourcing Decisions in the Context of Size, Interdependency and Risk," *Information Systems Journal*, 8(2), 1998.

Feeny, D., and Willcocks, L., "Redesigning the IS Function around Core Capabilities," *Long Range Planning*, 32(3), 354–367, June 1998.

Feeny, D., and Willcocks, L., "Core IS Capabilities for Exploiting Information Technology," *Sloan Management Review*, 39(3), 9–21, 1998.

Lacity, M., and Willcocks, L., "An Empirical Investigation of Information Technology Sourcing Practices: Lessons from Experience," *MIS Quarterly*, 22(3), 363–408, 1998.

Lacity, M., Willcocks, L., and Subramanian, A., "Client Server Implementation: New Technology, Lessons from History," *Journal of Strategic Information Systems*, March 1998.

Willcocks, L., and Currie, W., "IT Outsourcing in Public Service Contexts: Towards the Contractual Organization?" *British Journal of Management*, 8, S107–S120, June 1998.

Willcocks, L., and Kern, T., "IT Outsourcing as Strategic Partnering: The Case of the Inland Revenue," *European Journal of Information Systems*, 7, 29–45, 1998.

Lacity, M., and Willcocks, L., "IT Outsourcing: Examining the Privatization Option in U.S. Public Administration," *Information Systems Journal*, 7(2), June 1997.

Lacity, M., Willcocks, L., and Feeny, D., "The Value of Selective IT Sourcing," *Sloan Management Review*, 37(3), 13–25, 1997.

Subramanian, A., and Lacity, M., "Managing Client Server Implementations: Today's Technology, Yesterday's Lessons," *Journal of Information Technology*, 12(3), 169–186, 1997.

Lacity, M., and Willcocks, L., "Interpreting Information Technology Sourcing Decisions from a Transaction Cost Perspective: Findings and Critique," *Accounting, Management and Information Technology*, 5(3/4), 203–244, 1996.

Willcocks, L., Fitzgerald, G., and Lacity, M., "To Outsource IT or Not? Recent Research on Economics and Evaluation Practice," *European Journal of Information Systems*, 5(3), 143–160, 1996.

Willcocks, L., Lacity, M., and Fitzgerald, G., "IT Outsourcing in Europe and the USA: Assessment Issues," *International Journal of Information Management*, 15(5), 333–351, 1996. A less developed version won the Best Paper Award at the 3rd European Conference in Information Systems, Athens, June 1995.

Lacity, M., and Hirschheim, R., "Benchmarking as a Strategy for Managing Conflicting Stakeholder Perceptions of Information Systems," *Journal of Strategic Information Systems*, 4(2), 165–185, June 1995.

Lacity, M., Willcocks, L., and Feeny, D., "IT Outsourcing: Maximise Flexibility and Control," *Harvard Business Review*, 84–93, May/June 1995.

Willcocks, L., and Choi, C., "Cooperative Partnership and 'Total' IT Outsourcing: From Contractual Obligation to Strategic Alliance?" *European Management Journal*, 13(1), 67–78, 1995.

Willcocks, L., Fitzgerald, G., and Feeny, D., "IT Outsourcing: The Strategic Implications," *Long Range Planning*, 28(5), 59–70, 1995.

Lacity, M., Hirschheim, R., and Willcocks, L., "Realizing Outsourcing Expectations: Incredible Expectations, Credible Outcomes," *Information Systems Management*, 7–18, Fall 1994.

Willcocks, L., "Managing Information Systems in UK Public Administration: Trends and Future Prospects," *Public Administration*, 72(2), 3–32, 1994.

Lacity, M., and Hirschheim, R., "Implementing Information Systems Outsourcing: Key Issues and Experiences of an Early Adopter," *Journal of General Management*, 19(1), 17–31, Autumn 1993.

Lacity, M., and Hirschheim, R., "The Information Systems Outsourcing Bandwagon," *Sloan Management Review*, 35(1), 73–86, 1993.

REFEREED PAPERS: CONFERENCE PROCEEDINGS

Lacity, M., and Poppo, L., "The Normative Value of Transaction Cost Economics: What Managers Have Learned in the IT Context," *Proceedings of the 2nd International Conference on Outsourcing of Information Systems*, Bayreuth, Germany, June 23, 2001.

Kern, T., and Willcocks, L., "Presentation in Contracting for IT Outsourcing: A Study of Thirteen Organizations," *Proceedings of the 7th European Conference in Information Systems*, Copenhagen, June 23–25, 1999.

Willcocks, L., and Lacity, M., "IT Sourcing at Polaris: Risk, Creative Contracting and Business Advantage," Winner of the Best Case Paper Award, *Proceedings of the 7th European Conference in Information Systems*, Copenhagen, June 23–25, 1999.

Kern, T., and Willcocks, L., "Cooperative Relationship Strategy in Global Information Technology Outsourcing: The Case of Xerox Corporation," *Proceedings of the 5th International Conference on Multi-organizational Partnerships and Cooperative Strategy*, Balliol College, Oxford, July 1999.

Willcocks, L., Lacity, M., and Kern, T., "IT Outsourcing and Risk Mitigation: Recent Case Research," *Proceedings of the 5th Decision Sciences Conference*, Athens, July 5–7, 1999.

Currie, W., and Willcocks, L., "Large-Scale IT Outsourcing: The Case of British Aerospace plc," *Proceedings of the 3rd UK Association for Information Systems Conference*, Lincoln, Lincolnshire, England, April 1998.

Graeser, V., and Willcocks, L., "IT Projects and Benefit Funding: Case Research at the Californian Franchise Tax Board," *Proceedings of the 6th European Conference in Information Systems*, Aix-en-Provence, France, June 1998.

Currie, W., and Willcocks, L., "Analysing IT Outsourcing Decisions in the Context of Size, Interdependency and Risk," *UK Association for Information Systems Conference*, 1997.

Willcocks, L., and Currie, C., "Information Technology in Public Services: Towards the Contractual Organization?" *Proceedings of the 10th Annual Conference of the British Academy of Management*, Aston Business School, Birmingham, England, September 15–18, 1997.

Willcocks, L., and Currie, W., "IT Outsourcing and Risk Mitigation at the Logistic Information System Agency: A Case Research Study," *British Academy of Management Conference*, London, September 1997.

Willcocks, L., and Kern, T., "IT Outsourcing as Strategic Partnering: The Case of the UK Inland Revenue," Winner of the Officers' Prize for Excellence, *Proceedings of the 5th European Conference in Information Systems*, June 1997.

Currie, W., and Willcocks, L., "The Impact of Compulsive Competitive Tendering of IT Services in Local Government," *Proceedings of the 3rd Financial Information Systems Conference*, Sheffield, Yorkshire, England, September 9–10, 1996.

Kern, T., and Willcocks, L., "The Enabling and Determining Environment: Neglected Issues in IT Outsourcing Strategy," in J. Dias Coelho, T. Jelasi, et al. (eds.), *Proceedings of the 4th European Conference in Information Systems*, Lisbon, July 2–4, 1996.

Kumar, K., and Willcocks, L., "Offshore Outsourcing: A Country Too Far?" in J. Dias Coelho, T. Jelasi, et al. (eds.), *Proceedings of the 4th European Conference in Information Systems*, Lisbon, July 2–4, 1996.

Willcocks, L., and Feeny, D., "Reconfiguring the Information Systems Function: A Core Capabilities Approach," Keynote Speech, *Proceedings of the*

Australiasian Conference in Information Systems, Hobart, Tasmania, Australia, December 12–14, 1996.

Willcocks, L., Lacity, M., and Fitzgerald, G., "IT Outsourcing in Europe and the USA: Assessment Issues," Best Paper Award, *Proceedings of the 3rd European Conference in Information Systems*, 1995.

Willcocks, L., and Fitzgerald, G., "Towards the Residual IS Organization? Research on IT Outsourcing Experiences in the United Kingdom," *Conference Proceedings: IFIP WG8.2 Transactions on Computer Science and Technology*, R. Baskerville, et al. (eds.), *Transforming Organizations with Information Technology*, Elsevier/North-Holland, Amsterdam, 1994.

Willcocks, L., and Fitzgerald, G., "Relationships in Outsourcing: Contracts and Partnerships," *Proceedings of the 2nd European Conference on Information Systems*, Nijenrode, The Netherlands, May 30–31, 1994.

Willcocks, L., and Fitzgerald, G., "To Outsource IT or Not? Recent Research on Economics and Evaluation Practice," *Proceedings of the Evaluation of IT Investments Conference*, Henley Management College, Henley, England, September 13–14, 1994.

Willcocks, L., and Fitzgerald, G., "The Outsourcing of Information Technology," *Proceedings of the British Academy of Management Conference*, University of Lancaster, Lancaster, England, September 12–14, 1994.

Willcocks, L., and Fitzgerald, G., "Contracting for IT Outsourcing: Recent Research Evidence," J. Gross, et al. (eds.), *Proceedings of the 15th Annual International Conference in Information Systems*, Vancouver, British Columbia, Canada, 91–98, December 13–16, 1994.

Willcocks, L., Fitzgerald, G., and Feeny, D., "Information Technology Outsourcing: From Incrementalism to Strategic Intent," *Proceedings of the 2nd SISNET Conference*, Barcelona, September 26–28, 1994.

Fitzgerald, G., and Willcocks, L., "IT Outsourcing in the United Kingdom and Europe: Recent Research Evidence," *Proceedings of the 14th International Conference in Information Systems*, Orlando, Fla., 1993.

REPRINTS AND SHORTER PAPERS

Feeny, D., and Willcocks, L., "Selective Sourcing and Core Capabilities," *Financial Times*, February 15, 1999.

Willcocks, L., and Lacity, M., "Strategic Dimensions of IT Outsourcing," *Financial Times*, March 1999.

Willcocks, L., Lacity, M., and Fitzgerald, G., "IT Outsourcing in Europe and the USA: Assessment Issues," *Proceedings of the 3rd European Conference in Information Systems*, Athens, June 3–5, 1995. Best Paper Award.

Willcocks, L., and Fitzgerald, G., "Outsourcing in the United Kingdom: Vendor/Client Issues," *Proceedings of the Information Resources Management Association International Conference: Managing Social and Economic Change with Information Technology,* San Antonio, Texas, May 22–25, 1994.

Willcocks, L., and Fitzgerald, G., "Assessing IT Outsourcing Options: Recent UK Case Evidence," *Proceedings of the IT Outsourcing Conference,* University of Twente, The Netherlands, May 29–30, 1993.

CONTRIBUTIONS TO BOOKS

Feeny, D., and Willcocks, L., "Selective Sourcing and Core Capabilities," in *Mastering Information Management,* FT/Prentice Hall, London, 2000.

Kern, T., and Willcocks, L., "Cooperative Relationship Strategy in Global IT Outsourcing: The Case of Xerox Corporation's Relationship Locally," in D. Faulkner, et al. (eds.), *Cooperative Strategies,* Oxford University Press, Oxford, 2000.

Lacity, M., and Willcocks, L., "Relationships in IT Outsourcing: A Stakeholder Perspective," in R. Zmud (ed.), *Framing the Domains of IT Management,* Pinnaflex, 355–384, 2000.

Willcocks, L., and Lacity, M., "Experience of Information Technology Outsourcing," in J. Angel (ed.), *The Outsourcing Practice Manual,* Sweet and Maxwell, London, 2000.

Willcocks, L., and Lacity, M., "Strategic Dimensions of IT Outsourcing," in *Mastering Information Management,* FT/Prentice Hall, London, 2000.

Lacity, M., Willcocks, L., and Feeny, D., "IT Outsourcing: Maximizing Flexibility and Control," in *Business Value from IT,* Harvard Business Press, Cambridge, Mass., 1999.

Feeny, D., and Willcocks, L., "The Emerging IT Function: Changing Capabilities and Skills," in W. Currie and R. Galliers (eds.), *Rethinking MIS,* Oxford University Press, Oxford, 1998.

Willcocks, L., and Currie, W., "IT Outsourcing in Public Service Contexts: Towards the Contractual Organization?" reprinted in M. Mische (ed.), *The High Performance IT Organization,* Auerbach Publications, Oxford, 1998.

Lacity, M., Hirschheim, R., and Willcocks, L., "Realizing Outsourcing Expectations," reprinted in R. Umbaugh (ed.), *Handbook of IS Management,* Auerbach, Boston, 1997.

Lacity, M., Willcocks, L., and Feeny, D., "Sourcing Information Technology Capability: A Decision-Making Framework," reprinted in M. Earl (ed.), *Information Management: The Organizational Dimension,* Oxford University Press, Oxford, 1996.

Willcocks, L., and Fitzgerald, G., "The Changing Shape of the Information Systems Function," reprinted in M. Earl (ed.), *Information Management: The Organizational Dimension*, Oxford University Press, Oxford, 1996.

Willcocks, L., and Fitzgerald, G., "Pilkington PLC: A Major Multinational Outsources Its Head Office IT Function," in E. Turban, E. Mclean, and J. Wetherbe (eds.), *Information Technology for Management*, Wiley, New York, 1995.

Willcocks, L., Lacity, M., and Fitzgerald, G., "Information Technology Outsourcing: Economics, Contracting and Measurement," reprinted in B. Farbey, F. Land, and D. Targett, *Hard Money, Soft Outcomes: Evaluating and Managing the IT Investment*, Alfred Waller, Henley, Oxfordshire, England, 1995.

Feeny, D., Willcocks, L., and Fitzgerald, G., "Strategic Management of IT in the Nineties: When Outsourcing Equals Rightsourcing," in S. Rock (ed.), *Director's Guide to Outsourcing*, Institute of Directors, London, 1993.

Willcocks, L., Fitzgerald, G., and Feeny, D., "Effective IT Outsourcing: The Evidence in Europe," in *The Management of Change: Market Testing and Outsourcing of IT Services*, Elite/British Computer Society, London, 1993.

Willcocks, L., and Sauer, C., "Risk and Its Management in IT Outsourcing," in J. Pritchard (ed.), *Mastering Risk,* FT/Prentice Hall, London, 1993.

WORKING PAPERS

A variety of working papers is available from Oxford Institute of Information Management. Contact *Jenny.Peachey@templeton.oxford.ac.uk* or call UK (0)1865-422500.

INDEX

A

ABN Amro, 186

Accenture, 24, 120

Access, and sourcing of
information technology (IT), 36

Advantra, 40

A.E. Schmidt, 154–55

Agiliti, 21, 25

Agillion, 274

Alpha, 130–34

American Airlines, Sabre
reservation system, 41, 51

Anderson, 276

Application access level, 85–87

Application availability, 90

Application customization, 247,
248–49

Application operating
infrastructure, 87–89

Application performance, 90–91

Application Service Provider
Service Level Agreement
Guidelines, 285

Application service providers
(ASPs), 5–6

Application service provision
(ASP), 2, 86, 270

M

MadetoOrder.com, 117
 and Corio, 117
Maeli, Jennifer, 118
Mail.com, *See* EasyLink Services
MainPass Technologies, Inc., 103,
 143–49, 208
 better-value claims, 147–48
 company strategy, 146
 competitive moves, 147–48
 MainPass Virtual Desktop
  (MVD), 144
  best-of-breed software,
   144–45
  business-to-business
   services, 145
  communication
   services, 145
  intranet/extranet, 144
 marketing, 146–47
 operational benefits, 145
 overview, 105–6
 products offered, 111
 profile of, 108
 service essentials, 144–45
 strategic alliances, 143
Managed service providers
 (MSPs), 4
Management principles, 65–82
 core IT capabilities, 67–73
  business systems
   thinking, 69
  contract facilitation, 71
  contract monitoring, 71
  designing technical
   architecture, 69
  information management
   strategy, 67
  information systems
   strategy, 67

information technology
 strategy, 67
informed buying, 70
IT governance, 69
IT market sourcing
 strategy, 67–68
making technology work,
 69–70
relationship building, 69
supplier development,
 71–72
provider evaluation/contract-
 ing, 73–80
 detailed contracts, 76–80
 weaknesses in
  contracting, 74
Marconi Medical Systems, 4
Marketing Management
 (Kotler), 269
marviQ, 103, 207
 application and data
  coexistence, 182
 customer case studies, 184–87
  CareView, 186–87
  Identrus, 185–86
  QuoteOnWine, 184–85
 data migration, 181–82
 FSP strategy, 179–82
  connectivity, 180
  functionality, 181
  integration, 181–82
 growth of, 179
 n-tier architecture, 182–87
  business logic, 183–84
  content, functionality, and
   legacy, 184
  presentation, 182–83
 overview, 160–61
 products offered, 111
 profile of, 109
Mass customization, 278–79

8 reasons why you should read the Financial Times for 4 weeks RISK-FREE!

To help you stay current with significant developments in the world economy ...
and to assist you to make informed business decisions — the Financial Times brings you:

1 Fast, meaningful overviews of international affairs ... plus daily briefings on major world news.

2 Perceptive coverage of economic, business, financial and political developments with special focus on emerging markets.

3 More international business news than any other publication.

4 Sophisticated financial analysis and commentary on world market activity plus stock quotes from over 30 countries.

5 Reports on international companies and a section on global investing.

6 Specialized pages on management, marketing, advertising and technological innovations from all parts of the world.

7 Highly valued single-topic special reports (over 200 annually) on countries, industries, investment opportunities, technology and more.

8 The Saturday Weekend FT section — a globetrotter's guide to leisure-time activities around the world: the arts, fine dining, travel, sports and more.

FT FINANCIAL TIMES
World business newspaper

The *Financial Times* delivers a world of business news.

Use the Risk-Free Trial Voucher below!

To stay ahead in today's business world you need to be well-informed on a daily basis. And not just on the national level. You need a news source that closely monitors the entire world of business, and then delivers it in a concise, quick-read format.

With the *Financial Times* you get the major stories from every region of the world. Reports found nowhere else. You get business, management, politics, economics, technology and more.

Now you can try the *Financial Times* for 4 weeks, absolutely risk free. And better yet, if you wish to continue receiving the *Financial Times* you'll get great savings off the regular subscription rate. Just use the voucher below.

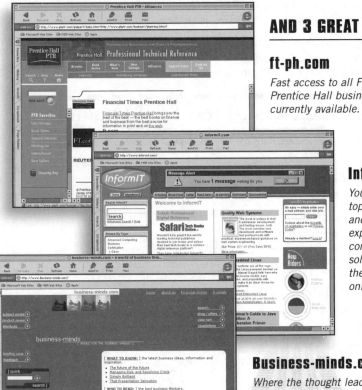